Off the Shelf
BAKING

Meredith Books®
Des Moines, Iowa

BETTER HOMES AND GARDENS® OFF THE SHELF BAKING
Editor: Tricia Laning
Contributing Project Editor: Mary Williams
Contributing Writer: Cynthia Pearson
Contributing Graphic Designer: The Design Office of Jerry J. Rank
Copy Chief: Terri Fredrickson
Publishing Operations Manager: Karen Schirm
Senior Editor, Asset & Information Management: Phillip Morgan
Edit and Design Production Coordinator: Mary Lee Gavin
Editorial Assistant: Cheryl Eckert
Book Production Managers: Pam Kvitne, Marjorie J. Schenkelberg,
    Rick von Holdt, Mark Weaver
Contributing Copy Editor: Caroline Stern
Contributing Proofreaders: Nicole Clausing, Stacie Gaylor, Gretchen Kauffman
Contributing Indexer: Elizabeth Parson
Test Kitchen Director: Lynn Blanchard
Test Kitchen Product Supervisor: Marilyn Cornelius
Test Kitchen Home Economists: Elizabeth Burt, R.D, L.D.; Juliana Hale;
    Laura Marzen, R.D.; Maryellyn Krantz; Greg Luna; Jill Moberly; Dianna Nolin;
    Colleen Weeden; Lori Wilson; Charles Worthington

MEREDITH® BOOKS
Executive Director, Editorial: Gregory H. Kayko
Executive Director, Design: Matt Strelecki
Managing Editor: Amy Tincher-Durik
Senior Editor/Group Manager: Jan Miller
Senior Associate Design Director: Ken Carlson
Marketing Product Manager: Gina Rickert
Publisher and Editor in Chief: James D. Blume
Editorial Director: Linda Raglan Cunningham
Executive Director, Marketing: Steve Malone
Executive Director, New Business Development: Todd M. Davis
Executive Director, Sales: Ken Zagor
Director, Operations: George A. Susral
Director, Production: Douglas M. Johnston
Director, Marketing: Amy Nichols
Business Director: Jim Leonard

Vice President and General Manager: Douglas J. Guendel

BETTER HOMES AND GARDENS® MAGAZINE
Deputy Editor, Food and Entertaining: Nancy Hopkins

MEREDITH PUBLISHING GROUP
President: Jack Griffin
Executive Vice President: Bob Mate

MEREDITH CORPORATION
Chairman and Chief Executive Officer: William T. Kerr
President and Chief Operating Officer: Stephen M. Lacy

In Memoriam: E.T. Meredith III (1933–2003)

All of us at Meredith® Books are dedicated to providing you with the information and ideas you need to create delicious foods. We welcome your comments and suggestions. Write to us at: Meredith Books, Cookbook Editorial Department, 1716 Locust St., Des Moines, IA 50309-3023.

Our seal assures you that every recipe in *Off the Shelf Baking* has been tested in the Better Homes and Gardens® Test Kitchen. This means that each recipe is practical and reliable, and meets our high standards of taste appeal. We guarantee your satisfaction with this book for as long as you own it.

Test Kitchen

Contents

Baked to Perfection! Treat yourself,

your family, and friends to the tastes and aromas of fresh-baked cookies, chewy bars, moist cakes, savory appetizers, and hearty casseroles—**without spending hours** in the kitchen. It's easy when you **combine convenience products** found at your local supermarket with **fresh ingredients.** You'll find dozens of **time-saving recipes** in this soon-to-be favorite cookbook.

Do you want to try something different with a store-bought cookie or basic cake mix? Do you crave the flavor of home-baked breads and rolls? Are you looking for a savory appetizer, crowd-pleasing casserole, or potluck favorite? The tips, tricks, and creative ideas for **using mixes and other prepared ingredients** will reduce prep time and yield baked-from-scratch results. And if you have children who love to help in the kitchen, there are some fun recipes just for them to make and enjoy.

> The secret ingredient to turning out delicious, mouthwatering baked goods that don't require a day in the kitchen is using the good stuff that's on your grocer's shelves.

Look for these icons throughout this book: **FAST** = start to finish in 30 minutes or less. EASY = prep time of 15 minutes or less.

Whether you are looking for the perfect holiday dessert, sweet after-school trest, or a delicious confection to share with a crowd, the recipes in this book are sure to please.

Warm up the oven—it's time to bake the Off the Shelf way!

Appetizers

Appetizer *Cheesecake*

PREP
35 MINUTES

BAKE
49 MINUTES

CHILL
6 TO 24 HOURS

OVEN
400°F/325°F

MAKES
16 APPETIZER SERVINGS

¼   cup butter or margarine, melted
6   sheets frozen phyllo dough
     (14×9-inch sheets), thawed
½   of a 6-ounce jar marinated
     artichoke hearts
3   8-ounce packages cream cheese,
     softened
1¼   cups crumbled feta cheese (5 ounces)
½   teaspoon dried oregano, crushed
¼   teaspoon garlic powder
3   eggs
¼   cup sliced green onion (2)
     Sliced roma tomatoes (optional)
     Whole Greek or ripe olives (optional)
     Fresh basil leaves (optional)

STEP 1   Preheat oven to 400°F. For crust, brush bottom and side of a 9-inch springform pan with some of the melted butter. Unfold phyllo dough; remove 1 sheet of phyllo. (As you work, cover the remaining phyllo dough with plastic wrap to prevent it from drying out.) Ease the phyllo sheet into the prepared pan off-center so that phyllo extends evenly up the side of the pan. Brush with melted butter. Repeat with remaining phyllo and butter, placing sheets off-center to cover bottom and side of pan. Trim off any phyllo that extends beyond the edge of the pan. Make 2 slits in the center of phyllo for steam to escape.

STEP 2   Bake in the preheated oven for 9 to 10 minutes or until light golden brown. Cool on a wire rack. Reduce oven temperature to 325°F.

STEP 3   Meanwhile, drain and chop artichokes, reserving 2 tablespoons of the marinade; set aside.

STEP 4   In a large mixing bowl beat cream cheese with an electric mixer on medium speed until smooth. Add feta cheese, oregano, and garlic powder; beat well. Add eggs; beat just until combined (do not overbeat). Stir in artichoke hearts, the reserved 2 tablespoons marinade, and the green onion. Pour into crust.

STEP 5   Bake in the 325° oven for 40 to 50 minutes or until center is soft-set and outside stays firm when gently shaken. Cool on a wire rack.

STEP 6   Cover and refrigerate for at least 6 hours or up to 24 hours. To serve, remove the side of the pan. (If desired, let stand to bring to room temperature.) If desired, garnish with tomato slices, olives, and basil.

PER SERVING: 239 cal., 21 g total fat (13 g sat. fat), 103 mg chol., 317 mg sodium, 6 g carbo., 0 g fiber, 6 g pro.
EXCHANGES: ½ Medium-Fat Meat, 4½ Fat

OFF THE SHELF TIP Rich, creamy cream cheese is available in fat-free, low-fat, and regular—plus an assortment of flavors.

Tapenade-Filled Palmiers

1   17.3-ounce package frozen puff
     pastry (2 sheets), thawed
2/3 cup purchased olive tapenade

PREP
40 MINUTES
FREEZE
1 HOUR
BAKE
12 TO 15 MINUTES
OVEN
400°F
MAKES
80 PALMIERS

STEP 1 On a lightly floured surface, unfold pastry sheets. Roll 1 pastry sheet into a 14×10-inch rectangle. Spread 1/3 cup of the tapenade over the rectangle, spreading to edges. Starting at a short side, roll up into a spiral, stopping at the center; repeat, starting at the other short side. Repeat with remaining pastry sheet and tapenade. Cover and quick-chill in the freezer about 1 hour.

STEP 2 Preheat oven to 400°F. Line baking sheets with parchment or clean, plain brown paper; set aside. Trim ends of pastry rolls. Cut the rolls crosswise into 1/4-inch slices. Place slices 1 inch apart on the prepared baking sheets.

STEP 3 Bake in the preheated oven for 12 to 15 minutes or until golden. Transfer to a wire rack; cool slightly. Serve warm.

MAKE-AHEAD DIRECTIONS: Bake and cool palmiers as directed. Layer cooled palmiers in a covered container with waxed paper between the layers. Cover and freeze for up to 3 months. Thaw at room temperature for 30 minutes. To serve, preheat oven to 400°F. Place palmiers on a baking sheet. Bake in the preheated oven for 5 minutes to crisp.

PER PALMIER: 39 cal., 3 g total fat (0 g sat. fat), 0 mg chol., 78 mg sodium, 2 g carbo., 0 g fiber, 0 g pro.
EXCHANGES: 1/2 Fat

OFF THE SHELF TIP Fetch olive tapenade from the condiment or ethnic aisle. It's a thick paste of chopped ripe olives, anchovies, capers, seasonings, olive oil, lemon juice.

SILICONE HOT PADS & TRIVETS These colorful trivets and pads are great—with heat resistance from 500 to 625 degrees—for their nonskid, no-slip properties and their ability to keep a pan of eagerly anticipated cinnamon rolls, for example, securely on the counter. The flexible varieties also multitask as hot pads and trivets.

Parmesan Pastry Spirals

Don't tell anyone how easy these are to make. Just accept the oohs, aahs, and yums when you serve them alongside fruit, with a salad, or as a crispy complement to simple baked chicken.

EASY

PREP
10 MINUTES
FREEZE
30 MINUTES
BAKE
12 MINUTES
OVEN
350°F
MAKES
ABOUT 24 SPIRALS

½   **of a 17.3-ounce package frozen puff pastry (1 sheet), thawed**
1   **tablespoon milk**
⅓   **cup grated Parmesan cheese**

STEP 1 On a lightly floured surface, roll puff pastry sheet into a 14x10-inch rectangle. Brush pastry with some of the milk; sprinkle with Parmesan cheese. Starting at a short side, loosely roll up into a spiral, stopping at center; repeat, starting at other short side. (Roll-ups should meet in center. Do not coil tightly.) Wrap in plastic wrap; quick-chill in the freezer for 30 minutes.

STEP 2 Preheat oven to 350°F. Line 2 baking sheets with parchment paper; set aside. Unwrap roll and place on a cutting board. Brush with remaining milk. Cut pastry roll crosswise into ³/₈-inch slices. Place slices on the prepared baking sheets, reshaping as necessary.

STEP 3 Bake in the preheated oven for 12 to 14 minutes or until golden and crisp. Transfer to a wire rack; cool slightly. Serve warm.

MAKE-AHEAD DIRECTIONS: Prepare as directed in Step 1, except freeze for up to 8 hours. Unwrap, cut, and bake as directed in Steps 2 and 3.

PER SPIRAL: 50 cal., 4 g total fat (0 g sat. fat), 1 mg chol., 59 mg sodium, 4 g carbo., 0 g fiber, 1 g pro.
EXCHANGES: 1 Fat

OFF THE SHELF TIP Check the freezer case for puff pastry. Choose shells or sheets, then store at home in the freezer. You can thaw just the sheets or shells that you need.

Ricotta Puffs

PREP
30 MINUTES

BAKE
20 MINUTES

COOL
5 MINUTES

OVEN
400°F

MAKES
18 PUFFS

RECIPE PICTURED ON PAGE 136.

1   **17.3-ounce package frozen puff pastry (2 sheets), thawed**
½   **cup ricotta cheese**
½   **cup chopped roasted red sweet peppers**
3   **tablespoons grated Romano or Parmesan cheese**
1   **tablespoon snipped fresh parsley**
1   **teaspoon dried oregano, crushed**
½   **teaspoon black pepper**
     Milk
     Grated Romano cheese

STEP 1   Preheat oven to 400°F. On a lightly floured surface, unfold the pastry sheets. Using a sharp knife, cut each pastry sheet into nine 3-inch squares.

STEP 2   For filling, in a medium bowl stir together ricotta cheese, roasted peppers, the 3 tablespoons Romano cheese, the parsley, oregano, and black pepper.

STEP 3   Moisten the edges of each pastry square with milk. Spoon about 2 teaspoons filling onto one-half of each pastry square. Fold the other half of the pastry over the filling, forming a rectangle. Seal edges by pressing with the tines of a fork. With a sharp knife, cut slits in the top of each pastry bundle. Brush with milk; sprinkle with additional Romano cheese. Arrange pastry bundles on an ungreased baking sheet.

STEP 4   Bake in the preheated oven about 20 minutes or until golden brown.

Transfer to a wire rack; cool slightly before serving.

PER PUFF: 137 cal., 10 g total fat (1 g sat. fat), 3 mg chol., 137 mg sodium, 10 g carbo., 0 g fiber, 3 g pro. **EXCHANGES:** ½ Starch, 2 Fat

OFF THE SHELF TIP Mild and sweet, roasted red sweet pepeprs are a real time-saver. They can be found in jars in the grocery aisle.

Cheese Puffs

PREP
30 MINUTES

BAKE
12 MINUTES

OVEN
400°F

MAKES
32 PUFFS

1   3-ounce package cream cheese, softened
1   egg yolk
1   teaspoon lemon juice
1   teaspoon snipped fresh chives
     Dash black pepper
½   cup shredded white cheddar cheese (2 ounces)
2   slices bacon, crisp-cooked, drained, and crumbled
1   17.3-ounce package frozen puff pastry (2 sheets), thawed
     Milk

STEP 1   Preheat oven to 400°F. For filling, in a small mixing bowl combine cream cheese, egg yolk, lemon juice, chives, and pepper; beat with an electric mixer on medium speed until nearly smooth. Stir in cheddar cheese and bacon.

STEP 2   On a lightly floured surface, roll 1 of the pastry sheets to a 12-inch square. Cut into sixteen 3-inch squares. Top each square with about 1 teaspoon of the filling. Brush edges of each square with milk. Fold each square in half diagonally. Seal edges by pressing with tines of a fork or fingers. Place on an ungreased baking sheet. Repeat with remaining pastry sheet and filling.

STEP 3   Bake in the preheated oven for 12 to 15 minutes or until golden.

MAKE-AHEAD DIRECTIONS: Prepare as directed through Step 2. Cover and refrigerate for up to 4 hours. Bake as directed in Step 3.

PER PUFF: 87 cal., 7 g total fat (1 g sat. fat), 12 mg chol., 83 mg sodium, 6 g carbo., 0 g fiber, 1 g pro. **EXCHANGES:** 2 Fat

OFF THE SHELF TIP   Rich, creamy cream cheese is available in fat-free, low-fat, and regular—plus an assortment of flavors.

Caraway-Cheese Crisps

EASY **FAST**

PREP
10 MINUTES

BAKE
10 MINUTES

OVEN
400°F

MAKES
18 CRISPS

½ of a 17.3-ounce package frozen puff pastry (1 sheet), thawed
1 egg, slightly beaten
1 tablespoon water
½ cup shredded Swiss cheese (2 ounces)
2 teaspoons caraway seeds, crushed

STEP 1 Preheat oven to 400°F. On a lightly floured surface, unfold pastry sheet. In a small bowl stir together egg and water. Brush pastry with egg mixture. Sprinkle with Swiss cheese and caraway seeds. Cut into desired shapes, making 18 pieces total. Place on a large ungreased baking sheet.

STEP 2 Bake in the preheated oven for 10 to 12 minutes or until puffed and golden. Cool.

PER CRISP: 76 cal., 5 g total fat (1 g sat. fat), 15 mg chol., 63 mg sodium, 5 g carbo., 2 g pro. **EXCHANGES:** 1½ Fat

OFF THE SHELF TIP Save time and mess by stocking up on a variety of ready-to-use shredded cheeses.

Shrimp & Cheese Crisps

PREP
25 MINUTES

BAKE
20 MINUTES

COOL
30 MINUTES

OVEN
375°F

MAKES
20 CRISPS

RECIPE PICTURED ON PAGE **136.**

½	of a 17.3-ounce package frozen puff pastry (1 sheet), thawed
1	recipe Tomato Tapenade
½	cup frozen peeled, cooked salad shrimp, thawed and well drained (3 ounces)
⅔	cup finely shredded pizza cheese blend
	Grape tomatoes, halved (optional)
	Cooked salad shrimp (optional)

STEP 1 Preheat oven to 375°F. On a lightly floured surface, unfold pastry sheet. Using a 2-inch fluted or round cutter, cut pastry into circles. Do not reroll pastry scraps. Place pastry rounds on an ungreased baking sheet.

STEP 2 Bake in the preheated oven about 15 minutes or until puffed and light brown. Transfer to a wire rack and let cool.

STEP 3 Split pastry rounds. Evenly spread ½ teaspoon of the Tomato Tapenade over the bottom half of each round. Top with some of the shrimp. Sprinkle with cheese. Replace tops. Return filled pastries to baking sheet. Bake about 5 minutes more or just until cheese is melted. Serve warm. If desired, garnish each serving with a grape tomato half and a shrimp.

PER CRISP: 98 cal., 7 g total fat (1 g sat. fat), 12 mg chol., 136 mg sodium, 6 g carbo., 0 g fiber, 3 g pro.
EXCHANGES: ½ Starch, 1 Fat

TOMATO TAPENADE: Finely chop ½ of a 7-ounce jar of oil-packed dried tomatoes, drained. In a small bowl combine the chopped tomatoes; 2 tablespoons oil from the tomatoes; 2 tablespoons drained capers, finely chopped; 1 teaspoon bottled minced garlic (2 cloves); 1 teaspoon anchovy paste; and ½ teaspoon black pepper. Mix well. Makes ⅓ cup.

OFF THE SHELF TIP You'll find shredded pizza cheese blends of Italian-style cheeses such as Parmesan, Asiago, mozzarella, Romano, and provolone. Simply sprinkle and bake.

Easy Artichoke Roll

Crescent dough rolls up with savory chopped artichokes and sweet pepper and a dusting of Parmesan for a melt-in-your-mouth appetizer that's full of flavor.

PREP
25 MINUTES
BAKE
30 MINUTES
COOL
5 MINUTES
OVEN
350°F
MAKES
16 SERVINGS

Nonstick cooking spray

1   **8-ounce package (8) refrigerated crescent rolls**

½   **cup finely shredded Parmesan cheese (2 ounces)**

¼   **cup mayonnaise or light mayonnaise dressing**

1   **6- to 6.5-ounce jar marinated artichoke hearts, drained and finely chopped**

½   **cup chopped red or green sweet pepper**

OFF THE SHELF TIP Crescent rolls are a flaky dough, ready to be shaped into rolls or used as the base of an appetizer, dessert, or main dish.

STEP 1   Preheat oven to 350°F. Coat a baking sheet with nonstick cooking spray; set aside.

STEP 2   On a lightly floured surface, unroll the crescent roll dough; seal perforations between rolls. With a lightly floured rolling pin, roll crescent roll dough into a 15x7½-inch rectangle. In a medium bowl stir together the Parmesan cheese and mayonnaise. Stir in the artichoke hearts. Spread mixture on dough, leaving ½ inch on each side. Sprinkle with sweet pepper. Roll up dough, beginning at one long edge. Moisten and pinch edges to seal. Place roll on the prepared baking sheet.

STEP 3   Bake in the preheated oven about 30 minutes or until golden brown. Let cool for a few minutes before slicing.

PER SERVING: 103 cal., 7 g total fat (2 g sat. fat), 5 mg chol., 200 mg sodium, 7 g carbo., 0 g fiber, 2 g pro.
EXCHANGES: ½ Starch, 1½ Fat

Focaccia Breadsticks

EASY **FAST**

PREP
15 MINUTES
BAKE
12 MINUTES
OVEN
350°F
MAKES
10 BREADSTICKS

¼   cup oil-packed dried tomatoes
¼   cup grated Romano or
        Parmesan cheese
2   teaspoons water
1½   teaspoons snipped fresh rosemary or
        ½ teaspoon dried rosemary, crushed
⅛   teaspoon cracked black pepper
1   10- to 13.8-ounce package
        refrigerated pizza dough

STEP 1   Preheat oven to 350°F. Lightly grease a baking sheet; set aside.

STEP 2   Drain dried tomatoes, reserving oil; finely snip tomatoes. In a small bowl combine tomatoes, 2 teaspoons of the reserved oil, the Romano cheese, water, rosemary, and pepper. Set aside.

STEP 3   On a lightly floured surface, unroll the pizza dough. Roll the dough into a 10x8-inch rectangle. Spread the tomato mixture crosswise over half of the dough. Fold plain half of dough over filling; press lightly to seal edges. Cut the folded dough lengthwise into ten ½-inch strips. Fold each strip in half and twist two or three times. Place 1 inch apart on a prepared baking sheet.

STEP 4   Bake in the preheated oven for 12 to 15 minutes or until golden brown. Cool on a wire rack.

PER BREADSTICK: 113 cal., 3 g total fat (1 g sat. fat), 3 mg chol., 263 mg sodium, 18 g carbo., 1 g fiber, 5 g pro.
EXCHANGES: 1 Starch, ½ Fat

OFF THE SHELF TIP Refrigerated pizza dough is commonly found in a tube with other refrigerated bread products. These unbaked crusts are ready to unroll, top, and bake for a perfect pizza.

Croque Monsieur Triangles

PREP
20 MINUTES
BAKE
12 MINUTES PER BATCH
COOL
5 MINUTES
OVEN
400°F
MAKES
18 APPETIZERS

1   **17.3-ounce package frozen puff pastry (2 sheets), thawed**
3   **tablespoons Dijon-style mustard**
4   **ounces shaved deli ham***
¾   **cup shredded Gruyère or Swiss cheese (3 ounces)**
1   **egg**
1   **tablespoon water**

STEP 1   Preheat oven to 400°F. Grease 2 large baking sheets or line with parchment paper; set aside. On a lightly floured surface, unfold pastry sheets. Roll each sheet into a 12-inch square. Cut each square into nine 4-inch squares.

STEP 2   Spoon ½ teaspoon mustard onto center of each square; spread slightly. Place a small pile of ham on mustard. Top evenly with Gruyère cheese.

STEP 3   In a small bowl beat together egg and water with a fork. Brush edges of squares with egg mixture. Fold one corner of each square over filling to opposite corner, forming a triangle. Press edges with the tines of a fork to seal. Place bundles on prepared baking sheets. Prick tops with a fork. Brush with egg mixture.

STEP 4   Bake, one baking sheet at a time, in the preheated oven about 12 minutes or until golden. Cool slightly before serving.

***NOTE:** Select a distinctly flavored ham such as Virginia ham or country ham.

MAKE-AHEAD DIRECTIONS: Cover filled triangles on each baking sheet with plastic wrap; refrigerate up to 2 hours. Bake as directed in Step 4.

PER APPETIZER: 157 cal., 11 g total fat (1 g sat. fat), 21 mg chol., 266 mg sodium, 11 g carbo., 0 g fiber, 4 g pro.
EXCHANGES: 1 Starch, 2 Fat

OFF THE SHELF TIP Save time and mess by stocking up on a variety of ready-to-use shredded cheeses.

Barbecue Beef Cups

Refrigerated biscuits in muffin cups cradle mounds of spiced ground beef and cheese for a hot, hearty snack.

PREP
15 MINUTES
BAKE
12 MINUTES
OVEN
400°F
MAKES
10 APPETIZERS

8	ounces ground beef
1/3	cup bottled barbecue sauce
1	tablespoon packed brown sugar
2	teaspoons dried minced onion
1	10- to 12-ounce package (10) refrigerated biscuits
1/2	cup shredded cheddar cheese (2 ounces)

OFF THE SHELF TIP Choose your favorite barbecue sauce from the condiment section—mild, sassy, or devilishly hot.

STEP 1 In a medium skillet cook ground beef over medium heat until brown. Drain off fat. Stir in barbecue sauce, brown sugar, and minced onion. Set aside.

STEP 2 Preheat oven to 400°F. Press a biscuit into the bottom and up the side of a 2 1/2-inch muffin cup; repeat with remaining biscuits to make a total of 10 biscuit-lined cups. Spoon ground beef mixture into biscuit-lined cups. Sprinkle with cheddar cheese.

STEP 3 Bake in the preheated oven about 12 minutes or until biscuit edges are golden brown. Loosen and carefully remove from muffin cups. Serve warm.

PER APPETIZER: 127 cal., 5 g total fat (2 g sat. fat), 20 mg chol., 295 mg sodium, 12 g carbo., 0 g fiber, 7 g pro.
EXCHANGES: 1 Starch, 1/2 High-Fat Meat

Mexicitos

PREP
50 MINUTES

BAKE
10 MINUTES PER BATCH

OVEN
350°F

RECIPE PICTURED
ON PAGE 142.

FOR **40** TURNOVERS

1¼	pounds lean ground beef
1	15-ounce can tomato sauce
2	teaspoons chili powder
2	teaspoons dried oregano, crushed
1	teaspoon garlic powder
1	tablespoon snipped fresh cilantro
2	10- to 12-ounce packages (20 total) refrigerated buttermilk biscuits
	Milk
	Salsa (optional)

FOR **20** TURNOVERS

12	ounces lean ground beef
1	8-ounce can tomato sauce
1	teaspoon chili powder
1	teaspoon dried oregano, crushed
½	teaspoon garlic powder
1½	teaspoons snipped fresh cilantro
1	10- to 12-ounce package (10) refrigerated buttermilk biscuits
	Milk
	Salsa (optional)

STEP 1 For filling, in a large skillet cook ground beef until brown; drain off fat. Stir in tomato sauce, chili powder, oregano, and garlic powder. Bring to boiling; reduce heat. Simmer, uncovered, for 5 minutes. Remove from heat. Stir in cilantro.

STEP 2 Preheat oven to 350°F. Grease a large baking sheet; set aside. Separate biscuits; cut each biscuit in half horizontally. On a lightly floured surface, roll each piece of biscuit dough into a 4-inch circle. Place about 1 tablespoon filling onto half of each circle. Fold opposite side of circle up and over filling. Brush edges with a little milk; seal edges with a fork. Place filled turnovers 1 inch apart on the prepared baking sheet; brush with milk.

STEP 3 Bake in the preheated oven for 10 to 12 minutes or until golden brown. Immediately remove from baking sheet. Cool slightly on a wire rack. Serve warm. If desired, serve with salsa for dipping.

MAKE-AHEAD DIRECTIONS: Prepare as directed. Cool turnovers completely on wire racks. Place in an airtight freezer container; freeze for up to 3 months. To reheat, transfer frozen turnovers to an ungreased cookie sheet. Bake, uncovered, in a 350° oven for 10 to 12 minutes or until heated through.

TIP: If making the 40-turnover recipe, remove only one package of biscuits from the refrigerator at a time.

PER TURNOVER: 60 cal., 2 g total fat (1 g sat. fat), 9 mg chol., 175 mg sodium, 7 g carbo., 0 g fiber, 4 g pro.
EXCHANGES: ½ Starch, ½ Fat

OFF THE SHELF TIP Refrigerated biscuits are available in a variety of sizes and shapes. They make a tasty base for an appetizer or topper for a casserole.

Mexican Snack Mix

Toss square cereal, nuts, and pretzels with hot pepper sauce and Mexican seasonings for fiesta-style party mix.

EASY

PREP
10 MINUTES
BAKE
30 MINUTES
COOL
15 MINUTES
OVEN
300°F
MAKES
10 CUPS (20 SERVINGS)

6   cups bite-size corn or rice square cereal
2   cups pretzel knots
2   cups sesame and cheese snack sticks
1   cup hot and spicy peanuts or salted peanuts
½   cup butter or margarine
1   tablespoon bottled hot pepper sauce (optional)
2   teaspoons Mexican seasoning

STEP 1   Preheat oven to 300°F. In a large roasting pan combine cereal, pretzels, snack sticks, and peanuts; set aside.

STEP 2   In a small saucepan combine butter, hot pepper sauce (if desired), and Mexican seasoning. Heat and stir over low heat until butter is melted. Drizzle butter mixture over cereal mixture, tossing to coat.

STEP 3   Bake, uncovered, in the preheated oven for 30 minutes, stirring twice. Spread mixture out onto a large piece of foil and let cool. Store mixture in an airtight container for up to 1 week.

PER ½ CUP: 171 cal., 10 g total fat (4 g sat. fat), 13 mg chol., 316 mg sodium, 17 g carbo., 1 g fiber, 4 g pro.
EXCHANGES: 1 Starch, 2 Fat

OFF THE SHELF TIP You'll find all sorts of salted and unsalted nuts in the baking aisle (look for pieces and already-chopped) or chips section.

Sweet & Spicy Spanish Mix

Shredded citrus peel, cinnamon, and coriander give this snack mix a Latin flair. Make extra to send home with friends.

PREP
25 MINUTES
BAKE
30 MINUTES
OVEN
300°F
MAKES
10 CUPS (20 SERVINGS)

RECIPE PICTURED
ON PAGE **136.**

½ cup butter
2 tablespoons packed brown sugar
1 teaspoon finely shredded lime or orange peel
1 teaspoon salt
¾ teaspoon ground coriander
½ teaspoon ground cinnamon
½ teaspoon crushed red pepper
4 cups crispy corn and rice cereal
3 cups bite-size shredded wheat biscuits
1 cup broken garlic-flavor crisp breadsticks
1 cup miniature pretzel twists
1 cup pecan halves

OFF THE SHELF TIP Crisp and salty miniature pretzel twists are the perfect size for a snack mix. You can snack on the leftovers!

STEP 1 Preheat oven to 300°F. In a small saucepan combine butter, brown sugar, lime peel, salt, coriander, cinnamon, and crushed red pepper. Heat and stir over low heat until butter melts and sugar is dissolved. Remove from heat.

STEP 2 In a large roasting pan, combine cereals, breadsticks, pretzels, and nuts. Drizzle butter mixture over cereal mixture; toss to coat.

STEP 3 Bake in the preheated oven for 30 minutes, stirring once. Spread mixture out onto a large piece of foil and let cool. Store in an airtight container for up to 1 week.

PER ½ CUP: 156 cal., 9 g total fat (3 g sat. fat), 13 mg chol., 283 mg sodium, 18 g carbo., 2 g fiber, 2 g pro.
EXCHANGES: 1 Starch, 2 Fat

Ham & Cheese
Crescent Snacks

A little mustard adds tang to this warm, pizza-sandwich, ideal for after-the-game gatherings.

FAST

PREP
15 MINUTES

BAKE
18 MINUTES

OVEN
375°F

MAKES
12 SERVINGS

1   8-ounce package (8) refrigerated crescent rolls
2   tablespoons butter or margarine, softened
1   to 2 teaspoons yellow mustard
1   cup cubed cooked ham (5 ounces)
⅓   cup chopped onion (1 small)
⅓   cup chopped green sweet pepper
1   cup shredded cheddar or American cheese (4 ounces)

STEP 1   Preheat oven to 375°F. Unroll crescent roll dough onto an ungreased baking sheet. Pat or roll dough to a 13x9-inch rectangle. Crimp edges of the dough.

STEP 2   In a small bowl combine butter and mustard; stir until smooth. Spread evenly over dough. Top with ham, onion, and sweet pepper. Sprinkle with cheddar cheese.

STEP 3   Bake in the preheated oven for 18 to 20 minutes or until edges are golden and cheese is melted. Serve warm.

MAKE-AHEAD DIRECTIONS: Prepare as directed through Step 2. Cover and refrigerate for up to 2 hours. Bake as directed in Step 3.

PER SERVING: 146 cal., 10 g total fat (4 g sat. fat), 22 mg chol., 386 mg sodium, 8 g carbo., 0 g fiber, 6 g pro.
EXCHANGES: ½ Starch, ½ Medium-Fat Meat, 1½ Fat

OFF THE SHELF TIP   Crescent rolls are a flaky dough, ready to be shaped into rolls or used as the base of an appetizer, dessert, or main dish.

Breads

Lemon-Basil Pull-Aparts

Lemon peel brightens the overall taste of most any dish, even if its flavor is subtle. In this bread, lemon's effect is magical.

EASY

PREP
15 MINUTES

BAKE
30 MINUTES

OVEN
350°F

MAKES
6 TO 8 SERVINGS

2   tablespoons butter, melted
1   16.3-ounce package (8) refrigerated
      large flaky biscuits
½   cup finely shredded Parmesan cheese
      (2 ounces)
1   teaspoon finely shredded lemon peel
1   teaspoon dried basil, crushed
¼   teaspoon onion powder
¼   teaspoon black pepper

STEP 1   Preheat oven to 350°F. Place melted butter in a 9x5x3-inch loaf pan; tilt to coat bottom of pan.

STEP 2   Meanwhile, separate biscuits; snip each into 4 pieces. In a large plastic bag combine Parmesan cheese, lemon peel, basil, onion powder, and pepper. Add biscuit pieces, 3 or 4 at a time, to cheese mixture; shake to coat each piece. Place coated pieces in prepared loaf pan. Sprinkle with any remaining cheese mixture.

STEP 3   Bake in the preheated oven for 30 minutes. Loosen edges; transfer to a serving plate. Cool slightly; serve warm.

PER SERVING: 307 cal., 17 g total fat (6 g sat. fat), 16 mg chol., 860 mg sodium, 31 g carbo., 1 g fiber, 8 g pro.
EXCHANGES: 2 Starch, ½ Lean Meat, 2½ Fat

OFF THE SHELF TIP   Refrigerated biscuits are available in a variety of sizes and shapes. They make a tasty base for an appetizer or topper for a casserole.

GOTTA-HAVE BAKEWARE

COOKIE SHEETS. Having at least four of the same size and material make it easy to rotate batches through the oven while others cool. Use cookie sheets for free-formed pizza, focaccia, and calzone baking, too.

CAKE PANS. Start with a pair of 9-inch pans. If your needs warrant, add sets of 8- or 10-inchers, or straight-sided square pans. You may also want a fluted bundt-style pan, and an angel food tube-cake pan. Springform cheesecake pans come in several sizes; 9-inch diameter is the most common variety.

PIE PLATES. Put two or three 9-inch pans in your cupboard, and they won't gather dust. Use them for pies, of course, but also for quiche, cornbread, and small batch brownies and bars as a stand-in for a 9-inch square pan.

TART PANS. The most useful tart pans have a bottom that lifts out of the scallop-edge side.

Savory Skillet Bread

Baking shaped dough in a skillet of hot olive oil gives this bread—loaded with dried tomato bits, onions, and herbs—a delicious soft crust.

PREP
20 MINUTES
COOK
20 MINUTES
OVEN
375°F
MAKES
8 SERVINGS

2   tablespoons olive oil
½   to ¾ cup coarsely chopped dried
        tomatoes (not oil-packed)
3   tablespoons chopped onion
3   tablespoons snipped fresh basil
2   tablespoons grated Parmesan cheese
¼   teaspoon garlic powder
¼   teaspoon crushed red pepper
1   16-ounce loaf frozen bread dough,
        thawed
        Parmesan cheese (optional)

OFF THE SHELF TIP Dried tomatoes come plain or packed in oil. Find them in the condiment section.

STEP 1 Preheat oven to 375°F. In a 10-inch cast-iron skillet heat 1 tablespoon of the oil over medium-low heat.

STEP 2 Meanwhile, in a small bowl combine the tomatoes, onion, basil, 2 tablespoons Parmesan cheese, garlic powder, and crushed red pepper. On a lightly floured surface, knead the tomato mixture into the bread dough until combined. Roll or pat dough into a 9-inch circle.

STEP 3 Remove skillet from heat. Place dough circle in the hot olive oil. Brush lightly with the remaining tablespoon olive oil.

STEP 4 Bake in the preheated oven about 20 minutes or until golden brown. If desired, sprinkle with additional Parmesan cheese. Serve warm.

PER SERVING: 191 cal., 6 g total fat (1 g sat. fat), 1 mg chol., 357 mg sodium, 29 g carbo., 1 g fiber, 4 g pro.
EXCHANGES: 2 Starch, 1 Fat

Broccoli Corn Bread

Fold chopped broccoli, onion, and shredded cheddar into corn muffin mix for a filled bread that makes a fine complement to roast beef or chicken.

EASY

PREP
10 MINUTES
BAKE
30 MINUTES
OVEN
350°F
MAKES
16 SERVINGS

RECIPE PICTURED
ON PAGE **142.**

1	8.5-ounce package corn muffin mix
3	eggs
1	8-ounce package shredded cheddar cheese (2 cups)
1	10-ounce package frozen chopped broccoli, thawed and well drained
½	cup chopped onion (1 medium)

STEP 1 Preheat oven to 350°F. Grease a 9x9x2-inch baking pan; set aside.

STEP 2 In a large bowl combine the corn muffin mix and eggs. Stir in cheddar cheese, broccoli, and onion. Spoon batter into the prepared pan, spreading evenly.

STEP 3 Bake in the preheated oven about 30 minutes or until a wooden toothpick inserted near the center comes out clean. Serve warm.

PER SERVING: 138 cal., 7 g total fat (3 g sat. fat), 55 mg chol., 209 mg sodium, 12 g carbo., 1 g fiber, 6 g pro.
EXCHANGES: 1 Starch, ½ High-Fat Meat

OFF THE SHELF TIP Find corn muffin mix, a versatile quick-cooking mix, on the baking aisle shelves.

GOTTA-HAVE BAKEWARE Though you'll find bakeware in several materials and composites, aluminum is terrific for its strong, rust-free service and even browning. Purchase the pebbled surface aluminum variety, and you'll have easy release, too.

SQUARE PANS. Many small-batch bar recipes call for a 9-inch square.

LOAF PANS. Get a set of two 9x3-inch pans; most bread recipes produce two loaves.

Corn Bread with *Dried Tomatoes*

⅓ cup bulgur or cracked wheat
¼ cup dried tomato bits*
1½ cups boiling water
¼ cup toasted wheat germ
1 8.5-ounce package corn muffin mix
¼ cup finely shredded Parmesan cheese (1 ounce)

OFF THE SHELF TIP Save time and mess by stocking up on a variety of ready-to-use shredded cheeses.

PREP
20 MINUTES
STAND
5 MINUTES
BAKE
20 MINUTES
OVEN
350°F
MAKES
9 SERVINGS

STEP 1 Preheat oven to 350°F. In a medium bowl combine bulgur and tomato bits. Pour boiling water over the bulgur mixture. Let stand for 5 minutes. Drain well.

STEP 2 Grease an 8x8x2-inch baking pan; sprinkle bottom of pan with half of the wheat germ.

STEP 3 Prepare corn muffin mix according to package directions for corn bread. Stir drained bulgur mixture and Parmesan cheese into the batter. Spoon batter into the prepared pan, spreading evenly. Sprinkle with remaining wheat germ.

STEP 4 Bake in the preheated oven for 20 to 25 minutes or until a wooden toothpick inserted in center comes out clean. Serve warm.

*NOTE: If you can't purchase dried tomato bits, finely snip dried tomatoes.

PER SERVING: 151 cal., 4 g total fat (1 g sat. fat), 26 mg chol., 269 mg sodium, 24 g carbo., 1 g fiber, 4 g pro.
EXCHANGES: 1½ Starch, ½ Fat

Zucchini Spoon Bread

Savory and soft enough that you'll need to eat it with a spoon, this zippy bread makes an unexpected side dish.

PREP
20 MINUTES

BAKE
35 MINUTES

OVEN
350°F

MAKES
8 TO 10 SERVINGS

3	cups shredded zucchini
1	8.5-ounce package corn muffin mix
1⅓	cups shredded Italian-style or Mexican-style cheese blend
4	eggs
½	cup cooking oil
½	cup finely chopped onion (1 medium)
¼	cup buttermilk
½	teaspoon dried Italian seasoning, crushed
	Dash bottled hot pepper sauce
⅔	cup chopped almonds

STEP 1 Preheat oven to 350°F. Grease a 2- to 2½-quart casserole; set aside.

STEP 2 In a large bowl combine zucchini, muffin mix, 1 cup of the cheese, the eggs, oil, onion, buttermilk, Italian seasoning, and hot pepper sauce. Spoon into prepared casserole. Sprinkle with almonds and the remaining ⅓ cup cheese.

STEP 3 Bake, uncovered, in the preheated oven about 35 minutes or until a knife inserted near the center comes out clean. To serve, spoon warm mixture onto plates.

PER SERVING: 416 cal., 30 g total fat (6 g sat. fat), 120 mg chol., 382 mg sodium, 26 g carbo., 2 g fiber, 13 g pro.
EXCHANGES: ½ Vegetable, 1½ Starch, 1 Medium-Fat Meat, 4½ Fat

OFF THE SHELF TIP Find corn muffin mix, a versatile quick-cooking mix, on the baking aisle shelves.

Charley Bread

An excellent choice to take to potlucks and gatherings, this corn bread is exceptionally moist, thanks to the inclusion of sour cream and creamed corn.

1	cup yellow cornmeal
1	cup all-purpose flour
2	tablespoons sugar
1	tablespoon baking powder
¾	teaspoon salt
1	8.25- to 8.5-ounce can cream-style corn
1	8-ounce carton dairy sour cream
½	cup cooking oil
2	eggs, slightly beaten
	Honey butter (optional)

OFF THE SHELF TIP Found in the baking aisle, cornmeal and/or polenta mix is often packaged in a tall cardboard cylinder and is the star ingredient in corn bread and polenta.

EASY

PREP
15 MINUTES
BAKE
25 MINUTES
OVEN
425°F
MAKES
12 SERVINGS

STEP 1 Preheat oven to 425°F. Grease the bottom and ½ inch up the sides of a 9x9x2-inch baking pan; set aside.

STEP 2 In a medium bowl stir together the cornmeal, flour, sugar, baking powder, and salt. Make a well in the center of the cornmeal mixture; set aside. In another bowl stir together the corn, sour cream, oil, and eggs. Add corn mixture all at once to the flour mixture. Stir just until moistened. Spoon batter into the prepared pan, spreading evenly.

STEP 3 Bake in the preheated oven about 25 minutes or until a wooden toothpick inserted near the center comes out clean. Cut into squares and serve warm. If desired, serve with honey butter.

PER SERVING: 232 cal., 14 g total fat (4 g sat. fat), 44 mg chol., 283 mg sodium, 23 g carbo., 1 g fiber, 4 g pro.
EXCHANGES: 1½ Starch, 2½ Fat

Orange Biscuit Ring

PREP
20 MINUTES
BAKE
35 MINUTES
COOL
30 MINUTES
OVEN
350°F
MAKES
10 SERVINGS

1¼   **cups sugar**
1   **tablespoon finely shredded**
     orange peel
⅓   **cup orange juice**
¼   **cup butter, melted**
2   **12-ounce packages (20 biscuits total)**
     refrigerated biscuits

STEP 1   Preheat oven to 350°F. Grease a 10-inch fluted tube pan; set aside.

STEP 2   In a small bowl combine sugar and orange peel, breaking up any orange peel clumps with a fork. In another small bowl combine orange juice and melted butter.

STEP 3   Separate biscuits. Dip each biscuit into the orange juice mixture, then roll in the sugar mixture to coat. Place biscuits on edge in the prepared pan. Pour any remaining orange juice mixture over biscuits.

STEP 4   Bake in the preheated oven for 35 to 40 minutes or until top is golden brown. Cool in pan on a wire rack for 1 minute. Invert pan onto a serving platter with slightly raised sides; remove pan. Cool for 30 to 45 minutes. Serve warm.

PER SERVING: 240 cal., 6 g total fat 13 mg chol., 410 mg sodium, 44 g carbo., 0 g fiber, 3 g pro.
EXCHANGES: 1½ Starch, 1½ Other Carbo., 1 Fat

OFF THE SHELF TIP Sold in cans in the refrigerator section, these biscuits are tasty and ready to pop into the oven.

Step-Saving Sweet Potato *Bread*

Pick up a fruit-based quick bread mix such as banana or cranberry, then stir in spices and canned sweet potatoes for a savory-sweet and nutrient-rich snack bread.

EASY

PREP
15 MINUTES

BAKE
55 MINUTES FOR
LARGE LOAF;
30 MINUTES FOR
SMALL LOAVES

COOL
10 MINUTES

OVEN
350°F

MAKES
1 LARGE LOAF OR
4 SMALL LOAVES
(16 SERVINGS)

1	14- to 16-ounce package banana, cranberry, or cranberry-orange quick bread mix
½	teaspoon ground cinnamon
⅛	teaspoon ground nutmeg
⅔	cup water
½	cup mashed, drained canned sweet potatoes
2	eggs, slightly beaten
2	tablespoons cooking oil
1	recipe Orange Icing

STEP 1   Preheat oven to 350°F. Grease and lightly flour bottom(s) and 1 inch up the side(s) of one 8x4x2-inch loaf pan or four 4½x2½x1½-inch loaf pans; set aside.

STEP 2   In a large bowl stir together quick bread mix, cinnamon, and nutmeg. Add the water, sweet potatoes, eggs, and oil. Stir just until moistened. Pour batter into the prepared pan(s), dividing evenly.

STEP 3   Bake in the preheated oven for 55 to 60 minutes for large loaf, 30 to 35 minutes for small loaves, or until a wooden toothpick inserted near center(s) comes out clean.

STEP 4   Cool in the pan(s) on wire rack(s) for 10 minutes. Remove from pan(s); cool completely on wire rack. If desired, for easier slicing wrap and store loaves overnight in a cool, dry place.

STEP 5   Before serving, drizzle loaves with Orange Icing.

ORANGE ICING: In a small bowl stir together ½ cup powdered sugar and enough orange juice to make icing of drizzling consistency (1 to 2 teaspoons).

PER SLICE: 143 cal., 3 g total fat (0 g sat. fat), 27 mg chol., 157 mg sodium, 25 g carbo., 1 g fiber, 2 g pro. **EXCHANGES:** 1½ Other Carbo., ½ Fat

OFF THE SHELF TIP   Stocked alongside other canned vegetables, canned sweet potatoes are available year-round and sometimes labeled as yams.

Fruited Pumpkin Loaf

Dried apricots, cranberries, and apricot nectar take this pumpkin bread in a fresh direction. Bake it in a single loaf to enjoy over a weekend or bake 5 mini loaves to share with friends and neighbors.

PREP
20 MINUTES

BAKE
55 MINUTES FOR LARGE LOAF;
30 MINUTES FOR SMALL LOAVES

OVEN
350°F

MAKES
1 LARGE OR
3 SMALL LOAVES
(16 TO 18 SERVINGS)

2   eggs
2/3   cup water
1/2   cup apricot nectar
3   tablespoons cooking oil
1   14-ounce package pumpkin quick bread mix
1   cup chopped pecans, toasted
1/2   cup snipped dried apricots
1/2   cup dried cranberries
1   recipe Apricot Icing (optional)
       Snipped dried apricots (optional)

STEP 1 Preheat oven to 350°F. Grease the bottom and 1/2 inch up sides of an 8x4x2-inch loaf pan or three 5³/₄x3x2-inch loaf pans; set aside.

STEP 2 In a large bowl beat eggs with a whisk; whisk in the water, nectar, and oil. Using a wooden spoon, stir bread mix into egg mixture until combined. Stir in pecans, the 1/2 cup apricots, and the cranberries. Spoon batter into prepared pan(s), dividing evenly.

STEP 3 Bake in the preheated oven for 55 to 65 minutes for large loaf, 30 to 35 minutes for small loaves, or until a wooden toothpick inserted near the center(s) comes out clean.

STEP 4 Cool in pan(s) on wire rack(s) for 10 minutes. Remove from pan(s). Cool completely on wire rack(s). Wrap and store overnight before slicing.

STEP 5 If desired, pour Apricot Icing over bread and sprinkle with additional snipped apricots.

PER SERVING: 202 cal., 9 g total fat (1 g sat. fat), 26 mg chol., 153 mg sodium, 27 g carbo., 2 g fiber, 3 g pro.
EXCHANGES: 1 Starch, 1 Other Carbo., 1½ Fat

APRICOT ICING: In a small bowl stir together ³/₄ cup powdered sugar and enough apricot nectar (3 to 4 teaspoons) to reach drizzling consistency.

OFF THE SHELF TIP This baking aisle gem is easy to dress up. Quick bread mix is available in a variety of flavors—banana, cranberry, pumpkin, and more!

Berry Good Banana Bread

The only thing better than soft, moist banana bread is banana bread loaded with fresh blueberries and tart dried cranberries. If you're looking for something new to take to a 4th of July gathering, this might be it.

PREP
15 MINUTES

BAKE
45 MINUTES

STAND
OVERNIGHT

OVEN
350°F

MAKES
2 LOAVES
(20 SLICES)

1	package 2-layer-size white cake mix
1¾	cups mashed ripe bananas (4 to 5)
2	eggs
1½	teaspoons apple pie spice
1	cup fresh blueberries
¾	cup dried cranberries

STEP 1 Preheat oven to 350°F. Grease the bottom and ½ inch up the sides of two 8x4x2-inch loaf pans; set aside.

STEP 2 In a large bowl combine cake mix, bananas, eggs, and apple pie spice; stir until moistened. Using a wooden spoon, beat for 1 minute (batter will be lumpy). Fold in blueberries and cranberries. Spoon batter into prepared loaf pans, dividing evenly.

STEP 3 Bake in the preheated oven for 45 to 50 minutes or until a wooden toothpick inserted near the centers comes out clean. Cool in pans on wire racks for 10 minutes. Remove loaves from pans and cool completely on wire racks. Wrap and store overnight before slicing.

PER SLICE: 154 cal., 3 g total fat (1 g sat. fat), 21 mg chol., 182 mg sodium, 30 g carbo., 1 g fiber, 2 g pro.
EXCHANGES: ½ Fruit, 1½ Other Carbo., ½ Fat

OFF THE SHELF TIP Available in dozens of flavors and most commonly packaged in boxes, cake mixes are a handy alternative to the made-from-scratch method.

Banana-Cinnamon Streusel Loaf

PREP
25 MINUTES
BAKE
45 MINUTES
OVEN
375°F
MAKES
1 LOAF
(12 TO 14 SLICES)

⅓   **cup all-purpose flour**
⅓   **cup packed brown sugar**
½   **teaspoon ground cinnamon**
¼   **cup cold butter**
½   **cup chopped pecans, toasted**
1   **14-ounce package banana quick bread mix**

STEP 1 Preheat oven to 375°F. Generously grease bottom and 1 inch up sides of a 9x5x3-inch loaf pan; set aside. For streusel, in a medium bowl combine flour, brown sugar, and cinnamon. Using a pastry blender, cut in butter until crumbly. Stir in pecans; set aside.

STEP 2 Prepare banana quick bread mix according to package directions. Spoon half of the batter into prepared pan; sprinkle with half of the streusel. Add remaining batter. Sprinkle with remaining streusel.

STEP 3 Bake in the preheated oven for 45 to 50 minutes or until a wooden toothpick inserted near the center comes out clean. Cool in pan on a wire rack for 10 minutes. Remove from pan; cool completely on wire rack. Wrap and store overnight before slicing.

PER SLICE: 233 cal., 9 g total fat (3 g sat. fat), 11 mg chol., 234 mg sodium, 35 g carbo., 1 g fiber, 3 g pro.
EXCHANGES: 2 Other Carbo., 2 Fat

OFF THE SHELF TIP This baking aisle gem is easy to dress up. Quick bread mix is available in a variety of flavors—banana, cranberry, pumpkin, and more!

Caramelized Onion & Brie *Focaccia*

This flatbread topped with sweet onions and salty Brie also makes a savory serve-along. Slice it in thin wedges so all your guests can enjoy it.

PREP
35 MINUTES
RISE
25 MINUTES
BAKE
25 MINUTES
OVEN
400°F
MAKES
12 SERVINGS

1   **16-ounce package hot roll mix**
1   **cup warm water (120°F to 130°F)**
1   **egg**
2   **tablespoons butter, softened**
2   **tablespoons butter**
2   **cups thinly sliced onion (4 medium)**
2   **teaspoons sugar**
2   **tablespoons balsamic vinegar or cider vinegar**
¼   **cup sliced almonds**
8   **ounces Brie cheese (remove rind, if desired), thinly sliced**

STEP 1   In a large bowl combine the flour mixture and yeast from hot roll mix. Stir in the warm water, egg, and 2 tablespoons softened butter, stirring until dough pulls away from side of bowl. Turn dough out onto a floured surface. With floured hands, shape dough into a ball. Knead dough about 5 minutes or until smooth. (If necessary, sprinkle additional flour over surface to reduce stickiness.) Cover; let rest for 5 minutes.

STEP 2   Grease a 12-inch pizza pan or a large baking sheet. Place dough on pan. Press into a circle 12 inches in diameter. Cover loosely; let rise in a warm place until double in size (about 25 minutes). After 15 minutes, preheat oven to 400°F.

STEP 3   In a large skillet melt 2 table-spoons butter over medium-low heat. Add onion; cover and cook for 10 to 12 minutes or until onion is tender and slightly golden, stirring occasionally. Stir in sugar. Cook and stir, uncovered, for

1 minute. Add vinegar; cook, uncovered, for 5 minutes more, stirring occasionally. Remove from heat.

STEP 4   Uncover dough. With fingers or wooden spoon handle, make deep indentations in the dough 1 inch apart.

STEP 5   Bake in the preheated oven for 10 minutes. Spoon onion mixture over partially baked dough. Sprinkle with almonds. Arrange Brie pieces on top. Bake about 15 minutes more or until bottom crust, when carefully lifted, is evenly brown. Cool slightly. Cut into wedges. Serve warm.

PER SERVING: 274 cal., 12 g total fat (6 g sat. fat), 47 mg chol., 417 mg sodium, 30 g carbo., 1 g fiber, 9 g pro.
EXCHANGES: 1½ Starch, ½ Other Carbo., ½ High-Fat Meat, 1½ Fat

OFF THE SHELF TIP   Shelved with other bread mixes, hot roll mix in a handy box helps you bake a homemade favorite in no time.

Cheese Bread

Fans of cheddar and herbs will appreciate this filled bread that's baked in a fluted tube pan and crusted with sesame seeds.

PREP
25 MINUTES

RISE
1 HOUR

BAKE
35 MINUTES

COOL
1 HOUR

OVEN
375°F

MAKES
16 SERVINGS

RECIPE PICTURED
ON PAGE **143.**

2	tablespoons sesame seeds
½	cup sliced green onion (4)
1	tablespoon butter or margarine
1	cup shredded cheddar cheese (4 ounces)
1	egg, slightly beaten
¼	cup snipped fresh parsley
2	tablespoons fine dry bread crumbs
½	teaspoon dried dill
⅛	teaspoon salt
	Few drops bottled hot pepper sauce
2	16-ounce loaves frozen white bread dough, thawed

STEP 1   Grease a 10-inch fluted tube pan. Sprinkle sesame seeds into pan to cover bottom and halfway up the side; set pan aside.

STEP 2   For filling, in a small saucepan cook the green onion in hot butter over medium heat for 2 to 3 minutes or until tender. Transfer to a small bowl. Stir in the cheddar cheese, egg, parsley, bread crumbs, dill, salt, and bottled hot pepper sauce; set aside.

STEP 3   Knead together both portions of dough and shape all the dough into one large ball. Place on a lightly floured surface; flatten slightly. Roll dough into an 18x12-inch rectangle. (Let dough rest for 5 to 10 minutes if it is difficult to roll.) Spread the filling over the dough. Roll up in a spiral, starting from a long side. Seal seam; pinch ends together lightly to seal. Place roll, seam side up, in prepared pan. Cover and let rise in a warm place until nearly double (about 1 hour). After 50 minutes, preheat oven to 375°F.

STEP 4   Bake in the preheated oven about 35 minutes or until golden brown and bread sounds hollow when lightly tapped. Remove bread from pan and let cool about 1 hour on a wire rack. Serve warm.

PER SERVING: 183 cal., 4 g total fat (2 g sat. fat), 23 mg chol., 92 mg sodium, 25 g carbo., 0 g fiber, 6 g pro.
EXCHANGES: 2 Starch, ½ Fat

OFF THE SHELF TIP Found in the freezer section in loaves, this bread dough is ready to thaw, re-form (if desired), and bake.

Easy Apricot Bread

PREP
30 MINUTES
RISE
40 MINUTES
BAKE
20 MINUTES
OVEN
350°F

Nonstick cooking spray
1   16-ounce loaf frozen white or whole wheat bread dough, thawed
½   cup low-calorie apricot, strawberry, or raspberry spread
½   cup chopped apricots, peeled and chopped peaches, blueberries, or raspberries
1   recipe Powdered Sugar Icing

STEP 1 Lightly coat 2 baking sheets with nonstick cooking spray. On a lightly floured surface, divide dough in half. Roll each half into a 12x7-inch rectangle. Carefully transfer each rectangle of dough to a prepared baking sheet.

STEP 2 Cut up any large pieces of fruit in the fruit spread. For each loaf, spoon ¼ cup of the fruit spread down the center third of the dough rectangle to within 1 inch of the ends. Sprinkle ¼ cup of the fresh fruit over the spread. On the long sides, make 2-inch-long cuts from the edges toward the center at 1-inch intervals. Starting at one end, alternately fold opposite strips of dough, at an angle, across fruit filling. Slightly press the ends together in the center to seal. Cover and let rise in a warm place until nearly double in size (about 40 minutes). After 30 minutes, preheat oven to 350°F.

STEP 3 Bake in the preheated oven about 20 minutes or until golden. Remove loaves from baking sheets; cool slightly on wire racks. Drizzle with Powdered Sugar Icing. Serve warm. Makes 2 loaves.

POWDERED SUGAR ICING: In a small bowl stir together ½ cup powdered sugar, 1 teaspoon lemon juice, and 1 to 2 teaspoons milk. Stir in enough additional milk, 1 teaspoon at a time, to make icing of drizzling consistency.

PER SERVING: 63 cal., 0 g total fat (0 g sat. fat), 0 mg chol., 5 mg sodium, 13 g carbo., 0 g fiber, 1 g pro.
EXCHANGES: ½ Starch, ½ Other Carbo.

OFF THE SHELF TIP Spreadable fruit is fruity and flavorful like jam or jelly without all of the sugar.

Easy Cranberry-Orange Ring

From holiday-scented cinnamon, nutmeg, and cloves to oranges and cranberries, this delightful bread is an edible symphony of flavors. Roll it with filling, ring it, bake it, and enjoy with guests or give it as a lovely gift.

PREP
40 MINUTES
RISE
1¼ HOURS
BAKE
20 MINUTES
COOL
1 HOUR
OVEN
350°F
MAKES
1 RING (16 SERVINGS)

¾   **cup snipped dried cranberries**
1   **teaspoon finely shredded orange peel (set aside)**
2   **tablespoons orange juice**
1   **16-ounce loaf frozen sweet roll dough, thawed**
2   **teaspoons butter, melted**
¼   **cup packed brown sugar**
2   **tablespoons finely chopped pecans**
1   **tablespoon all-purpose flour**
¼   **teaspoon ground cinnamon**
¼   **teaspoon ground nutmeg**
⅛   **teaspoon ground cloves**
1   **teaspoon butter, melted**
1   **recipe Orange Icing**

STEP 1   Line a large baking sheet with foil; grease foil. Set baking sheet aside. In a medium bowl stir together cranberries and orange juice; set aside.

STEP 2   On a lightly floured surface, roll dough into a 15x9-inch rectangle (if dough is difficult to roll, let rest a few minutes and try again). Brush with the 2 teaspoons melted butter.

STEP 3   Drain cranberries; return cranberries to bowl. Add orange peel, brown sugar, pecans, flour, cinnamon, nutmeg, and cloves to cranberries. Sprinkle cranberry mixture evenly over dough. Starting from a long side, roll up into a spiral; seal edge. Place, seam side down, on prepared baking sheet. Bring ends together to form a ring. Moisten ends; pinch together to seal ring. Using kitchen scissors or a sharp knife, cut from the outside edge toward center, leaving about 1 inch attached. Repeat around the edge at 1-inch intervals. Gently turn each slice slightly so the same side of all slices faces upward.

STEP 4   Cover; let rise in a warm place until nearly double (1¼ to 1½ hours). Brush ring with the 1 teaspoon melted butter. Preheat oven to 350°F.

STEP 5   Bake in the preheated oven about 20 minutes or until golden. Remove ring from foil and cool completely on a wire rack. Drizzle Orange Icing over ring. Let stand until icing sets.

ORANGE ICING: In a small bowl stir together ½ cup powdered sugar, ¼ teaspoon finely shredded orange peel, and enough orange juice (1 to 3 teaspoons) to make an icing of drizzling consistency.

PER SERVING: 140 cal., 3 g total fat (1 g sat. fat), 18 mg chol., 59 mg sodium, 26 g carbo., 1 g fiber, 2 g pro.
EXCHANGES: 1 Starch, ½ Other Carbo., ½ Fat

OFF THE SHELF TIP Sweet roll dough is available in both refrigerated and frozen varieties. This ready-made dough will provide plenty of sweet aroma and flavor without the hassle.

Cobblestone-Ranch Dinner Rolls

Diners biting into these soft, warm rolls will be rewarded with a filling of ranch-dressing-spiked Parmesan cheese. Will one batch be enough? Better make two.

PREP
40 MINUTES

RISE
30 MINUTES

BAKE
20 MINUTES

COOL
15 MINUTES

OVEN
350°F

MAKES
12 ROLLS

Nonstick cooking spray
⅓ cup butter or margarine, melted
⅓ cup finely shredded Parmesan cheese
1 0.4-ounce envelope ranch salad dressing mix
1 16-ounce package frozen white roll dough (12 rolls), thawed
1 tablespoon yellow cornmeal

STEP 1 Coat a 9x1½-inch round baking pan with nonstick cooking spray; set aside. In a small bowl combine 3 tablespoons of the melted butter, the Parmesan cheese, and dry ranch dressing mix; set aside.

STEP 2 On a lightly floured surface, roll each thawed roll to a 3- to 4-inch circle. Place about 1 rounded teaspoon of the cheese mixture in the center of each dough circle; pull edges to center and pinch to seal, shaping into a round ball. Place balls in the prepared pan. Drizzle rolls with remaining melted butter. Sprinkle with cornmeal. Cover and let rise in a warm place until rolls are nearly double (30 to 45 minutes). Preheat oven to 350°F.

STEP 3 Bake in the preheated oven for 20 to 25 minutes or until golden. Carefully invert to remove rolls. Invert again onto a serving platter. Let cool for 15 minutes before serving.

PER ROLL: 160 cal., 8 g total fat (4 g sat. fat), 16 mg chol., 261 mg sodium, 19 g carbo., 1 g fiber, 4 g pro.
EXCHANGES: 1 Starch, 2 Fat

OFF THE SHELF TIP Frozen white roll dough is already shaped into balls and is ready to thaw and bake.

Onion Rolls

PREP
25 MINUTES

RISE
20 MINUTES

BAKE
20 MINUTES

OVEN
375°F

MAKES
12 ROLLS

2	cups chopped onion (2 large)
1	teaspoon dried basil, crushed
1	teaspoon paprika
⅛	teaspoon salt
1	tablespoon butter
1	tablespoon sugar
⅓	cup pine nuts, toasted
1	16-ounce package hot roll mix
1	tablespoon butter, melted

STEP 1 In a large skillet cook onion, basil, paprika, and salt in 1 tablespoon hot butter until onion is tender. Add sugar; cook and stir for 1 minute. Remove from heat and stir in pine nuts; cool slightly.

STEP 2 Grease a 13x9x2-inch baking pan; set aside. Prepare hot roll mix and let stand according to package directions.

STEP 3 To shape rolls, on a lightly floured surface, roll dough into a 12x8-inch rectangle. Spread the onion mixture over dough to within 1 inch of long edges. Roll up rectangle, starting from a long side. Seal seams. Slice into 12 pieces. Place pieces, cut sides down, in the prepared pan.

STEP 4 Cover loosely with plastic wrap, leaving room for rolls to rise. Let rise in a warm place until double (20 to 30 minutes). Preheat oven to 375°F.

STEP 5 Uncover rolls. Bake in the preheated oven for 20 to 25 minutes or until golden. Brush with 1 tablespoon melted butter. Serve warm.

PER ROLL: 215 cal., 7 g total fat (2 g sat. fat), 22 mg chol., 293 mg sodium, 33 g carbo., 1 g fiber, 7 g pro. **EXCHANGES:** 1½ Starch, ½ Other Carbo., 1½ Fat

OFF THE SHELF TIP Shelved with other bread mixes, hot roll mix in a handy box helps you bake a homemade favorite in no time.

Parmesan Rosettes

Rolled out and tied into individual rosettes, this dough gets brushed with an Italian-inspired blend of cheese and seasonings. The shapely rosettes are pretty in a bread basket or on a bread plate.

EASY **FAST**

PREP
15 MINUTES

BAKE
15 MINUTES

OVEN
375°F

MAKES
12 ROSETTES

RECIPE PICTURED ON PAGE **142.**

1	**11-ounce package (12) refrigerated breadsticks**
3	**tablespoons grated Parmesan or Romano cheese**
1	**teaspoon sesame seeds**
½	**teaspoon dried Italian seasoning, crushed**
¼	**teaspoon garlic powder**
2	**tablespoons butter, melted**

STEP 1 Preheat oven to 375°F. Separate breadsticks and uncoil into individual pieces. On a lightly floured surface, roll each piece into a 12-inch-long rope.

STEP 2 Tie each rope in a loose knot, leaving 2 long ends. Tuck the top end of the rope under roll. Bring bottom end up and tuck into center of roll.

STEP 3 In a shallow dish combine Parmesan cheese, sesame seeds, Italian seasoning, and garlic powder. Brush top and sides of each rosette with melted butter. Carefully dip the top and sides of each rosette into the cheese mixture. Place rosettes 2 to 3 inches apart on an ungreased baking sheet.

STEP 4 Bake in the preheated oven about 15 minutes or until golden. Serve warm.

PER ROSETTE: 135 cal., 5 g total fat (2 g sat. fat), 6 mg chol., 334 mg sodium, 18 g carbo., 1 g fiber, 4 g pro.
EXCHANGES: 1 Starch, 1 Fat

OFF THE SHELF TIP A staple for any off-the-shelf cook, refrigerated breadsticks come in a variety of savory flavors such as garlic, Parmesan, and corn bread to make any meal special.

Cheese-Coated Rolls

PREP
20 MINUTES

RISE
30 MINUTES

BAKE
30 MINUTES

OVEN
375°F

MAKES
12 ROLLS

1   cup shredded aged (dry) Jack cheese or Parmesan cheese (4 ounces)

2   teaspoons chili powder

2   16-ounce packages frozen white roll dough (12 rolls per package), thawed

⅓   cup butter, melted

STEP 1   Generously grease twelve 3½-inch (jumbo) muffin cups. Set aside.

STEP 2   In a small bowl stir together cheese and chili powder.

STEP 3   Roll each roll in butter; coat with cheese mixture. Place 2 rolls in each prepared muffin cup. Drizzle tops of rolls with any remaining butter.

STEP 4   Cover and let rise in a warm place until nearly double (about 30 minutes). After 20 minutes, preheat oven to 375°F.

STEP 5   Bake in the preheated oven about 30 minutes or until rolls sound hollow when lightly tapped. Immediately remove from muffin cups. Cool slightly on a wire rack. Serve warm.

PER ROLL: 299 cal., 14 g total fat (5 g sat. fat), 18 mg chol., 415 mg sodium, 37 g carbo., 2 g fiber, 9 g pro.
EXCHANGES: 2½ Starch, 2 Fat

OFF THE SHELF TIP   Frozen white roll dough is already shaped into balls and is ready to thaw and bake.

Cheddar-Corn Bread Rolls

EASY

PREP
10 MINUTES

STAND
5 MINUTES

RISE
20 MINUTES

BAKE
20 MINUTES

OVEN
375°F

MAKES
15 ROLLS

RECIPE PICTURED
ON PAGE **142.**

1   **16-ounce package hot roll mix**
1   **cup shredded cheddar cheese**
     (4 ounces)
⅓   **cup cornmeal**
1¼   **cups hot water (120°F to 130°F)**
2   **tablespoons olive oil**
1   **egg, slightly beaten**
     Milk
     Cornmeal

OFF THE SHELF TIP Shelved with other bread mixes, hot roll mix in a handy box helps you bake a homemade favorite in no time.

STEP 1   In a large bowl stir together the flour mixture and yeast from the hot roll mix, the cheddar cheese, and the ⅓ cup cornmeal. Add the hot water, oil, and egg; stir until combined.

STEP 2   Turn dough out onto a well-floured surface. Knead dough for 5 minutes or until smooth and elastic. Cover and let rest 5 minutes. Lightly grease a 13x9x2-inch baking pan; set aside.

STEP 3   Divide dough into 15 pieces. Shape each piece into a ball by pulling and tucking the dough underneath. Arrange dough balls in prepared pan. Cover and let rise in a warm place for 20 minutes. After 10 minutes, preheat oven to 375°F.

STEP 4   Brush dough with milk and sprinkle with additional cornmeal. Bake in the preheated oven for 20 to 22 minutes or until golden.

PER ROLL: 176 cal., 5 g total fat (2 g sat. fat), 22 mg chol., 228 mg sodium, 26 g carbo., 0 g fiber, 7 g pro. **EXCHANGES:** 2 Starch, ½ Fat

Checkerboard Rolls

2   tablespoons poppy seeds

2   tablespoons sesame seeds

1   teaspoon lemon-pepper seasoning

2   tablespoons yellow cornmeal

2   tablespoons grated or finely shredded Parmesan cheese

3   tablespoons butter, melted

16   pieces (1.3 ounces each) frozen white roll dough

OFF THE SHELF TIP Frozen white roll dough is already shaped into balls and is ready to thaw and bake.

PREP
20 MINUTES

CHILL
8 TO 24 HOURS

STAND
45 MINUTES

BAKE
15 MINUTES

OVEN
375°F

MAKES
16 ROLLS

STEP 1 Grease a 9x9x2-inch square pan; set aside. In a shallow dish combine poppy seeds, sesame seeds, and lemon-pepper seasoning. In another shallow dish combine cornmeal and Parmesan cheese. Place butter in a third dish. Working quickly, roll dough pieces in butter, then in one of the seasoning mixtures to lightly coat. (Coat half of the rolls with one seasoning mixture, and the remaining rolls with the other seasoning mixture.) Alternate rolls in prepared pan. Cover rolls with greased plastic wrap. Let thaw in refrigerator for at least 8 hours or up to 24 hours.

STEP 2 Remove pan from refrigerator; uncover and let stand at room temperature for 45 minutes. After 35 minutes, preheat oven to 375°F.

STEP 3 Bake rolls in the preheated oven for 15 to 20 minutes or until golden. Remove rolls from pan to wire rack. Cool slightly.

PER ROLL: 137 cal., 5 g total fat (2 g sat. fat), 7 mg chol., 244 mg sodium, 19 g carbo., 1 g fiber, 4 g pro.
EXCHANGES: 1 Starch, 1 Fat

Mexican Fiesta Spoon Biscuits

PREP
20 MINUTES
BAKE
45 MINUTES
STAND
15 MINUTES
OVEN
350°F
MAKES
24 SERVINGS

1   **16.3-ounce package (8) refrigerated large buttermilk biscuits**
1   **10.2-ounce package (5) refrigerated large buttermilk biscuits**
1   **16-ounce jar (1¾ cups) chunky salsa**
2   **cups shredded Monterey Jack cheese (8 ounces)**
½   **cup chopped green sweet pepper**
½   **cup sliced green onion (4)**
1   **2.25-ounce can sliced, pitted ripe olives, drained**

STEP 1   Preheat oven to 350°F. Grease a 3-quart rectangular baking dish; set aside. Using kitchen scissors, cut each biscuit into 8 pieces and place in a large bowl. Add salsa and toss gently to coat the pieces. Spoon mixture evenly into prepared dish. Sprinkle with Monterey Jack cheese, sweet pepper, onion, and olives.

STEP 2   Bake, uncovered, in the preheated oven about 45 minutes or until edges are puffed and deep golden brown and center is no longer doughy. Let stand for 15 minutes before serving. Cut into squares to serve.

PER SERVING: 144 cal., 7 g total fat (3 g sat. fat), 8 mg chol., 534 mg sodium, 15 g carbo., 1 g fiber, 5 g pro.
EXCHANGES: 1 Starch, ½ Medium-Fat Meat, ½ Fat

TIP: For a smaller recipe, prepare as at left, except use one 16.3-ounce package (8) refrigerated large buttermilk biscuits, one 8-ounce jar (about ¾ cup) chunky salsa, 1 cup shredded Monterey Jack cheese (4 ounces), ¼ cup chopped green sweet pepper, ¼ cup sliced green onion (2), and ¼ cup sliced, pitted ripe olives. Layer mixture as at left in a greased 2-quart square baking dish. Bake and let stand as directed. Makes 8 to 10 servings.

OFF THE SHELF TIP   Refrigerated biscuits are available in a variety of sizes and shapes. They make a tasty base for an appetizer or topper for a casserole.

Garlic Dinner Rolls

Transform refrigerated breadsticks into pretty fleurs-de-lis, then brush them with a butter mix of grated Asiago, parsley, and cayenne pepper.

PREP
15 MINUTES
BAKE
13 MINUTES
OVEN
375°F
MAKES
12 ROLLS

1	11-ounce package (12) refrigerated breadsticks
2	tablespoons purchased garlic butter spread, melted
½	cup finely shredded or grated Asiago or Romano cheese (2 ounces)
1	teaspoon dried parsley flakes
⅛	teaspoon cayenne pepper

STEP 1   Preheat oven to 375°F. Line a large baking sheet with foil; set aside. On a lightly floured surface, separate dough into 12 breadsticks. Cut each piece lengthwise into three strips, leaving ¾ inch uncut at one end. For each fleur-de-lis roll, coil strips from cut end down toward uncut base, coiling outside strips away from the center and coiling the center strip in either direction. If necessary, pinch slightly to hold shape. Transfer to prepared baking sheet.

STEP 2   Brush rolls with melted garlic butter spread. In a small bowl combine Asiago cheese, parsley flakes, and cayenne pepper; sprinkle generously over rolls.

STEP 3   Bake in the preheated oven for 13 to 15 minutes or until golden. Serve warm.

PER ROLL: 112 cal., 5 g total fat (2 g sat. fat), 8 mg chol., 263 mg sodium, 12 g carbo., 0 g fiber, 3 g pro.
EXCHANGES: 1 Starch, ½ Fat

OFF THE SHELF TIP   A staple for any off-the-shelf cook, refrigerated breadsticks come in a variety of savory flavors such as garlic, Parmesan, and corn bread to make any meal special.

Easy Tapenade Rolls

A jar of luscious olive tapenade and grated Romano provide spoonfuls of tasty filling that await your palate within soft, warm white rolls.

PREP
20 MINUTES

RISE
30 MINUTES

BAKE
15 MINUTES

OVEN
350°F

MAKES
12 ROLLS

⅓   cup purchased olive tapenade
¼   cup finely shredded or grated Romano cheese (1 ounce)
1   16-ounce package frozen white roll dough (12 rolls), thawed
1   tablespoon butter, melted
2   tablespoons finely shredded or grated Romano cheese

STEP 1 Lightly grease an 11x7x1½-inch baking pan; set aside. In a small bowl combine tapenade and the ¼ cup Romano cheese.

STEP 2 On a lightly floured surface, pat each thawed roll into a 3-inch circle. Place a rounded teaspoon of the tapenade mixture onto the center of each dough circle. Bring up edge of each roll and pinch to seal and enclose filling. Place filled rolls, seam sides down, in the prepared pan. Cover and let rise in a warm place until nearly double (about 30 minutes). After 20 minutes, preheat oven to 350°F.

STEP 3 Brush tops of rolls with melted butter. Sprinkle with the 2 tablespoons Romano cheese.

STEP 4 Bake in the preheated oven for 15 to 20 minutes or until rolls are golden and sound hollow when lightly tapped. Remove rolls from pan. Cool on wire rack. Serve slightly warm or at room temperature.

PER ROLL: 156 cal., 8 g total fat (2 g sat. fat), 5 mg chol., 365 mg sodium, 18 g carbo., 1 g fiber, 4 g pro.
EXCHANGES: 1 Starch, 1½ Fat

OFF THE SHELF TIP Fetch olive tapenade from the condiment or ethnic aisle. It's a thick paste of chopped ripe olives, anchovies, capers, seasonings, olive oil, lemon juice.

Pesto Pinwheels

PREP
25 MINUTES
RISE
45 MINUTES
BAKE
30 MINUTES
OVEN
375°F
MAKES
16 ROLLS

1	cup packed fresh basil
¾	cup pine nuts or almonds
3	tablespoons olive oil
1	teaspoon bottled minced garlic (2 cloves)
½	teaspoon salt
¼	teaspoon black pepper
½	cup grated Parmesan cheese
½	cup grated Romano cheese
⅓	cup diced pimiento
2	16-ounce loaves frozen bread dough, thawed
	Fresh basil sprigs (optional)

STEP 1 For filling, in a blender or food processor combine the 1 cup basil, the pine nuts, 2 tablespoons of the olive oil, the garlic, salt, and pepper. Cover and blend or process until mixture is finely minced. Place mixture in a bowl; stir in Parmesan cheese, Romano cheese, and pimiento. Set aside.

STEP 2 Lightly grease a 13x9x2-inch baking pan. On a lightly floured surface, roll each of the loaves into an 8-inch square. Brush squares lightly with the remaining olive oil. Spread half of the filling on each of the squares. Roll up each square. Seal seams. Slice each roll into 8 pieces (16 total). Place, cut sides up, in the prepared pan. Cover and let rise until nearly double (45 to 60 minutes). Preheat oven to 375°F.

STEP 3 Uncover rolls. Bake in the preheated oven about 30 minutes or until golden brown. Cool slightly; remove from pan. Serve warm.

PER ROLL: 224 cal., 8 g total fat (1 g sat. fat), 5 mg chol., 147 mg sodium, 26 g carbo., 0 g fiber, 7 g pro. **EXCHANGES:** 2 Starch, ½ Lean Meat, 1 Fat

OFF THE SHELF TIP Packed in oil and found in the grocery aisle, bottled minced garlic couldn't get much easier to use.

Sticky Red Raspberry Rolls

EASY

PREP
10 MINUTES
BAKE
25 MINUTES
OVEN
350°F
MAKES
8 ROLLS

½   cup seedless red raspberry jam
1   11-ounce package refrigerated French bread dough
2   tablespoons sugar
¼   of an 8-ounce tub cream cheese
1   tablespoon milk

STEP 1   Preheat oven to 350°F. In a small saucepan heat and stir jam until melted. Set aside 2 tablespoons of the jam. Pour remaining jam into an 8x8x2-inch baking pan.

STEP 2   Cut bread dough into 16 slices. Lay bread dough slices on top of the jam in the baking pan; brush tops of dough with reserved jam. Sprinkle tops of dough slices with sugar.

STEP 3   Bake in the preheated oven for 25 to 30 minutes or until brown. Invert onto a serving platter. Scrape any remaining jam from baking pan and spread over rolls.

STEP 4   In a small saucepan cook and stir cream cheese and milk over medium-low heat until mixture reaches drizzling consistency. Drizzle over rolls. Serve warm.

PER ROLL: 186 cal., 4 g total fat (2 g sat. fat), 7 mg chol., 276 mg sodium, 34 g carbo., 1 g fiber, 4 g pro. **EXCHANGES:** 1 Starch, 1 Other Carbo., 1 Fat

OFF THE SHELF TIP   Red raspberry jam and preserves from the condiment section are the taste of summer and available with seeds or without.

Caramel-Pecan Rolls

EASY

PREP
15 MINUTES

CHILL
8 TO 24 HOURS

STAND
30 MINUTES

BAKE
20 MINUTES

COOL
5 MINUTES

OVEN
350°F

MAKES
12 ROLLS

½   cup powdered sugar
2   tablespoons whipping cream
½   teaspoon ground cinnamon
¾   cup pecan pieces, toasted, if desired
1   16-ounce package frozen white roll dough (12 rolls)
1   tablespoon butter or margarine, melted

STEP 1   Grease a 9x1½-inch round baking pan; set aside. In a small bowl stir together powdered sugar, whipping cream, and cinnamon; spread into prepared pan. Sprinkle pecans evenly over powdered sugar mixture. Place rolls on mixture in pan. Brush rolls with melted butter. Cover and chill for at least 8 hours or up to 24 hours.

STEP 2   Before baking, let rolls stand at room temperature for 30 minutes. After 20 minutes, preheat oven to 350°F.

STEP 3   Uncover rolls and bake in the preheated oven for 20 to 25 minutes or until light brown. Cool in pan on a wire rack for 5 minutes. Carefully invert rolls onto a serving platter. Serve warm.

PER ROLL: 181 cal., 9 g total fat (2 g sat. fat), 6 mg chol., 158 mg sodium, 23 g carbo., 1 g fiber, 4 g pro.
EXCHANGES: 1 Starch, ½ Other Carbo., 1½ Fat

OFF THE SHELF TIP Frozen white roll dough is already shaped into balls and is ready to thaw and bake.

Honey-Pecan Crescent Rolls

Using refrigerated crescent roll dough means that you can bake these sticky, gooey, ooh-yum delights over a campfire away from home or over the backyard fire pit.

FAST

PREP
20 MINUTES
BAKE
12 MINUTES
OVEN
375°F
MAKES
8 SERVINGS

1   8-ounce package (8) refrigerated crescent rolls
1   tablespoon butter, melted
⅓   cup finely chopped pecans (toasted, if desired)
2   tablespoons packed brown sugar
½   teaspoon ground cinnamon
2   tablespoons honey

STEP 1   Preheat oven to 375°F. Lightly grease a baking sheet; set aside.

STEP 2   Unroll crescent roll dough and divide into 8 triangles. Brush triangles with melted butter. Set aside 2 tablespoons of the pecans for the topping. In a small bowl combine remaining pecans, the brown sugar, and cinnamon; sprinkle evenly over the triangles. Roll up triangles, starting with the wide end. Place rolls, point sides down, on the prepared baking sheet.

STEP 3   Bake in the preheated oven 12 to 15 minutes or until golden. Drizzle rolls with honey; sprinkle with remaining pecans. Serve warm.

PER SERVING: 173 cal., 11 g total fat (2 g sat. fat), 4 mg chol., 242 mg sodium, 19 g carbo., 1 g fiber, 2 g pro.
EXCHANGES: 1 Starch, 2 Fat

OFF THE SHELF TIP Crescent rolls are a flaky dough, ready to be shaped into rolls or used as the base of an appetizer, dessert, or main dish.

Baked Doughnut *Twists*

Packaged biscuit mix makes these coffee-flavored, spice-kissed twists simple to stir together.

PREP
25 MINUTES

BAKE
10 MINUTES

OVEN
400°F

MAKES
8 TO 10 DOUGHNUTS

2   cups packaged biscuit mix
2   tablespoons sugar
2   teaspoons instant coffee crystals
¼   cup milk
1   egg, slightly beaten
1   teaspoon finely shredded orange peel
2   tablespoons butter or margarine, melted
⅓   cup sugar
½   teaspoon ground cinnamon
⅛   teaspoon ground nutmeg

PER DOUGHNUT: 213 cal., 8 g total fat (3 g sat. fat), 35 mg chol., 407 mg sodium, 31 g carbo., 0 g fiber, 3 g pro.
EXCHANGES: 1 Starch, 1 Other Carbo., 1½ Fat

OFF THE SHELF TIP Look for sparkling instant coffee crystals in a jar on the coffee shelf.

STEP 1   Preheat oven to 400°F. In a medium bowl stir together biscuit mix and the 2 tablespoons sugar; set aside. In a small bowl dissolve coffee crystals in milk; stir in egg and orange peel. Add coffee mixture all at once to biscuit mixture. Stir just until moistened.

STEP 2   Turn dough out onto a well-floured surface. Quickly knead by gently folding and pressing for 10 to 20 strokes or until nearly smooth. Pat or lightly roll dough to ½-inch thickness. Cut dough with a floured 2½-inch doughnut cutter, dipping the cutter into flour between cuts. Holding opposite sides of the doughnut, twist once, forming a figure 8. Place on an ungreased baking sheet.

STEP 3   Bake in the preheated oven for 10 to 12 minutes or until golden brown. Brush each twist with melted butter. In a shallow dish stir together the ⅓ cup sugar, the cinnamon, and nutmeg. Dip each twist into sugar mixture. Serve warm.

Muffins, Biscuits & Scones

good

Cherry-Nut Muffins

1¾   cups all-purpose flour
½   cup sugar
2   teaspoons baking powder
¼   teaspoon salt
1   egg white, slightly beaten
¾   cup fat-free milk
3   tablespoons cooking oil
1   teaspoon finely shredded orange peel
½   cup snipped dried tart cherries
2   tablespoons chopped walnuts

OFF THE SHELF TIP With stronger, more intense flavor than their fresh counterparts, nearly every fruit is available in its dried form and is most commonly packaged in bags or boxes.

PREP
15 MINUTES
BAKE
18 MINUTES
COOL
5 MINUTES
OVEN
400°F
MAKES
12 MUFFINS

STEP 1   Preheat oven to 400°F. Line twelve 2½-inch muffin pans with paper bake cups; set aside. In a medium bowl stir together flour, sugar, baking powder, and salt. Make a well in the center of the flour mixture; set aside.

STEP 2   In another bowl combine egg white, milk, oil, and orange peel. Add milk mixture all at once to flour mixture. Stir just until moistened (batter should be lumpy). Gently fold in cherries and nuts. Spoon batter into prepared muffin cups, filling each two-thirds full.

STEP 3   Bake in the preheated oven for 18 to 20 minutes or until golden and a wooden toothpick inserted in centers comes out clean. Cool in muffin cups on a wire rack for 5 minutes. Remove from muffin cups; serve warm.

PER MUFFIN: 154 cal., 4 g total fat (1 g sat. fat), 0 mg chol., 128 mg sodium, 26 g carbo., 1 g fiber, 3 g pro.
EXCHANGES: 1½ Starch, ½ Fat

Refrigerator Bran Muffins

PREP
15 MINUTES

COOK
18 MINUTES

CHILL
2 HOURS

OVEN
375°F

MAKES
12 MUFFINS

1½ cups packaged low-fat biscuit mix
1 cup whole bran cereal
1 teaspoon ground cinnamon
½ cup refrigerated or frozen egg product, thawed
1 cup fat-free milk
⅓ cup packed brown sugar
2 tablespoons cooking oil
¾ cup snipped dried fruit, such as cherries, raisins, or apricots

OFF THE SHELF TIP Usually found in boxes or bags, biscuit mixes often only require the addition of water or milk.

STEP 1 In a large bowl combine biscuit mix, cereal, and cinnamon. Make a well in the center. In a small bowl combine egg product, milk, brown sugar, and oil. Add egg mixture all at once to cereal mixture. Stir just until moistened (batter will be lumpy). Gently stir in fruit. To store, place batter in a covered container and refrigerate at least 2 hours or up to 3 days.

STEP 2 To bake, preheat oven to 375°F. Spray the desired number of 2½-inch muffin cups with nonstick cooking spray. Gently stir batter; spoon batter into prepared muffin cups, filling each two-thirds full. Bake in the preheated oven for 18 to 20 minutes or until golden. Remove from pans and cool on a wire rack.

PER MUFFIN: 143 cal., 4 g total fat (1 g sat. fat), 0 mg chol., 241 mg sodium, 26 g carbo., 3 g fiber, 4 g pro.
EXCHANGES: 1½ Starch, 1 Fat

Harvest Bran *Muffins*

Shredded carrot, dried fruit, and nuts load these muffins with harvest flavor.

1	**14-ounce package oat bran muffin mix**
⅓	**cup finely shredded carrot**
¼	**cup snipped dried apples**
¼	**cup dried cranberries or coarsely chopped dried tart cherries**
3	**tablespoons finely chopped walnuts**

OFF THE SHELF TIP You'll find all sorts of salted and unsalted nuts in the baking aisle (look for pieces and already-chopped) or chips section.

PREP
15 MINUTES
BAKE
15 MINUTES
COOL
5 MINUTES
OVEN
400°F
MAKES
12 MUFFINS

STEP 1 Preheat oven to 400°F. Grease twelve 2½-inch muffin cups; set aside.

STEP 2 Prepare muffin mix according to package directions, except gently stir in carrot, dried apples, and cranberries. Divide evenly among prepared muffin cups. Sprinkle with nuts.

STEP 3 Bake in the preheated oven for 15 to 18 minutes or until golden. Cool in pan on wire rack for 5 minutes; loosen edges and remove from muffin cups. Serve slightly warm or at room temperature.

PER MUFFIN: 161 cal., 4 g total fat (1 g sat. fat), 0 mg chol., 206 mg sodium, 28 g carbo., 2 g fiber, 3 g pro. **EXCHANGES:** 1 Starch, 1 Other Carbo., ½ Fat

Lemon Muffins

Thick, intensely flavored lemon curd produces a lush muffin that wears a crown of toasted coconut.

PREP
25 MINUTES

BAKE
18 MINUTES

COOL
5 MINUTES

OVEN
400°F

MAKES
6 MUFFINS

1½   cups all-purpose flour
½   cup granulated sugar
¼   cup whole wheat flour
2   teaspoons baking powder
¼   teaspoon salt
1   egg
¾   cup milk
¼   cup cooking oil
⅔   cup purchased lemon curd or
      apricot preserves
2   tablespoons toasted coconut

STEP 1 Preheat oven to 400°F. Grease 6 popover pans and line with paper bake cups; set aside.* In a medium bowl stir together the all-purpose flour, sugar, whole wheat flour, baking powder, and salt. Make a well in the center of the flour ingredients; set aside.

STEP 2 In a small bowl combine egg, milk, and oil. Add egg mixture all at once to flour mixture. Stir just until moistened (batter should be lumpy).

STEP 3 Spoon half of the batter into prepared popover pans (2 rounded tablespoons in each cup). Spoon 2 rounded teaspoons of the lemon curd on top of the batter in each cup. (There will be some remaining lemon curd for topping.) Spoon remaining batter into popover pans, filling each cup two-thirds full.

STEP 4 Bake in the preheated oven for 18 to 20 minutes or until golden brown. Cool in popover pans on a wire rack for 5 minutes. Remove from popover pans.

Top with remaining lemon curd and toasted coconut. Serve warm or cool.

*NOTE: To make in muffin cups, grease twelve 2½-inch muffin cups and line with paper bake cups; set aside. Prepare muffin batter through Step 2. Spoon half the batter into prepared muffin cups (a rounded tablespoon in each muffin cup). Spoon a rounded teaspoon of lemon curd on top of the batter in each cup. (There will be some remaining lemon curd for topping.) Spoon remaining batter into muffin cups, filling each cup two-thirds full. Bake and cool as directed. Makes 12 muffins.

PER MUFFIN: 319 cal., 13 g total fat (4 g sat. fat), 65 mg chol., 291 mg sodium, 47 g carbo., 5 g fiber, 6 g pro.
EXCHANGES: 2 Starch, 1 Other Carbo., 2 Fat

OFF THE SHELF TIP Look for lemon curd near jams and jellies. The thick, intensely flavored spread of lemons, butter, eggs, and sugar is delicious on its own and in baked goods.

Sweet Potato Muffins

PREP
20 MINUTES
BAKE
18 MINUTES
COOL
25 MINUTES
OVEN
400°F
MAKES
12 MUFFINS

RECIPE PICTURED
ON PAGE **136.**

1¾   **cups all-purpose flour**
⅓   **cup packed brown sugar**
1½   **teaspoons baking powder**
½   **teaspoon baking soda**
1   **teaspoon apple pie spice or ground cinnamon**
¼   **teaspoon salt**
½   **of a 17-ounce can sweet potatoes, drained (about 1 cup)**
1   **egg, slightly beaten**
½   **cup milk**
⅓   **cup fruit jam or preserves (such as plum, strawberry, peach, or apricot)**
¼   **cup cooking oil**
1   **recipe Jam Icing**

STEP 1   Preheat oven to 400°F. Lightly grease twelve 2½-inch muffin cups or line with paper bake cups; set aside.

STEP 2   In a large bowl combine flour, brown sugar, baking powder, baking soda, apple pie spice, and salt. Make a well in the center of the flour mixture; set aside.

STEP 3   In another bowl mash the drained sweet potatoes with a fork. Stir in egg, milk, jam, and oil. Add sweet potato mixture all at once to flour mixture. Stir just until moistened (batter should be lumpy). Spoon batter into prepared muffin cups, filling each about three-fourths full.

STEP 4   Bake in the preheated oven for 18 to 20 minutes or until golden and a wooden toothpick inserted in centers comes out clean. Cool in muffin cups on a wire rack for 5 minutes. Remove from muffin cups. Cool slightly. Drizzle muffins with Jam Icing and, if desired, top with additional jam or preserves.

JAM ICING: In a small bowl stir together ¾ cup powdered sugar, 1 tablespoon fruit jam or preserves (such as plum, strawberry, peach, or apricot), ¼ teaspoon vanilla, and enough milk (2 to 3 teaspoons) to make icing of drizzling consistency. Makes about ¼ cup.

PER MUFFIN: 215 cal., 6 g total fat (1 g sat. fat), 19 mg chol., 174 mg sodium, 39 g carbo., 1 g fiber, 3 g pro.
EXCHANGES: 1 Starch, 1½ Other Carbo., 1 Fat

OFF THE SHELF TIP Stocked alongside other canned vegetables, canned sweet potatoes are available year-round and sometimes labeled as yams.

Honey-Nut Corn Muffins

Corn muffin mix goes uptown with the addition of honey and chopped pecans. These pair beautifully with grilled vegetables, meats, or barbecue.

EASY **FAST**

PREP
10 MINUTES

BAKE
15 MINUTES

OVEN
400°F

MAKES
6 TO 8 MUFFINS

1   8.5-ounce package corn muffin mix
½   cup chopped pecans
2   tablespoons honey
      Honey butter (optional)

STEP 1   Preheat oven to 400°F. Grease six to eight 2½-inch muffin cups; set aside.

STEP 2   Prepare corn muffin mix according to package directions, except stir in nuts and honey. Spoon batter into prepared muffin cups, filling each about three-fourths full.

STEP 3   Bake in the preheated oven about 15 minutes or until golden brown. Serve warm. If desired, serve with honey butter.

PER MUFFIN: 262 cal., 12 g total fat (1 g sat. fat), 36 mg chol., 298 mg sodium, 36 g carbo., 1 g fiber, 5 g pro.
EXCHANGES: 2 Starch, 2 Fat

OFF THE SHELF TIP Find corn muffin mix, a versatile quick-cooking mix, on the baking aisle shelves.

Pesto *Biscuits*

PREP
20 MINUTES

BAKE
8 MINUTES

OVEN
450°F

MAKES
10 BISCUITS

2	cups all-purpose flour
3	tablespoons dry buttermilk powder or nonfat dry milk powder
2	teaspoons baking powder
½	teaspoon baking soda
¼	teaspoon salt
⅓	cup butter-flavored shortening or regular shortening
2	tablespoons purchased pesto
½	cup water

STEP 1   Preheat oven to 450°F. In a large bowl stir together flour, buttermilk powder, baking powder, baking soda, and salt. Using a pastry cutter, cut in shortening and pesto until mixture resembles coarse crumbs. Make a well in the center; add the water all at once. Stir just until dough clings together.

STEP 2   Turn dough out onto a lightly floured surface. Knead by folding and gently pressing dough for 10 to 12 strokes or until dough is nearly smooth. Roll or pat to ½-inch thickness. Cut with a 2½-inch biscuit cutter, dipping cutter into flour between cuts. Place biscuits on an ungreased baking sheet.

STEP 3   Bake in the preheated oven for 8 to 10 minutes or until golden. Serve warm.

MAKE-AHEAD DIRECTIONS: Prepare as directed. Wrap cooled biscuits in foil; place in airtight freezer containers or plastic freezer bags. Seal, label, and freeze for up to 1 month. To serve, preheat oven to 350°F. Bake foil-wrapped biscuits in preheated oven for 15 to 20 minutes or until warm.

PER BISCUIT: 173 cal., 8 g total fat (2 g sat. fat), 2 mg chol., 236 mg sodium, 20 g carbo., 1 g fiber, 4 g pro.
EXCHANGES: 1½ Starch, 1½ Fat

OFF THE SHELF TIP From the condiment aisle or ethnic shelves, pesto is a spread of basil leaves blended with olive oil, garlic, pine nuts, and Parmesan cheese.

Cheddar Garlic
Biscuits

Invite your guests to prepare this easy and appealing bread—and collect the rave reviews.

PREP
10 MINUTES

BAKE
8 MINUTES

OVEN
425°F

MAKES
10 TO 12 BISCUITS

2 cups packaged biscuit mix
½ cup shredded cheddar cheese (2 ounces)
⅔ cup milk
¼ cup butter or margarine, melted
½ teaspoon garlic powder

OFF THE SHELF TIP Usually found in boxes or bags, biscuit mixes often only require the addition of water or milk.

STEP 1 Preheat oven to 425°F. Grease a baking sheet; set aside.

STEP 2 In a large bowl combine biscuit mix and cheddar cheese; add milk. Stir to combine. Drop dough from a well-rounded tablespoon onto the prepared baking sheet.

STEP 3 Bake in the preheated oven for 8 to 10 minutes or until golden. In a small bowl combine melted butter and garlic powder; brush over hot biscuits. Serve warm.

PER BISCUIT: 178 cal., 11 g total fat (5 g sat. fat), 21 mg chol., 402 mg sodium, 16 g carbo., 1 g fiber, 4 g pro.
EXCHANGES: 1 Starch, 2 Fat

Bacon & Chive Biscuits

Serve this lightly salty biscuit along with a green salad or with eggs for breakfast.

EASY **FAST**

PREP
10 MINUTES

BAKE
8 MINUTES

OVEN
450°F

MAKES
6 TO 8 BISCUITS

Nonstick cooking spray

1   **7.75-ounce package buttermilk or cheese-garlic biscuit mix**

½   **cup finely shredded sharp cheddar cheese (2 ounces)**

4   **slices packaged ready-to-serve cooked bacon, finely chopped**

2   **tablespoons snipped fresh chives or chopped green onion**

STEP 1   Preheat oven to 450°F. Lightly coat a baking sheet with nonstick cooking spray; set aside.

STEP 2   Prepare biscuit mix according to package directions, except stir cheese, bacon, and chives into the dry mix before adding water. Drop batter into 6 or 8 mounds onto prepared baking sheet.

STEP 3   Bake in the preheated oven for 8 to 10 minutes or until golden brown. Serve warm.

PER BISCUIT: 211 cal., 10 g total fat (4 g sat. fat), 14 mg chol., 586 mg sodium, 23 g carbo., 1 g fiber, 6 g pro.
EXCHANGES: 1½ Starch, ½ Medium-Fat Meat, 1 Fat

OFF THE SHELF TIP Usually found in boxes or bags, biscuit mixes often only require the addition of water or milk.

Green Onion Parker House Biscuits

Boursin cheese elevates a simple biscuit from plain to sophisticated. Turn to this recipe when elegant is what you're after.

EASY **FAST**

PREP
10 MINUTES

BAKE
8 MINUTES

OVEN
400°F

MAKES
10 BISCUITS

RECIPE PICTURED ON PAGE 137.

1   **5.2-ounce container semisoft cheese with garlic and herbs**
¼   **cup sliced green onion (2)**
1   **12-ounce package (10) refrigerated biscuits**
1 . **egg yolk**
1   **tablespoon water**
2   **tablespoons grated Parmesan cheese**
       Sliced green onions

OFF THE SHELF TIP Refrigerated biscuits are available in a variety of sizes and shapes. They make a tasty base for an appetizer or topper for a casserole.

STEP 1   Preheat oven to 400°F. Grease a baking sheet; set aside. In a small bowl stir together semisoft cheese and the ¼ cup green onions; set aside.

STEP 2   Unwrap biscuits. Using your fingers, gently split the biscuits horizontally. Place the biscuit bottoms on prepared baking sheet. Spread about 1 tablespoon of the cheese mixture over each biscuit bottom. Replace biscuit tops.

STEP 3   In a small bowl use a fork to beat together egg yolk and the water. Brush biscuit tops with egg yolk mixture. Sprinkle with Parmesan cheese and additional sliced green onions.

STEP 4   Bake in the preheated oven for 8 to 10 minutes or until golden. Serve warm.

PER BISCUIT: 149 cal., 8 g total fat (5 g sat. fat), 23 mg chol., 394 mg sodium, 16 g carbo., 0 g fiber, 4 g pro.
EXCHANGES: 1 Starch, 1½ Fat

Beer Bites

Nonstick cooking spray
1   **cup packaged biscuit mix**
1   **tablespoon snipped fresh chives**
⅓   **cup beer**

EASY **FAST**

PREP
10 MINUTES
BAKE
6 MINUTES
OVEN
450°F
MAKES
24 BISCUITS

STEP 1   Preheat oven to 450°F. Lightly coat a baking sheet with nonstick cooking spray; set aside.

STEP 2   In a small bowl combine biscuit mix and chives. Stir in beer until a soft dough forms. Drop by well-rounded measuring teaspoons onto the prepared baking sheet.

STEP 3   Bake in the preheated oven for 6 to 8 minutes or until tops are light brown. Serve warm.

PER BISCUIT: 22 cal., 1 g total fat (0 g sat. fat), 0 mg chol., 62 mg sodium, 3 g carbo., 0 g fiber, 0 g pro. **EXCHANGES:** ½ Fat

OFF THE SHELF TIP   Usually found in boxes or bags, biscuit mixes often only require the addition of water or milk.

Biscuits with Berry-Cherry Filling

If you don't make a snack of the leftover fruit mixture, whip out another batch of biscuits or thin the fruit with water and serve with turkey or pork (or even pancakes).

PREP
20 MINUTES

BAKE
25 MINUTES

OVEN
375°F

MAKES
12 BISCUITS

1   **26-ounce package (12) frozen unbaked biscuits**

2   **4-inch sprigs fresh thyme**

1   **6-ounce package dried cranberries (1⅓ cups)**

2   **3-ounce packages dried cherries (1⅓ cups)**

⅔   **cup pure maple or maple-flavored syrup**
    Cayenne pepper (optional)
    Pure maple syrup or maple-flavored syrup

STEP 1   Preheat oven to 375°F. Place biscuits on a large baking sheet. Bake in the preheated oven for 20 minutes.

STEP 2   Meanwhile, remove leaves from thyme sprigs, discarding stems (you should have about 1 teaspoon leaves). In a food processor* combine cranberries, cherries, ⅔ cup maple syrup, and the thyme leaves. Cover and process until mixture is a coarse paste. If desired, add cayenne pepper to taste.

STEP 3   Remove biscuits from oven. Using a fork, carefully split the warm biscuits horizontally. Spread 1 to 2 tablespoons of the fruit mixture onto bottom half of each biscuit. Replace biscuit tops. Brush biscuits with additional maple syrup. Bake for 5 minutes more. Serve warm.

*NOTE: If you do not have a food processor, chop dried fruit and place in a medium bowl. Stir in the ⅔ cup syrup, thyme, and, if desired, cayenne pepper.

PER BISCUIT: 344 cal., 9 g total fat (3 g sat. fat), 0 mg chol., 608 mg sodium, 60 g carbo., 2 g fiber, 5 g pro.
EXCHANGES: ½ Fruit, 1½ Starch, 2 Other Carbo., 1½ Fat

OFF THE SHELF TIP   Dried Fruit: With stronger, more intense flavor than their fresh counterparts, nearly every fruit is available in its dried form and is most commonly packaged in bags or boxes.

Pumpkin & Raisin Scones

PREP
10 MINUTES

BAKE
12 MINUTES

OVEN
375°F

MAKES
8 SCONES

2   cups packaged biscuit mix
⅓   cup raisins or dried cranberries
¼   cup granulated sugar
2   teaspoons pumpkin pie spice
½   cup canned pumpkin
¼   cup milk
1   tablespoon coarse or granulated
       sugar
1   tablespoon very finely snipped
       crystallized ginger

STEP 1   Preheat oven to 375°F. Grease a baking sheet; set aside.

STEP 2   In a large bowl combine biscuit mix, raisins, the ¼ cup granulated sugar, and the pumpkin pie spice. In a small bowl combine canned pumpkin and 3 tablespoons of the milk. Add pumpkin mixture all at once to dry mixture; stir until combined.

STEP 3   Turn dough out onto a lightly floured surface. Knead by folding and gently pressing dough for 10 to 12 strokes or until dough is nearly smooth. Pat or lightly roll into a ½-inch-thick circle. Cut into 8 wedges. Place wedges 1 inch apart on the prepared baking sheet. In a small bowl combine the 1 tablespoon coarse sugar and the crystallized ginger. Brush dough wedges with remaining 1 tablespoon milk; sprinkle with ginger mixture.

STEP 4   Bake in the preheated oven for 12 to 15 minutes or until a toothpick inserted near center comes out clean. Cool slightly on a wire rack. Serve warm.

PER SCONE: 189 cal., 5 g total fat (1 g sat. fat), 1 mg chol., 377 mg sodium, 34 g carbo., 1 g fiber, 3 g pro. **EXCHANGES:** 2 Starch, 1 Fat

OFF THE SHELF TIP   Not just for pumpkin pie, canned pumpkin adds moistness and texture to many baked goods.

Cakes

Triple-Chocolate Cake

PREP
20 MINUTES

BAKE
45 MINUTES

COOL
1 HOUR

OVEN
350°F

MAKES
16 SERVINGS

Nonstick cooking spray

2 tablespoons unsweetened cocoa powder (optional)

1 package 2-layer-size devil's food cake mix

1 package 4-serving-size instant chocolate fudge pudding mix

1 cup plain fat-free yogurt

1 2.5-ounce jar pureed dried plums (prunes) (baby food)

½ cup water

2 eggs

2 egg whites

¼ cup light mayonnaise dressing or salad dressing

1 teaspoon vanilla

½ cup semisweet chocolate pieces

Powdered sugar

STEP 1 Preheat oven to 350°F. Coat a 10-inch fluted tube pan with nonstick cooking spray. Coat the inside of the pan with cocoa powder (if desired) or flour the pan; shake out excess cocoa powder or flour. Set aside.

STEP 2 In a large mixing bowl combine the cake mix, pudding mix, yogurt, plums, water, eggs, egg whites, mayonnaise dressing, and vanilla. Beat with an electric mixer on low speed until combined; beat on medium speed until smooth. Stir in chocolate pieces. Spoon the batter into the prepared pan, spreading evenly.

STEP 3 Bake in the preheated oven about 45 minutes or until a wooden toothpick inserted near the center comes out clean. Cool in pan on a wire rack for 10 minutes. Remove from pan and cool completely on wire rack. Sift powdered sugar over cake before serving.

PER SERVING: 216 cal., 5 g total fat (2 g sat. fat), 28 mg chol., 385 mg sodium, 39 g carbo., 1 g fiber, 4 g pro.
EXCHANGES: 2½ Other Carbo., 1 Fat

OFF THE SHELF TIP Available in dozens of flavors and most commonly packaged in boxes, cake mixes are a handy alternative to the made-from-scratch method.

PERFECT PREHEATING Regardless of what your oven tells you, allow at least 15 minutes for it to fully preheat before baking.

Orange-Chocolate Cake

Swap the water in a chocolate cake mix for orange liqueur, then dress the frosted cake with candied orange slices for a sophisticated and refreshing chocolate indulgence.

PREP
20 MINUTES

BAKE
ACCORDING TO PACKAGE DIRECTIONS

MAKES
12 SERVINGS

RECIPE PICTURED ON PAGE 140.

1   package 2-layer-size devil's food cake mix
¼   cup orange liqueur
1   16-ounce can chocolate frosting
     Candied orange slices (optional)

STEP 1   Preheat oven and prepare cake according to package directions, except replace ¼ cup of the water with the ¼ cup orange liqueur. Use desired pan size. Bake and cool as directed.

STEP 2   Frost cooled cake with the chocolate frosting. If desired, garnish with candied orange slices.

PER SERVING: 475 cal., 24 g total fat (6 g sat. fat), 55 mg chol., 469 mg sodium, 56 g carbo., 1 g fiber, 4 g pro.
EXCHANGES: 3½ Other Carbo., 5 Fat

OFF THE SHELF TIP Canned frosting is now available in a rainbow of flavors and colors and makes putting the icing on the cake a snap!

White Russian Cake

PREP
20 MINUTES
BAKE
ACCORDING TO PACKAGE DIRECTIONS
MAKES
12 SERVINGS

1 package 2-layer-size chocolate cake mix
⅓ cup coffee liqueur
½ of an 8-ounce container frozen whipped dessert topping, thawed
1 tablespoon coffee liqueur
Powdered sugar

OFF THE SHELF TIP Grab a tub of whipped dessert topping, a light, fluffy topper from your grocer's freezer.

STEP 1 Prepare cake mix according to package directions using two 8x1½- or 9x1½-inch round cake pans, except replace ⅓ cup of the water with ⅓ cup coffee liqueur.

STEP 2 In a medium bowl fold together whipped dessert topping and 1 tablespoon liqueur. Spread one of the cake layers with whipped topping mixture. Top with remaining cake layer. Sift powdered sugar over top of cake.

PER SERVING: 305 cal., 13 g total fat (4 g sat. fat), 35 mg chol., 281 mg sodium, 40 g carbo., 1 g fiber, 3 g pro.
EXCHANGES: 2½ Other Carbo., 3½ Fat

Chocolate Fleck Cake

Everyday cake mix goes glam with chocolate sprinkles, cocoa-spiked whipped cream frosting, and a topping of nuts for a luscious ending to a special meal.

PREP
20 MINUTES

BAKE
ACCORDING TO PACKAGE DIRECTIONS

COOL
1 HOUR

OVEN
350°F

MAKES
12 SERVINGS

1   package 2-layer-size white or yellow cake mix
⅓   cup chocolate-flavored sprinkles
1½   cups whipping cream
⅔   cup presweetened cocoa powder
¼   cup finely chopped pecans or walnuts

OFF THE SHELF TIP Available in dozens of flavors and most commonly packaged in boxes, cake mixes are a handy alternative to the made-from-scratch method.

STEP 1   Preheat oven to 350°F. Grease and lightly flour two 8x1½- or 9x1½-inch round cake pans; set aside. Prepare cake mix according to package directions, except stir chocolate sprinkles into batter. Pour batter into the prepared pans, spreading evenly.

STEP 2   Bake in the preheated oven as directed on package. Cool cake layers in pans on wire racks for 10 minutes. Remove cake layers from pans. Cool on wire racks.

STEP 3   In a chilled medium mixing bowl, combine whipping cream and cocoa powder. Beat with chilled beaters of electric mixer on medium speed until soft peaks form (tips curl).

STEP 4   Fill and frost cake with whipped cream mixture. Sprinkle pecans over top. If desired, refrigerate cake for up to 2 hours. Store leftover cake, covered, in the refrigerator.

PER SERVING: 395 cal., 21 g total fat (10 g sat. fat), 41 mg chol., 339 mg sodium, 46 g carbo., 1 g fiber, 3 g pro.
EXCHANGES: 3 Other Carbo., 4½ Fat

Double Chocolate Chip Cookie-Crusted Cake

Have your cookie and your cake and enjoy them both beneath a drizzle of chocolate sauce. Mugs of coffee or glasses of milk make the perfect accompaniment.

PREP
30 MINUTES

BAKE
50 MINUTES

COOL
1 HOUR

OVEN
350°F

MAKES
9 TO 12 SERVINGS

1	package 2-layer-size yellow or French vanilla cake mix
2/3	cup sugar
1/3	cup unsweetened cocoa powder
1/2	cup butter
1	cup chopped walnuts
1 1/2	cups semisweet chocolate pieces
1/4	cup cooking oil
2/3	cup water
2	eggs
3	tablespoons light cream or milk

STEP 1 Preheat oven to 350°F. Grease and flour a 9x9x2-inch baking pan. Set pan aside.

STEP 2 For crust, in a medium bowl combine 1½ cups of the cake mix, sugar, and cocoa powder. Using a pastry blender, cut in butter until crumbly. Add walnuts and 1 cup of the chocolate pieces; toss to mix. Press the crumb mixture onto bottom of the prepared pan. Bake in the preheated oven for 15 minutes. Cool on a wire rack for 15 minutes.

STEP 3 Meanwhile, in a large mixing bowl combine remaining cake mix, oil, water, and eggs. Beat with an electric mixer on medium speed for 2 minutes. Pour batter over the partially baked crust. Bake in the 350° oven about 35 minutes more or until a wooden toothpick inserted near the center of the cake layer only comes out clean. Cool completely on a wire rack.

STEP 4 In a small saucepan combine the remaining ½ cup chocolate pieces and the light cream; heat and stir over low heat until smooth. Drizzle over cake.

PER SERVING: 669 cal., 39 g total fat (15 g sat. fat), 76 mg chol., 464 mg sodium, 83 g carbo., 3 g fiber, 8 g pro.
EXCHANGES: 2½ Starch, 3 Other Carbo., 7 Fat

OFF THE SHELF TIP Semisweet chocolate pieces are melt-in-your-mouth chips of chocolate and ready to be melted or mixed into your bread, cookie, cake, or bar recipe.

Chocolate-Graham Peanut Butter *Snack Cake*

The nutty cracker bottom ends up on top of this rectangular cake, which is then spread with chocolate frosting to make a very satisfying crowd-pleaser.

PREP
20 MINUTES
BAKE
30 MINUTES
COOL
1 HOUR
OVEN
350°F
MAKES
18 SERVINGS

1   package 2-layer-size white cake mix
1   cup finely crushed chocolate graham crackers
1   10-ounce package peanut butter-flavor pieces
²/₃ cup honey-roasted peanuts, chopped
1   16-ounce can chocolate frosting

STEP 1   Preheat oven to 350°F. Grease a 13x9x2-inch baking pan; set aside.

STEP 2   Prepare cake according to package directions, except stir in crushed graham crackers, 1 cup of the peanut butter pieces, and ¹/₃ cup of the peanuts. Pour batter into prepared pan, spreading evenly.

STEP 3   Bake in the preheated oven for 30 to 35 minutes or until a wooden toothpick inserted in center comes out clean. Cool in pan on a wire rack. Spread frosting over cooled cake. Sprinkle with remaining peanut butter pieces and peanuts.

PER SERVING: 355 cal., 14 g total fat (7 g sat. fat), 12 mg chol., 345 mg sodium, 54 g carbo., 1 g fiber, 4 g pro.
EXCHANGES: 1 Starch, 2½ Other Carbo., 3 Fat

OFF THE SHELF TIP Packaged in bags, peanut butter-flavored pieces can be found next to chocolate pieces in the baking aisle.

Cream Cheese-Filled Chocolate Cupcakes

PREP
20 MINUTES
BAKE
ACCORDING TO PACKAGE DIRECTIONS
MAKES
ABOUT 30 CUPCAKES

1   8-ounce package cream cheese, softened
⅓   cup sugar
1   egg
     Dash salt
1   cup semisweet chocolate pieces (6 ounces)
1   package 2-layer-size chocolate cake mix
     Favorite frosting (optional)

STEP 1   In a medium mixing bowl, combine the cream cheese and sugar; beat with an electric mixer on medium-high speed until combined. Beat in egg and salt. Stir in chocolate pieces. Set aside.

STEP 2   Preheat oven and prepare cake mix according to package directions. Line thirty 2½-inch muffin cups with paper bake cups. Divide batter among muffin cups, filling each about half full. Drop a rounded teaspoon of the cream cheese mixture into each batter-filled muffin cup.

STEP 3   Bake in the preheated oven according to package directions. Remove cupcakes from muffin cups; cool on wire racks. If desired, frost with favorite frosting.

PER CUPCAKE: 161 cal., 9 g total fat (4 g sat. fat), 29 mg chol., 141 mg sodium, 20 g carbo., 1 g fiber, 2 g pro.
EXCHANGES: 1 Starch, ½ Other Carbo., 1½ Fat

OFF THE SHELF TIP Rich, creamy cream cheese is available in fat-free, low-fat, and regular—plus an assortment of flavors.

Brownie Surprise *Cupcakes*

Tuck a mini candy in a brownie cupcake beneath a layer of frosting and enjoy the molten goodness.

EASY

PREP
15 MINUTES
BAKE
22 MINUTES
OVEN
350°F
MAKES
15 CUPCAKES

RECIPE PICTURED ON PAGE 134.

1   **21-ounce package fudge brownie mix**
15   **miniature-size chocolate-coated caramel-topped nougat bars with peanuts or 15 dark-chocolate-covered mint creams**
     Canned vanilla frosting
     Small multicolored decorative candies (optional)

OFF THE SHELF TIP Fudge brownie mix is a boxed, warm, chocolaty dessert and is usually shelved with other dessert mixes.

STEP 1   Preheat the oven to 350°F. Line fifteen 2½-inch muffin cups with paper bake cups. Prepare the fudge brownie mix according to package directions. Spoon 1 tablespoon of the batter into each paper bake cup. Place a miniature-size candy bar or mint cream in each cup. Divide the remaining batter among the cups.

STEP 2   Bake in the preheated oven for 22 minutes. Cool in pans on a wire rack. Cupcakes may dip slightly in center. Remove cupcakes from pans. Frost with vanilla frosting and, if desired, sprinkle with decorative candies.

TIP: If all of the cupcakes do not fit in the oven at one time, refrigerate the unbaked extras until the first ones finish baking.

PER CUPCAKE: 348 cal., 17 g total fat (4 g sat. fat), 30 mg chol., 171 mg sodium, 49 g carbo., 1 g fiber, 3 g pro.
EXCHANGES: 3½ Other Carbo., 3 Fat

Marbled Angel Food Cake

Cocoa powder, powdered sugar, and milk are all you need to transform an angel food cake mix into a marbled and glazed light treat.

PREP
20 MINUTES

BAKE
ACCORDING TO
PACKAGE DIRECTIONS

COOL
1 HOUR

MAKES
12 SERVINGS

1   16-ounce package angel food
      cake mix
¼   cup unsweetened cocoa powder
2   cups powdered sugar
2   tablespoons unsweetened
      cocoa powder
3   to 4 tablespoons milk

STEP 1   Preheat oven and prepare cake mix according to package directions. Transfer 4 cups of the batter to a large bowl; sift the the ¼ cup cocoa powder over batter and fold in until combined. Alternately pour white and chocolate batters into an ungreased 10-inch tube pan; cut through batter with a knife or spatula to marble. Bake and cool according to package directions

STEP 2   For icing, in a medium bowl stir together powdered sugar and the 2 tablespoons cocoa powder. Stir in enough milk to make drizzling consistency. Drizzle over top and down sides of cake.

PER SERVING: 219 cal., 1 g total fat 256 mg sodium, 51 g carbo., 4 g pro.
EXCHANGES: 3½ Other Carbo.

OFF THE SHELF TIP Available in dozens of flavors and most commonly packaged in boxes, cake mixes are a handy alternative to the made-from-scratch method.

Coffee-Chocolate Angel Food Cake

Cocoa powder infuses an angel food cake topped with coffee cream and crushed toffee for a light bite with a rich kick.

PREP
20 MINUTES
BAKE
35 MINUTES
COOL
ABOUT 2 HOURS
OVEN
350°F
MAKES
12 SERVINGS

1 **16-ounce package angel food cake mix**
¼ **cup unsweetened cocoa powder**
1¼ **cups water**
1 **recipe Coffee Cream**
2 **1.4-ounce bars chocolate-covered English toffee, crushed**

STEP 1 Preheat oven to 350°F. In a large mixing bowl stir together cake mix and cocoa powder. Add the water. Beat with an electric mixer on low speed for 30 seconds. Beat on medium speed for 1 minute. Pour into an ungreased 10-inch tube pan. Gently cut through batter with a knife or narrow metal spatula to remove any large air pockets.

STEP 2 Bake on lowest oven rack in the preheated oven for 35 to 45 minutes or until top springs back when lightly touched. Immediately invert cake; cool completely in pan. Loosen sides of cake from pan; remove cake.

STEP 3 Place cake, upside down, on serving plate. Spread top of cake with Coffee Cream. Sprinkle with crushed candy. Store leftover cake, covered, in refrigerator.

COFFEE CREAM: In a medium bowl dissolve 2 teaspoons instant coffee crystals in 1 tablespoon hot water. Add one 7-ounce jar marshmallow creme and ½ teaspoon vanilla. Beat with an electric mixer on medium to high speed until smooth. In a chilled small bowl beat 1 cup whipping cream on medium to high speed until stiff peaks form (tips stand straight). Gently fold whipped cream into marshmallow mixture.

PER SERVING: 295 cal., 10 g total fat (5 g sat. fat), 29 mg chol., 299 mg sodium, 48 g carbo., 0 g fiber, 4 g pro.
EXCHANGES: 3 Other Carbo., 2½ Fat

OFF THE SHELF TIP Grab a bar or a bag of chocolate-covered English toffee from the grocery checkout or candy aisle. It makes a tasty topping for many desserts.

Apricot Cakes For Two

PREP
1 HOUR
BAKE
15 MINUTES
COOL
40 MINUTES
STAND
1 HOUR
OVEN
350°F
MAKES
6 CAKES
(2 SERVINGS PER CAKE)

1   **16-ounce package pound cake mix**
½   **cup water**
¼   **cup apricot brandy, raspberry liqueur, apricot nectar, or raspberry juice blend**
2   **eggs**
1   **recipe Apricot Butter Frosting**

STEP 1   Preheat oven to 350°F. Grease and lightly flour a 15x10x1-inch baking pan. Set aside.

STEP 2   In a large mixing bowl combine cake mix, water, brandy, and eggs. Beat with an electric mixer on low speed for 30 seconds; beat on medium speed for 3 minutes. Pour batter into the prepared pan, spreading evenly.

STEP 3   Bake about 15 minutes or until a wooden toothpick inserted near the center comes out clean. Cool in a pan on a wire rack for 10 minutes. Remove cake from pan and cool completely.

STEP 4   Transfer cake to a large cutting board. Using a 2- to 2½-inch round cutter, cut cake into 12 rounds. (Cut remaining cake scraps into cubes and serve with fruit, ice cream, or yogurt.) For each cake, spread 1 tablespoon of the frosting on top of one cake round. Top with a second cake round. Spread a thin coating of frosting* on the sides of the cake to seal in any crumbs. Let cakes stand, uncovered, for 1 hour or until first coat is set. To frost cake, carefully pick up each cake and add a thicker coating of frosting around the sides. Place cake on serving plate and frost top.

APRICOT BUTTER FROSTING: In a very large mixing bowl beat ¾ cup softened butter with an electric mixer on medium speed until smooth. Gradually add 2 cups powdered sugar, beating well. Slowly beat in ⅓ cup apricot nectar or raspberry juice blend. Gradually beat in 7 cups powdered sugar. Beat in enough additional apricot nectar to reach spreading consistency. If desired, tint frosting a pale peach or pink color.

*NOTE: For the thin coating of frosting, transfer ¾ cup of the prepared frosting to a small bowl. Stir in enough apricot nectar or raspberry juice blend (about 1 tablespoon) to make frosting of glazing consistency.

PER SERVING: 588 cal., 17 g total fat (9 g sat. fat), 66 mg chol., 227 mg sodium, 108 g carbo., 0 g fiber, 2.5 g pro.
EXCHANGES: 7 Other Carbo., 3½ Fat

OFF THE SHELF TIP Available in dozens of flavors and most commonly packaged in boxes, cake mixes are a handy alternative to the made-from-scratch method.

Neapolitan Pound Cake

1   **16-ounce package pound cake mix**
½   **cup strawberry or seedless raspberry preserves**
5   **or 6 drops red food coloring**
¼   **cup presweetened cocoa powder**
½   **cup canned chocolate frosting**

OFF THE SHELF TIP Red raspberry jam and preserves from the condiment section are the taste of summer and available with seeds or without.

PREP
30 MINUTES
BAKE
35 MINUTES
COOL
1 HOUR
OVEN
350°F
MAKES
12 SERVINGS

STEP 1 Preheat oven to 350°F. Generously grease and flour a 10-inch fluted tube pan or a 9x5x3-inch loaf pan.

STEP 2 Prepare cake mix according to package directions. Divide batter into thirds and place in 3 separate bowls. Stir preserves and red food coloring into 1 portion of the batter. Stir presweetened cocoa powder into another portion of the batter. Leave the remaining portion plain. Alternately spoon batters into the prepared pan.

STEP 3 Bake in the preheated oven for 35 to 40 minutes for the fluted tube pan, 60 to 70 minutes for the loaf pan, or until a toothpick inserted in center of cake comes out clean. Cool in pan on wire rack for 10 minutes. Remove cake from pan. Cool completely on wire rack.

STEP 4 Place frosting in a small microwave-safe bowl; microwave on 100% (high) power for 10 to 20 seconds or just until drizzling consistency. Drizzle frosting over cake.

PER SERVING: 223 cal., 5 g total fat (2 g sat. fat), 24 mg chol., 145 mg sodium, 43 g carbo., 1 g fiber, 2 g pro.
EXCHANGES: 3 Other Carbo., 1 Fat

Lemon-Lime Cake

A luscious limey cream cheese layer bakes into a lemon cake drizzled with a lime glaze for a sure hit with those who love citrus.

PREP
25 MINUTES
BAKE
45 MINUTES
OVEN
350°F
MAKES
12 SERVINGS

1   package 2-layer-size lemon cake mix
2   3-ounce packages cream cheese, softened
2   tablespoons butter, softened
1   tablespoon cornstarch
½   cup sweetened condensed milk
1   egg
3   teaspoons finely shredded lime peel
4   tablespoons lime juice
     Several drops green food coloring (optional)
1   cup powdered sugar
     Water

STEP 1   Preheat oven to 350°F. Generously grease and flour a 10-inch fluted tube pan; set aside.

STEP 2   Prepare cake mix according to package directions; pour batter into the prepared pan. In a medium mixing bowl combine cream cheese, butter, and cornstarch; beat with an electric mixer on low to medium speed until smooth. Gradually beat in sweetened condensed milk, egg, 2 teaspoons of the lime peel, 3 tablespoons of the lime juice, and, if desired, green food coloring. Spoon cream cheese mixture evenly over batter in pan.

STEP 3   Bake in the preheated oven about 45 minutes or until a wooden toothpick inserted near the center comes out clean. Cool in pan on a wire rack for 10 minutes. Remove cake from pan. Cool completely on wire rack.

STEP 4   For icing, in a small bowl stir together powdered sugar, the remaining 1 teaspoon lime peel, the remaining 1 tablespoon lime juice, and, if desired, additional green food coloring. Stir in enough water (2 to 3 teaspoons) to make drizzling consistency. Drizzle over cooled cake.

PER SERVING: 321 cal., 12 g total fat (6 g sat. fat), 43 mg chol., 354 mg sodium, 52 g carbo., 0 g fiber, 4 g pro.
EXCHANGES: 3½ Other Carbo., 2½ Fat

OFF THE SHELF TIP   Available in dozens of flavors and most commonly packaged in boxes, cake mixes are a handy alternative to the made-from-scratch method.

Lemonade Cake

Crazy for lemon?
Layer it on by
blending lemon peel
into a lemon cake
mix that you'll
frost with lemon-
infused whipped
cream topping.
The taste is divine.

EASY

PREP
15 MINUTES
BAKE
ACCORDING TO
PACKAGE DIRECTIONS
MAKES
12 SERVINGS

1   package 2-layer-size lemon cake mix
1   teaspoon finely shredded lemon peel
1   8-ounce container frozen whipped
      dessert topping, thawed
1   tablespoon finely chopped lemon peel
      Thin lemon slices or lemon peel curls
      (optional)

STEP 1   Preheat oven and prepare cake mix according to package directions using two 8x1½-inch or 9x1½-inch round cake pans, except stir the 1 teaspoon finely shredded lemon peel into the batter.

STEP 2   In a medium bowl place whipped topping. Fold in the 1 tablespoon finely chopped lemon peel until combined. Frost cooled cake. Garnish with lemon slices or lemon peel curls, if desired.

PER SERVING: 303 cal., 14 g total fat (6 g sat. fat), 54 mg chol., 292 mg sodium, 39 g carbo., 1 g fiber, 3 g pro.
EXCHANGES: 1 Starch, 1½ Other Carbo., 3 Fat

OFF THE SHELF TIP Grab a tub of whipped dessert topping, a light, fluffy topper from your grocer's freezer.

Lemon Cream-Filled Coffee Cake

PREP
25 MINUTES

BAKE
45 MINUTES

COOL
45 MINUTES

OVEN
350°F

MAKES
12 SERVINGS

1	8-ounce package cream cheese, softened
¼	cup sugar
1	cup lemon yogurt
1½	teaspoons finely shredded lemon peel
3	cups all-purpose flour
1	cup sugar
1	tablespoon baking powder
¼	teaspoon salt
¼	teaspoon ground nutmeg or mace
1	cup butter
2	eggs, slightly beaten
1	cup milk
½	teaspoon almond extract
½	cup sugar
½	cup all-purpose flour
¼	cup butter
½	cup chopped pecans or sliced almonds

STEP 1 Preheat oven to 350°F. Grease a 13x9x2-inch baking pan; set aside.

STEP 2 In a medium mixing bowl beat cream cheese with an electric mixer on medium speed until fluffy. Beat in ¼ cup sugar; fold in lemon yogurt and lemon peel. Set aside.

STEP 3 In a large mixing bowl stir together 3 cups flour, 1 cup sugar, baking powder, salt, and nutmeg. Using a pastry blender, cut in the 1 cup butter until mixture resembles fine crumbs. Combine eggs, milk, and almond extract. Add to flour mixture, stirring until mixed. Pour half of the batter into the prepared pan, spreading evenly.

STEP 4 Spoon the cream cheese mixture over the batter. Spoon the remaining batter in small mounds over the cream cheese mixture, spreading out as much as possible.

STEP 5 Combine the ½ cup sugar and ½ cup flour; using the pastry blender, cut in the ¼ cup butter until mixture resembles coarse crumbs. Stir in pecans. Sprinkle nut mixture over batter in pan.

STEP 6 Bake in the preheated oven for 45 to 50 minutes or until cake is golden and a wooden toothpick inserted in dough mounds comes out clean (do not test in filling). Cool on a wire rack for at least 45 minutes before serving. Store, covered, in the refrigerator.

PER SERVING: 559 cal., 32 g total fat (18 g sat. fat), 114 mg chol., 447 mg sodium, 61 g carbo., 1 g fiber, 8 g pro.
EXCHANGES: 1½ Starch, 2½ Other Carbo., 6½ Fat

OFF THE SHELF TIP Rich, creamy cream cheese is available in fat-free, low-fat, and regular—plus an assortment of flavors.

Coconut-Orange Cake

Orange juice concentrate and coconut join cake mix and fluffy frosting mix to produce a cake that tastes like sunshine.

1	package 2-layer-size white cake mix
1	cup milk
2	egg whites
½	of a 6-ounce can (⅓ cup) frozen orange juice concentrate, thawed
½	cup flaked coconut
1	package fluffy white frosting mix (for 2-layer cake)
⅓	cup flaked coconut or large coconut flakes, toasted

PREP
30 MINUTES

BAKE
30 MINUTES

COOL
1 HOUR

OVEN
350°F

MAKES
12 SERVINGS

**RECIPE PICTURED
ON PAGE 140.**

OFF THE SHELF TIP From the baking aisle, coconut is packaged in bags or cans and is available shredded, flaked, and even toasted.

STEP 1 Preheat oven to 350°F. Grease and flour two 9x1½-inch round cake pans; set aside. In a large mixing bowl combine cake mix, milk, egg whites, and orange juice concentrate. Beat with an electric mixer on medium speed for 2 minutes. Using a rubber scraper, gently fold in the ½ cup coconut. Divide batter evenly between prepared pans, spreading evenly.

STEP 2 Bake in the preheated oven for 30 to 35 minutes or until a wooden toothpick inserted near centers comes out clean. Cool in pans on wire racks for 10 minutes. Remove cakes from pans. Cool thoroughly on wire racks.

STEP 3 Prepare frosting according to package directions. Fill and frost cake. Sprinkle toasted coconut on top of cake. Store frosted cake, covered, in the refrigerator.

PER SERVING: 291 cal., 6 g total fat (3 g sat. fat), 2 mg chol., 361 mg sodium, 57 g carbo., 0 g fiber, 3 g pro.
EXCHANGES: 4 Other Carbo., 1 Fat

Apple-Walnut Cake

A splash of apple brandy or juice spikes this frosted spice cake that packs a crunch with chopped fresh apples and walnuts.

1 package 2-layer-size spice cake mix
1 cup finely chopped, peeled apple
2 tablespoons apple brandy or apple juice
¾ cup chopped black walnuts or walnuts
1 16-ounce can vanilla frosting
Apple slices and/or chopped black walnuts or walnuts (optional)

OFF THE SHELF TIP Canned frosting is now available in a rainbow of flavors and colors and makes putting the icing on the cake a snap!

PREP
30 MINUTES
BAKE
ACCORDING TO PACKAGE DIRECTIONS
MAKES
12 SERVINGS

STEP 1 Preheat oven and prepare cake mix according to package directions, except stir the 1 cup chopped apple, brandy, and the ¾ cup chopped walnuts into the batter. Use desired pan size. Cool as directed on package.

STEP 2 Frost cooled cake. If desired, garnish with apple slices and/or additional walnuts.

PER SERVING: 411 cal., 17 g total fat (5 g sat. fat), 0 mg chol., 372 mg sodium, 60 g carbo., 1 g fiber, 3 g pro.
EXCHANGES: 1 Starch, 3 Other Carbo., 3 Fat

Peachy Pecan Cake

Celebrate the stone fruit season by sliding chopped fresh peaches and nuts over a citrusy whipped frosting between the layers of a spice cake. Delicious!

PREP
40 MINUTES

BAKE
ACCORDING TO
PACKAGE DIRECTIONS

COOL
1 HOUR

MAKES
12 SERVINGS

1   package 2-layer-size butter pecan cake mix
1   10½-ounce package tiny marshmallows
2   tablespoons orange juice
1   tablespoon lemon juice
1   8-ounce container frozen whipped dessert topping, thawed
3   medium fresh peaches, peeled and chopped
½   cup chopped pecans, toasted

OFF THE SHELF TIP Bags of fluffy, sweet marshmallows are available in regular and miniature sizes and in traditional white or pastel colors.

STEP 1   Preheat oven and prepare cake mix according to package directions using two 9x1½-inch round cake pans. Cool layers as directed.

STEP 2   For frosting, in a medium saucepan cook and stir marshmallows, orange juice, and lemon juice over low heat until smooth. Let cool for 15 minutes. Fold whipped topping into marshmallow mixture.

STEP 3   Frost the top of one cake layer with some of the frosting. Top with chopped peaches and half of the nuts. Place remaining cake layer on top of the frosted layer. Frost top and sides of cake. Sprinkle remaining nuts over top of cake.

PER SERVING: 370 cal., 12 g total fat (5 g sat. fat), 53 mg chol., 306 mg sodium, 64 g carbo., 1 g fiber, 4 g pro.
EXCHANGES: 1 Starch, 3 Other Carbo., 2 Fat

Pecan-Praline Treat

PREP

20 MINUTES

BAKE

ACCORDING TO
PACKAGE DIRECTIONS

MAKES

16 SERVINGS

1   package 2-layer-size butter pecan
       cake mix
1   cup caramel ice cream topping
1   cup chopped pecans, toasted

STEP 1   Preheat oven and prepare cake
according to package directions using
a 13x9x2-inch baking pan. Cool cake in
pan on a wire rack.

STEP 2   Drizzle caramel topping over
cooled cake. Sprinkle with chopped pecans.

PER SERVING: 275 cal., 11 g total fat (2 g sat. fat),
40 mg chol., 271 mg sodium, 43 g carbo., 1 g fiber,
3 g pro.
EXCHANGES: 3 Other Carbo., 2 Fat

OFF THE SHELF TIP Grocers vary
in where they stock ice cream toppings.
Look by pancake syrups or near the ice
cream freezer.

Praline Crunch Cake

PREP
25 MINUTES

BAKE
40 MINUTES

OVEN
350°F

MAKES
16 SERVINGS

2   **tablespoons molasses**

     Water

1   **tablespoon instant coffee crystals**

1   **package 2-layer-size yellow cake mix**

3   **eggs**

⅓   **cup cooking oil**

⅓   **cup all-purpose flour**

1   **tablespoon packed brown sugar**

½   **teaspoon ground cinnamon**

3   **tablespoons butter**

⅓   **cup chopped pecans**

¼   **cup butter, softened**

3½   **cups powdered sugar**

¼   **cup half-and-half, light cream, or milk**

1   **teaspoon instant coffee crystals**

1   **teaspoon vanilla**

STEP 1   Preheat oven to 350°F. Grease a 13x9x2-inch baking pan; set aside. Place molasses in a 2-cup glass measuring cup; add enough water to measure 1⅓ cups total mixture and stir to combine. Transfer to a large mixing bowl. Add the 1 tablespoon coffee crystals; stir to dissolve. Add cake mix, eggs, and oil. Beat with an electric mixer on low speed until combined. Beat on medium speed for 2 minutes. Pour into the prepared pan, spreading evenly.

STEP 2   Bake in the preheated oven about 30 minutes or until a wooden toothpick inserted near the center comes out clean. Cool in pan on a wire rack.

STEP 3   In a small bowl stir together flour, brown sugar, and cinnamon. Using a pastry blender, cut in the 3 tablespoons butter until crumbly. Stir in pecans. Knead with fingers until mixture starts to cling together. Spread clumps in a 15x10x1-inch baking pan. Bake in the 350° oven about 10 minutes or until light golden. Transfer to a piece of foil to cool.

STEP 4   For frosting, in a large mixing bowl beat the ¼ cup butter with an electric mixer on medium speed for 30 seconds. Add 1 cup of the powdered sugar; beat until combined. In a small bowl stir together the ¼ cup half-and-half and the 1 teaspoon instant coffee crystals until dissolved. Add to powdered sugar mixture along with vanilla. Beat until combined (mixture may appear curdled). Gradually add remaining 2½ cups powdered sugar, beating until smooth and spreadable. If necessary, beat in additional half-and-half to make spreadable. Frost cooled cake with frosting; sprinkle with baked pecan mixture.

PER SERVING: 354 cal., 15 g total fat (5 g sat. fat), 56 mg chol., 272 mg sodium, 53 g carbo., 0 g fiber, 3 g pro.
EXCHANGES: 3½ Other Carbo., 3 Fat

OFF THE SHELF TIP   Available in dozens of flavors and most commonly packaged in boxes, cake mixes are a handy alternative to the made-from-scratch method.

Maple-Macadamia Snack

PREP
20 MINUTES
BAKE
ACCORDING TO
PACKAGE DIRECTIONS
MAKES
16 SERVINGS

½   **cup all-purpose flour**
3   **tablespoons sugar**
¼   **cup butter**
1   **cup chopped macadamia nuts**
1   **package 2-layer-size spice cake mix**
¼   **cup maple-flavor syrup**

STEP 1   For topping, in a medium bowl combine flour and sugar. Using a pastry blender, cut in butter until crumbly; stir in nuts. Set aside.

STEP 2   Preheat oven and prepare cake mix according to package directions using a 13x9x2-inch baking pan, except replace ¼ cup of the water with the maple-flavor syrup. Pour batter into prepared pan, spreading evenly. Sprinkle the topping over cake batter.

STEP 3   Bake in the preheated oven and cool cake according to package directions.

PER SERVING: 309 cal., 18 g total fat (4 g sat. fat), 49 mg chol., 244 mg sodium, 37 g carbo., 1 g fiber, 3 g pro.
EXCHANGES: 2½ Other Carbo., 3½ Fat

OFF THE SHELF TIP   Available in dozens of flavors and most commonly packaged in boxes, cake mixes are a handy alternative to the made-from-scratch method.

Oatmeal Cake

PREP
30 MINUTES
BAKE
30 MINUTES
STAND
20 MINUTES
COOL
1 HOUR
OVEN
350°F

1	cup quick-cooking rolled oats
1½	cups boiling water
1½	cups all-purpose flour
1½	teaspoons ground cinnamon
1	teaspoon baking soda
½	teaspoon salt
½	cup shortening
1	cup granulated sugar
1	cup packed brown sugar
2	eggs
6	tablespoons butter or margarine
1	cup coconut
⅔	cup packed brown sugar
2	tablespoons milk
⅔	cup chopped walnuts

STEP 1 Grease a 13x9x2-inch baking pan; set aside. In a small bowl combine oats and boiling water; let stand for 20 minutes. Meanwhile, in a medium bowl combine flour, cinnamon, baking soda, and salt.

STEP 2 Preheat oven to 350°F. In a mixing bowl beat shortening, granulated sugar, and the 1 cup brown sugar with an electric mixer on medium speed until combined. Beat in eggs. Beat in oatmeal mixture. Add flour mixture; beat until combined. Pour batter into the prepared pan, spreading evenly.

STEP 3 Bake in the preheated oven for 30 to 35 minutes or until a wooden toothpick inserted near center comes out clean. Place pan on a wire rack.

STEP 4 For topping, in a saucepan combine butter, coconut, the ⅔ cup brown sugar, and the milk; cook and stir until boiling. Stir in nuts. Spoon topping over hot cake; cool completely.

PER SERVING: 358 cal., 17 g total fat (6 g sat. fat), 39 mg chol., 218 mg sodium, 80 g carbo., 2 g fiber, 4 g pro.
EXCHANGES: 3½ Other Carbo., 3 Fat

OFF THE SHELF TIP From the baking aisle, coconut is packaged in bags or cans and is available shredded, flaked, and even toasted.

Rosemary Mini Cupcakes

PREP
20 MINUTES

BAKE
12 MINUTES

COOL
30 MINUTES

OVEN
350°F

MAKES
36 MINI CUPCAKES

1   **package 1-layer-size white cake mix**
1   **teaspoon snipped fresh rosemary or**
     ¼ teaspoon dried rosemary, crushed
½   **teaspoon finely shredded orange peel**
½   **cup powdered sugar**
1   **tablespoon orange juice**

STEP 1   Preheat the oven to 350°F. Line thirty-six 1¾-inch muffin cups with miniature paper bake cups;* set aside.

STEP 2   Prepare cake mix according to package directions, except stir in rosemary and orange peel. Spoon a well-rounded teaspoon of the batter into each prepared muffin cup.

STEP 3   Bake cupcakes in the preheated oven about 12 minutes or until tops spring back when lightly touched and cupcakes are golden brown. Cool in muffin cups on a wire rack for 5 minutes.

STEP 4   Meanwhile, for glaze, in a small bowl stir together powdered sugar and orange juice; set aside. Remove cupcakes from muffin cups. Dip tops in the glaze mixture. Cool completely on wire rack.

*TIP: If you don't have 1¾-inch muffin cups, line twelve 2½-inch muffin cups with paper bake cups. Prepare batter as directed for Rosemary Mini Cupcakes. Spoon batter into prepared muffin cups, filling each ⅔ full. Bake in a 350°F oven about 15 minutes or until golden brown. Cool and glaze as directed. Makes twelve 2½-inch cupcakes.

PER MINI CUPCAKE: 34 cal., 1 g total fat (0 g sat. fat), 0 mg chol., 46 mg sodium, 7 g carbo., 0 g fiber, 0 g pro.
EXCHANGES: ½ Other Carbo.

OFF THE SHELF TIP   Available in dozens of flavors and most commonly packaged in boxes, cake mixes are a handy alternative to the made-from-scratch method.

Cookies & Bars

Peanut Butter Chocolate Cookies

Fast, simple, and satisfying, these drop cookies will put your craving sweets to rest.

FAST

PREP
20 MINUTES

BAKE
9 MINUTES PER BATCH

OVEN
375°F

MAKES
ABOUT 30 COOKIES

1   package 1-layer-size devil's food cake mix
½   cup peanut butter
1   egg
2   tablespoons water
1   tablespoon cooking oil
½   cup miniature candy-coated semisweet chocolate pieces or miniature semisweet chocolate pieces

STEP 1 Preheat oven to 375°F. In a large mixing bowl combine cake mix, peanut butter, egg, water, and cooking oil. Beat with an electric mixer on medium speed until combined. Stir in chocolate pieces. Drop dough by rounded teaspoons 2 inches apart onto ungreased cookie sheets.

STEP 2 Bake in the preheated oven for 9 to 11 minutes or until edges are firm. Transfer cookies to a wire rack and let cool. To store, place cookies in layers separated by waxed paper in an airtight container; cover. Store at room temperature up to 3 days or freeze up to 3 months.

PER COOKIE: 121 cal., 6 g total fat (1 g sat. fat), 7 mg chol., 168 mg sodium, 16 g carbo., 1 g fiber, 2 g pro. **EXCHANGES:** 1 Other Carbo., 1½ Fat

OFF THE SHELF TIP Sold in smooth and chunky forms, peanut butter is often found in plastic jars or plastic tubs next to the jelly or in glass jars in the refrigerated section.

GO SHORT (OR SHORTENING) ON GREASE OR NEED GREASE?

Most cookies have enough butter or shortening in them that they don't require a nonstick or a greased cookie sheet. Bake a couple of cookies on an ungreased sheet first, let them cool two minutes but no longer, then slide a spatula underneath to remove them. If the cookie sticks, bake the remainder of the batch on sheets lightly greased with solid shortening. Shortening has a high burn point and doesn't result in the sticky buildup that aerosol non-stick sprays can produce.

Chocolate Cappuccino Cookies

PREP
30 MINUTES

BAKE
8 MINUTES PER BATCH

COOL
2 MINUTES

OVEN
350°F

MAKES
ABOUT 48 COOKIES

3	**tablespoons water**
1	**tablespoon instant espresso coffee powder**
1	**19.5- or 19.8-ounce package fudge brownie mix**
1	**egg**
3	**tablespoons cooking oil**
1/4	**teaspoon ground cinnamon**
1 1/2	**cups dark chocolate pieces, semisweet chocolate pieces, and/or white baking pieces**
	Milk chocolate kisses (optional)

STEP 1   Preheat oven to 350°F. Lightly grease a baking sheet or line a baking sheet with parchment paper; set aside. In a small bowl combine water and espresso coffee powder; stir until dissolved. Set aside.

STEP 2   In a large mixing bowl combine brownie mix, egg, oil, cinnamon, and the espresso mixture. Beat with an electric mixer on low speed until combined, scraping sides of bowl occasionally. Using a wooden spoon, stir in chocolate pieces. Drop dough by rounded teaspoons 1 inch apart onto prepared baking sheet or shape into 1-inch balls and place 1 inch apart on prepared baking sheet.

STEP 3   Bake in the preheated oven about 8 minutes or until edges are just set (centers will appear doughy). Do not overbake. Cool on cookie sheet for 2 minutes. If desired, place a chocolate kiss on each cookie. Transfer to a wire rack and let cool. Store cookies in an airtight container at room temperature up to 24 hours. Freeze for longer storage.

PER COOKIE: 85 cal., 4 g total fat (1 g sat. fat), 5 mg chol., 34 mg sodium, 13 g carbo., 1 g fiber, 1 g pro.
EXCHANGES: 1 Other Carbo., 1/2 Fat

OFF THE SHELF TIP Fudge brownie mix is a boxed, warm, chocolaty dessert and is usually shelved with other dessert mixes.

Candy Bar Cookies

PREP
30 MINUTES

BAKE
10 MINUTES

OVEN
375°F

RECIPE PICTURED ON PAGE 138.

FOR 48 BARS

1	cup packed brown sugar
⅔	cup butter or margarine
¼	cup dark- or light-colored corn syrup
¼	cup peanut butter
1	teaspoon vanilla
3½	cups quick-cooking rolled oats
1	12-ounce package semisweet chocolate pieces (2 cups)
1	cup butterscotch pieces
⅔	cup peanut butter
½	cup chopped peanuts

FOR 32 BARS

½	cup packed brown sugar
⅓	cup butter or margarine
2	tablespoons dark- or light-colored corn syrup
2	tablespoons peanut butter
½	teaspoon vanilla
1¾	cups quick-cooking rolled oats
1	cup semisweet chocolate pieces
½	cup butterscotch pieces
⅓	cup peanut butter
¼	cup chopped peanuts

STEP 1 Preheat oven to 375°F. Line a 13x9x2-inch baking pan with foil, extending foil over edges of pan; set pan aside. In a medium saucepan cook and stir brown sugar, butter, and corn syrup over medium-low heat until combined. Remove saucepan from heat; stir in the ¼ cup peanut butter and the vanilla until smooth.

STEP 2 For crust, place rolled oats in a very large bowl. Pour brown sugar mixture over oats, stirring gently until combined. Press oat mixture evenly onto bottom of prepared baking pan. Bake in the preheated oven for 10 to 12 minutes or until edges are light brown.

STEP 3 Meanwhile, in the same saucepan cook and stir chocolate pieces and butterscotch pieces together over low heat until melted. Stir in the ⅔ cup peanut butter until mixture is smooth. Slowly pour mixture over the hot crust, spreading evenly; sprinkle with peanuts.

STEP 4 Cool in pan on a wire rack for several hours or until chocolate layer is firm. (If necessary, refrigerate until chocolate is set.) When firm, use foil to lift out of pan. Cut into bars.

PER BAR: 166 cal., 9 g total fat (4 g sat. fat), 7 mg chol., 64 mg sodium, 16 g carbo., 2 g fiber, 3 g pro. **EXCHANGES:** 1 Other Carbo., 2 Fat

FOR 32 BARS: Prepare using method above, except press crust into a foil-lined 8x8x2-inch baking pan.

OFF THE SHELF TIP Semisweet chocolate pieces are melt-in-your-mouth chips of chocolate and ready to be melted or mixed into your bread, cookie, cake, or bar recipe.

Mocha Cookies

EASY

PREP
10 MINUTES

BAKE
10 MINUTES PER BATCH

OVEN
350°F

MAKES
20 COOKIES

3   tablespoons sugar
2   tablespoons unsweetened cocoa powder
1   tablespoon instant espresso coffee powder or 2 tablespoons instant coffee crystals, crushed
1   18-ounce package refrigerated portioned sugar cookie dough
2   tablespoons milk

STEP 1   Preheat oven to 350°F. In a small bowl stir together sugar, cocoa powder, and espresso powder. Break cookie dough into portions. Roll each cookie dough portion in milk, then in the sugar mixture. Place cookie dough portions on an ungreased large baking sheet.

STEP 2   Bake in the preheated oven for 10 to 12 minutes or until edges are set. Transfer to a wire rack and let cool.

PER COOKIE: 123 cal., 5 g total fat (1 g sat. fat), 10 mg chol., 82 mg sodium, 18 g carbo., 1 g fiber, 1 g pro.
EXCHANGES: 1½ Other Carbo., 1 Fat

OFF THE SHELF TIP   Cookie dough is sold in a roll or 18-ounce package from the refrigerator section. Choose your favorite flavor to make baking cookies a breeze.

Carrot Cake Cookies

PREP
30 MINUTES

BAKE
10 MINUTES PER BATCH

OVEN
350°F

MAKES
ABOUT 36 COOKIES

2	eggs, slightly beaten
½	cup cooking oil
½	teaspoon vanilla
1	package 2-layer-size spice or carrot cake mix
½	cup finely shredded carrot (1 medium)
½	cup golden raisins
½	cup finely chopped walnuts or pecans, toasted if desired (optional)
½	teaspoon vanilla
1	16-ounce can cream cheese frosting
¼	cup finely chopped walnuts or pecans, toasted if desired (optional)

OFF THE SHELF TIP Canned frosting is now available in a rainbow of flavors and colors and makes putting the icing on the cake a snap!

STEP 1   Preheat oven to 350°F. In a large mixing bowl combine eggs, oil, and vanilla. Add cake mix, carrot, raisins, the ½ cup nuts (if desired), and vanilla. Stir until combined and no lumps of cake mix remain. Drop dough by rounded teaspoonfuls 2 inches apart onto an ungreased baking sheet.

STEP 2   Bake in the preheated oven for 10 to 12 minutes or until edges are light brown. Transfer to a wire rack and let cool. Frost with cream cheese frosting. If desired, sprinkle with the ¼ cup nuts.

PER COOKIE: 152 cal., 6 g total fat (2 g sat. fat), 12 mg chol., 129 mg sodium, 22 g carbo., 0 g fiber, 1 g pro.
EXCHANGES: 1½ Other Carbo., 1½ Fat

Banana-Nut Sandwich Cookies

For fun, cut these sandwich cookies with a football-shape cutter for fall tailgate parties, but you can use a scalloped round or a biscuit cutter too.

FAST

PREP
20 MINUTES

BAKE
9 MINUTES PER BATCH

OVEN
350°F

MAKES
TWELVE 2½- TO 3-INCH SANDWICH COOKIES

Nonstick cooking spray
1   **7- to 8.1-ounce package banana nut muffin mix**
¾   **cup all-purpose flour**
¼   **cup packed brown sugar**
½   **cup butter or margarine, melted and cooled slightly**
1   **to 2 tablespoons milk (optional)**
1½   **cups powdered sugar**
½   **cup butter or margarine, softened**
1   **teaspoon vanilla**
½   **cup white baking pieces or semisweet chocolate pieces**
2   **teaspoons shortening**

STEP 1 Preheat oven to 350°F. Lightly coat a large baking sheet with nonstick cooking spray; set aside. In a large bowl stir together muffin mix, flour, and brown sugar. Add the ½ cup melted butter all at once. Using a fork, stir just until a soft dough forms. (If necessary, add enough milk to form dough.)

STEP 2 Turn dough out onto a lightly floured surface. Pat or lightly roll dough until ⅛ to ¼ inch thick. Using a 2½- to 3-inch cookie cutter, cut out cookies. Place 2 inches apart on the prepared baking sheet.

STEP 3 Bake in the preheated oven for 9 to 10 minutes or until cookies begin to brown. Remove cookies to a wire rack to cool completely.

STEP 4 For butter cream filling, in a medium bowl beat powdered sugar, the ½ cup softened butter, and vanilla with an electric mixer on medium speed until creamy. Spread a scant tablespoon of filling on the bottom of 1 cookie; top with another cookie, bottom side down, to make a cookie "sandwich." Repeat with remaining cookies and filling.

STEP 5 In a small microwave-safe bowl place white baking pieces and shortening. Microwave on medium (50%) power for 1 to 2 minutes or until pieces are melted and smooth, stirring every 30 seconds. Cool slightly (about 5 minutes). Carefully transfer melted chocolate to a heavy resealable plastic bag. Cut off tip of one corner of bag. Pipe melted chocolate onto cookies.

PER SERVING: 359 cal., 22 g total fat (12 g sat. fat), 46 mg chol., 266 mg sodium, 38 g carbo., 0 g fiber, 2 g pro.
EXCHANGES: 2½ Other Carbo., 4½ Fat

OFF THE SHELF TIP This baking aisle gem is easy to dress up. Quick bread mix is available in a variety of flavors—banana, cranberry, pumpkin, and more!

Little Lemon Snowbites

PREP
25 MINUTES
BAKE
7 MINUTES PER BATCH
OVEN
375°F
MAKES
ABOUT 24 SANDWICH
COOKIES

**RECIPE PICTURED
ON PAGE 132.**

1	17.5-ounce package sugar cookie mix
¼	cup crushed hard lemon candies
⅔	cup purchased lemon curd
⅔	cup frozen whipped dessert topping, thawed
2	tablespoons powdered sugar

STEP 1 Preheat the oven to 375°F. Line a cookie sheet with foil or parchment paper; set aside. Prepare cookie mix according to package directions. Stir in the crushed candies. If necessary, cover and chill dough about 1 hour or until easy to handle. Roll dough into 1-inch balls. Place balls 2 inches apart on prepared cookie sheet.

STEP 2 Bake in the preheated oven for 7 to 9 minutes or until edges are firm and cookies are light brown on bottoms. Cool on cookie sheet for 1 minute. Transfer to a wire rack and let cool.

STEP 3 For filling, in small bowl stir together lemon curd and whipped topping; set aside. To assemble cookies, place a rounded teaspoon of filling on the bottom side of a cookie; top with another cookie, top side up. Repeat with remaining cookies and filling. Sprinkle tops of cookies with powdered sugar. Store filled cookies in the refrigerator for up to 3 days or freeze for up to 1 month.

PER SANDWICH COOKIE: 169 cal., 7 g total fat (3 g sat. fat), 26 mg chol., 87 mg sodium, 25 g carbo., 1 g fiber, 1 g pro.
EXCHANGES: 1½ Other Carbo., 1½ Fat

OFF THE SHELF TIP Look for lemon curd near jams and jellies. The thick, intensely flavored spread of lemons, butter, eggs, and sugar is delicious on its own and in baked goods.

Maple-Cinnamon *Wedges*

EASY

PREP
15 MINUTES
BAKE
20 MINUTES
OVEN
350°F
MAKES
30 WEDGES

1	**18-ounce roll refrigerated sugar cookie dough**
¼	**cup all-purpose flour**
3	**tablespoons butter, melted**
2	**tablespoons pure maple syrup or maple-flavor syrup**
¼	**cup packed brown sugar**
¼	**cup finely chopped pecans**
½	**teaspoon ground cinnamon**

STEP 1   Preheat oven to 350°F. Line a 13x9x2-inch baking pan with foil. Lightly grease the foil; set aside.

STEP 2   In a large bowl combine cookie dough and flour; stir or knead until well mixed. Press dough evenly into the prepared pan.

STEP 3   In a small bowl combine melted butter and maple syrup. Drizzle syrup mixture over dough, spreading evenly. In another small bowl combine brown sugar, pecans, and cinnamon. Sprinkle over syrup layer in pan.

STEP 4   Bake in the preheated oven about 20 minutes or until edges are firm (center will be soft). Cool on a wire rack. When cool, use foil to lift from pan. Cut into 15 bars; cut each bar in half diagonally to make wedges. Store in a tightly covered container up to 3 days.

PER WEDGE: 105 cal., 5 g total fat (2 g sat. fat), 8 mg chol., 81 mg sodium, 14 g carbo., 0 g fiber, 1 g pro.
EXCHANGES: 1 Other Carbo., 1 Fat

OFF THE SHELF TIP   You'll find all sorts of salted and unsalted nuts in the baking aisle (look for pieces and already-chopped) or chips section.

Chili Powder & Pecan Crackles

Surprise! The secret's out: Chili powder puts the snap in these nut-crunchy goodies.

PREP
25 MINUTES

BAKE
8 MINUTES PER BATCH

OVEN
375°F

MAKES
ABOUT 20

RECIPE PICTURED ON PAGE 135.

1	package 1-layer size devil's food cake mix
2	tablespoons unsweetened cocoa powder
¼	to ½ teaspoon ground dried chipotle chili powder
1	egg, slightly beaten
1	tablespoon butter, softened
2	tablespoons milk
½	cup finely chopped pecans

STEP 1   Preheat oven to 375°F. In a medium bowl stir together cake mix, cocoa powder, chipotle chili powder, egg, and butter until all is moistened (dough will be stiff).

STEP 2   Roll dough into 1-inch balls. Place milk in a shallow dish. Place nuts in another shallow dish. Dip balls in milk, then in nuts to coat. Place 2 inches apart on an ungreased baking sheet.

STEP 3   Bake in the preheated oven for 8 to 9 minutes or until tops are crackled. Cool on cookie sheet for 1 minute. Transfer to a wire rack and let cool completely. To store, place cookies in layers separated by waxed paper in an airtight container; cover. Store at room temperature for up to 24 hours or freeze for up to 3 months.

PER SERVING: 133 cal., 5 g total fat (1 g sat. fat), 12 mg chol., 207 mg sodium, 22 g carbo., 1 g fiber, 2 g pro.
EXCHANGES: 1½ Other Carbo., 1 Fat

OFF THE SHELF TIP Available in dozens of flavors and most commonly packaged in boxes, cake mixes are a handy alternative to the made-from-scratch method.

Piecrust Cookies

PREP
15 MINUTES

BAKE
8 MINUTES

OVEN
400°F

MAKES
ABOUT 25 COOKIES

½   **of a 15-ounce package rolled refrigerated unbaked piecrusts (1 crust)**

1   **tablespoon butter or margarine, melted**

2   **tablespoons packed brown sugar**

½   **to 1 teaspoon pumpkin pie spice or apple pie spice**

STEP 1   Preheat oven to 400°F. Unroll piecrust according to package directions using the microwave method. Place on a lightly floured surface. Brush piecrust with melted butter. Sprinkle with brown sugar and pumpkin pie spice. Use a pastry wheel or pizza cutter to cut dough into 1½- to 2-inch square cookies (some of the edges may be smaller). Place on an ungreased large baking sheet, leaving a small space between cookies.

STEP 2   Bake in the preheated oven about 8 minutes or until golden brown. Serve warm or let cool.

PER COOKIE: 47 cal., 3 g total fat (1 g sat. fat), 3 mg chol., 35 mg sodium, 5 g carbo., 0 g fiber, 0 g pro.
EXCHANGES: ½ Other Carbo., ½ Fat

OFF THE SHELF TIP   Refrigerated rolled unbaked piecrust puts the fun back in baking pies or any dessert that requires a pastry crust.

Mocha-Chocolate Chip Cheesecake Bars

Instant coffee yields a pleasing note to this union of cheesecake and chocolate chip cookie.

PREP
15 MINUTES

BAKE
20 MINUTES

OVEN
350°F

MAKES
36 BARS

1   18-ounce package refrigerated
    chocolate chip cookie dough
1   8-ounce package cream cheese
    or reduced-fat cream cheese
    (Neufchâtel), softened
⅓   cup sugar
1   egg
1   tablespoon instant coffee crystals
1   teaspoon vanilla
1   teaspoon water
½   cup miniature semisweet
    chocolate pieces

OFF THE SHELF TIP Look for these sparkling instant coffee crystals in a jar on the coffee shelf.

STEP 1   Preheat oven to 350°F. For crust, in a 13x9x2-inch baking pan, crumble cookie dough. Press evenly onto bottom of pan; set aside.

STEP 2   In a medium bowl combine cream cheese, sugar, and egg; beat with a wooden spoon until smooth. In a small bowl or custard cup, stir together coffee crystals, vanilla, and water until crystals are dissolved. Stir coffee mixture into cream cheese mixture. Spread evenly over crust; sprinkle with chocolate pieces.

STEP 3   Bake in the preheated oven about 20 minutes or until completely set. Cool in pan on a wire rack; cut into bars. To store, tightly cover pan and store in the refrigerator up to 3 days or freeze up to 1 month.

PER BAR: 109 cal., 6 g total fat (3 g sat. fat), 15 mg chol., 71 mg sodium, 12 g carbo., 0 g fiber, 1 g pro.
EXCHANGES: 1 Other Carbo., 1 Fat

Chocolate Chip Cream Bars

With a cheesecake-like spread over chocolate chip cookie dough, these bars will become a classic born of beloved dessert favorites.

PREP
20 MINUTES

BAKE
28 MINUTES

OVEN
350°F

MAKES
30 BARS

1   **18-ounce package or roll refrigerated chocolate chip cookie dough**

1   **8-ounce package cream cheese, softened**

½   **cup sugar**

1   **egg**

½   **teaspoon vanilla**

STEP 1   Preheat oven to 350°F. Line a 9x9x2-inch baking pan with foil, extending foil over edges of the pan; grease the foil. Set aside. Using a sharp knife, cut the cookie dough into 4 equal portions. For crust, press 3 portions of the cookie dough evenly into the bottom of the prepared pan; set aside.

STEP 2   For filling, in a medium mixing bowl beat cream cheese with an electric mixer on medium speed until smooth. Add sugar, egg, and vanilla, beating on low speed until combined. Spread filling evenly over crust. Dot filling with the remaining portion of cookie dough.

STEP 3   Bake in the preheated oven for 28 to 30 minutes or until top is light brown and filling is set. Cool on a wire rack. Cut into bars. Cover and store in refrigerator.

DOUBLE CHOCOLATE CREAM BARS: Prepare as above, except beat ¼ cup unsweetened cocoa powder into the filling before spreading over the crust. Continue as directed above.

PER BAR: 120 cal., 6 g total fat (3 g sat. fat), 18 mg chol., 76 mg sodium, 14 g carbo., 0 g fiber, 1 g pro. EXCHANGES: 1 Other Carbo., 1½ Fat

OFF THE SHELF TIP Cookie dough is sold in a roll or 18-ounce package from the refrigerator section. Choose your favorite flavor to make baking cookies a breeze.

Chocolate Goody Bars

Frosting dresses up a brownie, but here, the frosting-dressed brownie is the base for layers of chopped nuts, chocolate chips, cereal, and peanut butter.

1	19.8-ounce package fudge brownie mix
½	cup cooking oil
2	eggs
¼	cup water
1	16-ounce can vanilla frosting
¾	cup chopped peanuts
1	12-ounce package semisweet chocolate pieces (2 cups)
1	cup creamy peanut butter
3	cups crisp rice cereal

PER BAR: 264 cal., 14 g total fat (4 g sat. fat), 12 mg chol., 140 mg sodium, 28 g carbo., 2 g fiber, 4 g pro.
EXCHANGES: 2 Other Carbo., ½ High-Fat Meat, 2 Fat

OFF THE SHELF TIP Fudge brownie mix is a boxed, warm, chocolaty dessert and is usually shelved with other dessert mixes.

PREP
20 MINUTES
BAKE
30 MINUTES
CHILL
1 ½ HOURS
OVEN
350°F
MAKES
36 BARS

RECIPE PICTURED ON PAGE **139.**

STEP 1 Preheat oven to 350°F. Line a 13x9x2-inch baking pan with foil, extending foil over edges of the pan. Grease foil; set pan aside.

STEP 2 In a large bowl stir together the brownie mix, oil, eggs, and water. Spread batter into the prepared pan. Bake in the preheated oven for 30 minutes. Cool completely in pan on a wire rack.

STEP 3 Frost bars with vanilla frosting. Sprinkle with peanuts. Cover and refrigerate about 45 minutes or until frosting is firm.

STEP 4 Meanwhile, in a medium saucepan combine chocolate pieces and peanut butter. Cook and stir over low heat until chocolate is melted; stir in cereal. Spread over frosting. Cover and refrigerate about 45 minutes more or until chocolate layer is set. Use foil to lift out of pan. Cut into bars. Store in a single layer in a covered container in the refrigerator.

Chocolate Caramel-Nut Bars

White cake mix and lower-fat cream cheese form a lush base for peanut, milk chocolate, and caramel flavors.

PREP
20 MINUTES
BAKE
30 MINUTES
OVEN
350°F
MAKES
24 BARS

Nonstick cooking spray

1   package 2-layer-size white cake mix

1   cup quick-cooking rolled oats

½   cup peanut butter

1   egg

2   tablespoons milk

1   8-ounce package reduced-fat cream
       cheese (Neufchâtel)

1   12.25-ounce jar caramel
       ice cream topping

1   11.5-ounce package milk
       chocolate pieces

1   cup cocktail peanuts

STEP 1   Preheat oven to 350°F. Coat a 13x9x2-inch baking pan with nonstick cooking spray; set aside.

STEP 2   For crumb mixture, in a large bowl combine cake mix and oats. Using a pastry blender, cut in peanut butter until mixture resembles fine crumbs. In a small bowl beat egg and milk with a fork; add to peanut butter mixture, stirring until well mixed. Set aside ¾ cup of the crumb mixture. Press remaining crumb mixture into the bottom of the prepared baking pan.

STEP 3   For filling, in a medium mixing bowl beat cream cheese with an electric mixer on medium speed until smooth. Add caramel topping; beat until combined. Spread over crumb mixture in baking pan. Sprinkle chocolate pieces on top; sprinkle with peanuts. Sprinkle evenly with reserved crumb mixture.

STEP 4   Bake in the preheated oven for 30 minutes. Cool completely on a wire rack. Cut into 24 bars. Store, covered, in the refrigerator.

PER BAR: 311 cal., 14 g total fat (5 g sat. fat), 16 mg chol., 273 mg sodium, 41 g carbo., 1 g fiber, 7 g pro. **EXCHANGES:** 2½ Other Carbo., 1 High-Fat Meat, 1½ Fat

OFF THE SHELF TIP Grocers vary in where they stock ice cream toppings. Look by pancake syrups, or near the ice cream freezer.

Chocolate-Mint Bars

Sweet, coconut-chocolate mint cream tops a chocolate crumb crust.

PREP
10 MINUTES

BAKE
20 MINUTES

OVEN
350°F

MAKES
48 BARS

1 tablespoon butter
1½ cups packaged chocolate cookie crumbs
1 cup chopped nuts
1 cup mint-flavored semisweet chocolate pieces
1 cup flaked coconut
1 14-ounce can sweetened condensed milk

OFF THE SHELF TIP Sweetened condensed milk is a thick and syrupy milk-and-sugar combo sold in 14-ounce cans on the baking aisle shelves.

STEP 1 Preheat oven to 350°F. Generously grease the bottom of a 13x9x2-inch baking pan with the butter. Sprinkle crumbs evenly onto the bottom of pan; sprinkle with nuts, chocolate pieces, and coconut. Drizzle sweetened condensed milk evenly over all.

STEP 2 Bake in the preheated oven for 20 to 25 minutes or until coconut is golden brown around edges. Cool in pan on a wire rack. Cut into squares. To store, tightly cover pan and store in the refrigerator up to 3 days.

PER BAR: 84 cal., 5 g total fat (2 g sat. fat), 3 mg chol., 41 mg sodium, 11 g carbo., 1 g fiber, 2 g pro.
EXCHANGES: ½ Other Carbo., 1 Fat

Easy Pecan Bars

You'll think of pecan pie with each bite of the cake-mix-based pecan bars.

PREP
20 MINUTES
BAKE
37 MINUTES
OVEN
350°F
MAKES
32 BARS

1   package 2-layer-size white or chocolate cake mix
¼   cup butter, softened
1   egg, slightly beaten
3   eggs
¾   cup packed brown sugar
¾   cup dark-colored corn syrup
1   teaspoon vanilla
1¼   cups coarsely chopped pecans

STEP 1   Preheat oven to 350°F. Lightly grease a 13x9x2-inch baking pan; set aside. Set aside 1 cup cake mix for the filling.

STEP 2   For crust, in a medium bowl combine remaining cake mix, butter, and the slightly beaten egg. Stir with a fork until crumbly. With lightly floured hands, press mixture evenly onto the bottom of the prepared pan. Bake in the preheated oven for 12 minutes.

STEP 3   Meanwhile, for filling, in a medium bowl combine the 3 eggs, brown sugar, corn syrup, and vanilla. Add the 1 cup reserved cake mix; stir with a fork just until blended. (Some tiny cake mix clumps will remain.) Spread filling evenly over baked crust; sprinkle pecans on top.

STEP 4   Bake in the 350° oven for 25 to 30 minutes more or until filling appears set when pan is gently shaken. Cool completely in the pan on a wire rack. Cut into bars. To store, tightly cover pan and store in the refrigerator up to 3 days.

PER BAR: 165 cal., 8 g total fat (2 g sat. fat), 30 mg chol., 168 mg sodium, 23 g carbo., 1 g fiber, 2 g pro. **EXCHANGES:** 1 Starch, ½ Other Carbo., 1 Fat

OFF THE SHELF TIP   Available in dozens of flavors and most commonly packaged in boxes, cake mixes are a handy alternative to the made-from-scratch method.

Coconut-Cashew Bars

Call this scrumptious six-layer bar with dried pineapple a taste of the tropics. With cookie dough as the base, this recipe goes together quickly.

EASY

PREP
15 MINUTES

BAKE
20 MINUTES

OVEN
350°F

MAKES
72 BARS

RECIPE PICTURED ON PAGE **138.**

Nonstick cooking spray
1   18-ounce roll or package refrigerated sugar cookie dough
1   14-ounce can sweetened condensed milk
1½   cups chopped dried pineapple
1   cup semisweet chocolate pieces
1⅓   cups flaked coconut
1⅓   cups cashew halves or coarsely chopped macadamia nuts

STEP 1 Preheat oven to 350°F. Lightly coat a 15x10x1-inch baking pan with nonstick cooking spray. With floured hands, press cookie dough into bottom of prepared pan. Spread evenly with sweetened condensed milk. Sprinkle with pineapple, chocolate pieces, coconut, and nuts. Press down firmly.

STEP 2 Bake in the preheated oven about 20 minutes or until light brown. Cool in pan on a wire rack; cut into bars. To store, tightly cover pan and store in the refrigerator up to 3 days.

PER BAR: 93 cal., 4 g total fat (2 g sat. fat), 4 mg chol., 38 mg sodium, 12 g carbo., 1 g fiber, 1 g pro. **EXCHANGES:** 1 Other Carbo., 1 Fat

OFF THE SHELF TIP Cookie dough is sold in a roll or 18-ounce package from the refrigerator section. Choose your favorite flavor to make baking cookies a breeze.

Maui Wowie Bars

PREP
20 MINUTES

BAKE
30 MINUTES

OVEN
350°F

MAKES
25 BARS

1   cup quick-cooking rolled oats
1   cup all-purpose flour
1   3.5-ounce jar macadamia nuts, finely chopped (¾ cup)
¼   cup sugar
½   cup butter, melted
2   teaspoons vanilla
¾   cup white baking pieces
1   12-ounce jar pineapple ice cream topping (1 cup)
¾   cup dried pineapple, finely chopped
¾   cup flaked coconut

STEP 1   Preheat oven to 350°F. Line a 9x9x2-inch baking pan with foil, extending foil over the edges of the pan. Grease the foil on the bottom and sides of pan. Set aside.

STEP 2   For crumb mixture, in a medium bowl stir together oats, flour, nuts, and sugar. Stir in ½ cup melted butter and vanilla until combined (mixture will be crumbly). Press 2 cups of the crumb mixture into the bottom of the prepared pan. Set remaining crumb mixture aside. Sprinkle crust mixture in the pan with white baking pieces.

STEP 3   In a medium bowl stir together the pineapple topping, dried pineapple, and coconut. Spoon evenly over the white-baking-piece layer. Sprinkle with the reserved crumb mixture.

STEP 4   Bake in the preheated oven about 30 minutes or until bubbly around the edges and crumb topping is lightly golden. Cool in pan on a wire rack. Use the foil to lift the bars out of the pan onto a cutting surface; cut into bars.

PER BAR: 200 cal., 10 g total fat (6 g sat. fat), 10 mg chol., 53 mg sodium, 26 g carbo., 1 g fiber, 1 g pro. **EXCHANGES:** ½ Starch, 1 Other Carbo., 2 Fat

OFF THE SHELF TIP From the baking aisle, coconut is packaged in bags or cans and is available shredded, flaked, and even toasted.

Salted Peanut Bars

PREP
20 MINUTES

BAKE
25 MINUTES

COOL
1 HOUR

OVEN
350°F

MAKES
32 BARS

1   package 2-layer-size white or yellow cake mix
½   cup butter, melted
1   egg, slightly beaten
1   10-ounce package peanut butter-flavor pieces
1   cup chopped salted peanuts
2   cups tiny marshmallows

OFF THE SHELF TIP You'll find all sorts of salted and unsalted nuts in the baking aisle (look for pieces and already-chopped) or chips section.

STEP 1   Preheat oven to 350°F. In a large bowl stir together cake mix and melted butter. Stir in egg (dough will be stiff). Press dough into the bottom of an ungreased 13x9x2-inch baking pan. Sprinkle with peanut butter pieces and peanuts.

STEP 2   Bake in the preheated oven about 20 minutes or until edges are light brown. Remove from oven. Sprinkle with marshmallows. Return to oven and bake about 5 minutes more or until marshmallows are puffed and just starting to brown.

STEP 3   Cool in pan on a wire rack for 1 hour. Cut into triangles or rectangles. To store, place in layers separated by waxed paper in an airtight container; cover. Store at room temperature up to 3 days or freeze up to 3 months.

PER BAR: 175 cal., 9 g total fat (4 g sat. fat), 14 mg chol., 171 mg sodium, 21 g carbo., 1 g fiber, 4 g pro. **EXCHANGES:** 1 Starch, ½ Other Carbo., 1½ Fat

Almond-Toffee Bars

This rich treat is super simple—just layer and bake. No bowl, no stirring, no leftovers!

EASY

PREP
15 MINUTES
BAKE
25 MINUTES
OVEN
325°F
MAKES
48 BARS

½ cup butter
1½ cups quick-cooking rolled oats
½ cup graham cracker crumbs
1 cup semisweet chocolate pieces (6 ounces)
1 cup almond brickle pieces
1 cup sliced or chopped almonds
1 14-ounce can sweetened condensed milk

OFF THE SHELF TIP Look for packaged graham cracker crumbs next to prepared crumb crusts. Or finely crush 24 cracker squares to make 1½ cups.

STEP 1 Preheat oven to 325°F. In a 13x9x2-inch baking pan, melt butter in the oven (about 6 minutes). Remove pan from oven. Sprinkle oats and crumbs evenly over melted butter; press lightly onto the bottom of the pan using the back of a large metal spoon. Sprinkle chocolate pieces, brickle pieces, and almonds evenly over crumb mixture. Drizzle with sweetened condensed milk.

STEP 2 Bake in the preheated oven for 25 to 30 minutes or until edges are bubbly and center is just light brown. Remove from oven and immediately run a narrow metal spatula or table knife around edges of pan to loosen the cookie. Cool completely in pan on a wire rack; cut into bars. To store, tightly cover pan and store in the refrigerator for up to 3 days.

PER BAR: 107 cal., 6 g total fat (2 g sat. fat), 9 mg chol., 44 mg sodium, 12 g carbo., 1 g fiber, 2 g pro. **EXCHANGES:** 1 Other Carbo., 1 Fat

TOFFEE-FRUIT BARS: Prepare as above, except substitute ½ cup snipped dried apricots for ½ cup chocolate pieces.

Banana Brownie Bars

A bite into these brownies gets a blast of flavor: Banana chips and other treats lurk within.

EASY

PREP
15 MINUTES
BAKE
20 MINUTES
OVEN
325°F
MAKES
24 BARS

RECIPE PICTURED ON PAGE **138.**

Nonstick cooking spray
1   8- or 10-ounce package brownie mix
1   cup quick-cooking rolled oats
1   egg
2   to 3 tablespoons water
1   cup broken banana chips
1   cup milk chocolate pieces (6 ounces)
1   cup tiny marshmallows
¾   cup chopped walnuts

STEP 1   Preheat oven to 325°F. Lightly coat a 13x9x2-inch baking pan with nonstick cooking spray; set aside.

STEP 2   In a medium bowl stir together brownie mix, oats, egg, and water. Using floured hands, spread evenly into bottom of prepared pan.

STEP 3   Bake in the preheated oven for 5 minutes. Layer banana chips, chocolate pieces, marshmallows, and nuts over partially baked crust; press down gently. Bake for 15 minutes more. Cool in pan on a wire rack; cut into bars. To store, tightly cover pan and store at room temperature up to 3 days.

PER BAR: 136 cal., 7 g total fat (3 g sat. fat), 10 mg chol., 38 mg sodium, 18 g carbo., 1 g fiber, 2 g pro.
EXCHANGES: 1 Other Carbo., 1½ Fat

OFF THE SHELF TIP   Banana chips are crunchy dried slices of sweet bananas shelved with other dried fruit.

Banana Crunch Bars

PREP
20 MINUTES

BAKE
10 MINUTES

CHILL
4 HOURS

STAND
20 MINUTES

OVEN
350°F

MAKES
16 TO 20 BARS

1¾   cups crushed chocolate wafers
       (about 36 wafers)
½   cup sugar
¼   cup unsweetened cocoa powder
1   teaspoon vanilla
½   cup butter, melted
3   tablespoons light-colored corn syrup
2   tablespoons butter
2   medium bananas, sliced (1½ cups)
1   teaspoon rum flavoring
½   cup semisweet chocolate pieces
½   cup peanut butter-flavor pieces
1   teaspoon shortening

PER BAR: 253 cal., 14 g total fat (8 g sat. fat), 22 mg chol., 204 mg sodium, 31 g carbo., 1 g fiber, 3 g pro. **EXCHANGES:** 2 Other Carbo., 3 Fat

OFF THE SHELF TIP Packaged in bags, peanut butter-flavored pieces can be found next to chocolate pieces in the baking aisle.

STEP 1   Preheat oven to 350°F. In a medium bowl combine the crushed wafers, sugar, cocoa powder, and vanilla. Stir in the ½ cup melted butter. Press into bottom of a greased 8x8x2-inch baking pan. Bake in the preheated oven for 10 minutes. Cool slightly on a wire rack, about 10 minutes.

STEP 2   In a small saucepan combine corn syrup and the 2 tablespoons butter. Stir over medium heat until melted and bubbly. Remove from heat; stir in bananas and rum flavoring. Spoon banana mixture in an even layer over baked crust.

STEP 3   In a small saucepan combine the chocolate pieces, peanut butter-flavored pieces, and shortening. Stir over low heat until melted. Drizzle over the banana mixture. Cover and refrigerate until set. Let stand at room temperature 20 minutes before cutting into bars. Serve the same day.

Easy Butter Bars

Oh-so-rich cream-cheesy bars boast a big butter flavor. Add a garnish of sugared cranberries and fresh mint, if you like.

PREP
20 MINUTES
BAKE
25 MINUTES
OVEN
350°F
MAKES
36 BARS

Nonstick cooking spray
1 **package 2-layer-size yellow or white cake mix**
½ **cup butter, softened**
1 **egg**
1 **8-ounce package cream cheese, softened**
2 **eggs**
1 **teaspoon butter flavoring**
3½ **cups powdered sugar**

STEP 1 Preheat oven to 350°F. Lightly coat a 15x10x1-inch baking pan with nonstick cooking spray.

STEP 2 For the crust, in a large mixing bowl combine cake mix, butter, and 1 egg. Beat with an electric mixer on low speed until mixture is crumbly. Pat mixture evenly into the bottom of the prepared pan; set aside.

STEP 3 In another large mixing bowl, beat cream cheese with the electric mixer on medium speed until smooth. Add 2 eggs and butter flavoring; beat until smooth. Add the powdered sugar; beat on low speed until well combined. Spread on top of crust in pan.

STEP 4 Bake in the preheated oven for 25 to 30 minutes or until the filling is set and golden brown. Cool in pan on a wire rack. (The filling may fall as it cools.) Using a sharp knife,* cut into bars.

*TIP: Dip the knife in hot water and lightly pat dry between cuts to make cleaner cuts.

PER BAR: 153 cal., 6 g total fat (4 g sat. fat), 31 mg chol., 136 mg sodium, 23 g carbo., 0 g fiber, 1 g pro. **EXCHANGES:** 1½ Other Carbo., 1½ Fat

OFF THE SHELF TIP Rich, creamy cream cheese is available in fat-free, low-fat, and regular—plus an assortment of flavors.

Gooey Pizza Brownies

PREP
20 MINUTES
BAKE
25 MINUTES
OVEN
350°F
MAKES
24 BROWNIES

**RECIPE PICTURED
ON PAGE 134.**

1   **19.8- to 21.5-ounce package
brownie mix**
1½   **cups tiny marshmallows**
½   **cup miniature semisweet
chocolate pieces**
½   **cup miniature candy-coated
semi-sweet chocolate pieces**
½   **cup toffee pieces**
⅓   **to ½ cup caramel ice cream topping**

OFF THE SHELF TIP Grocers vary
in where they stock ice cream toppings.
Look by pancake syrups or near the ice
cream freezer.

STEP 1   Preheat oven to 350°F. Grease
the bottom of a 13x9x2-inch baking pan;
set aside.

STEP 2   Prepare brownie mix according
to package directions. Spread batter into
the prepared pan.

STEP 3   Bake in the preheated oven
for 24 to 27 minutes or until edges are
firm. Remove pan from oven. Top with
marshmallows, chocolate pieces, and
candy pieces. Drizzle with the caramel
topping. Bake for 1 to 2 minutes more or
until marshmallows are puffy. Cool in pan
on wire rack.

PER BROWNIE: 245 cal., 10 g total fat (3 g sat. fat),
18 mg chol., 123 mg sodium, 35 g carbo., 0 g fiber,
2 g pro.
EXCHANGES: 2 Fat

Fudgy Brownies

EASY

PREP
15 MINUTES

BAKE
35 MINUTES

OVEN
350°F

RECIPE PICTURED ON PAGE 138.

9   ounces unsweetened chocolate, coarsely chopped
1   cup butter
⅓   cup water
4   teaspoons instant coffee crystals
1½   cups granulated sugar
1½   cups packed brown sugar
5   eggs
1½   teaspoons vanilla
2   cups all-purpose flour
¾   cup ground almonds
½   teaspoon ground cinnamon
¼   teaspoon salt
3   tablespoons powdered sugar (optional)
¼   teaspoon unsweetened cocoa powder (optional)

STEP 1 Preheat oven to 350°F. Line a 13x9x2-inch baking pan with foil, extending foil over edges of pan. Grease foil; set pan aside.

STEP 2 In a large microwave-safe mixing bowl combine the chocolate, butter, water, and coffee crystals. Microwave, uncovered, on 100% power (high) for 2 to 4 minutes or until butter is melted, stirring once or twice. Remove bowl from microwave oven. Stir until chocolate is completely melted.

STEP 3 Beat in granulated sugar and brown sugar with an electric mixer on low to medium speed until combined. Add eggs and vanilla; beat on medium speed for 2 minutes. Add flour, almonds, cinnamon, and salt. Beat on low speed until combined. Spread batter into the prepared pan.

STEP 4 Bake in the preheated oven about 35 minutes or until top appears set and dry. Cool in pan on a wire rack. Use foil to lift brownies out of pan. Cut into bars. If desired, stir together the powdered sugar and cocoa powder; sift over brownies.

PER BROWNIE: 302 cal., 17 g total fat (9 g sat. fat), 66 mg chol., 127 mg sodium, 37 g carbo., 2 g fiber, 4 g pro.
EXCHANGES: 1½ Starch, 1 Other Carbo., 3 Fat

OFF THE SHELF TIP Look for sparkling instant coffee crystals in a jar on the coffee shelf.

Desserts

Banana-Pecan Streusel *Bread Pudding*

PREP
20 MINUTES

BAKE
40 MINUTES

COOL
30 MINUTES

OVEN
350°F

MAKES
10 TO 12 SERVINGS

1   12-ounce can (1½ cups) evaporated milk
1⅓ cups mashed ripe banana (4 medium)
3   eggs, slightly beaten
½   cup granulated sugar
2   teaspoons vanilla
1   teaspoon ground cinnamon
¼   teaspoon almond extract
2   large croissants or five 1-inch slices French bread, cut or torn into 1-inch pieces (about 4 cups)
¼   cup packed brown sugar
2   tablespoons all-purpose flour
1   tablespoon butter, melted
1   teaspoon ground cinnamon
½   cup chopped pecans
    Whipped cream or ice cream (optional)

STEP 1 Preheat oven to 350°F. Lightly grease a 2-quart rectangular baking dish; set aside.

STEP 2 In a large bowl stir together milk, banana, eggs, granulated sugar, vanilla, 1 teaspoon cinnamon, and the almond extract. Place croissant pieces in the prepared baking dish. Pour egg mixture evenly over croissants, pressing pieces down to be sure they are all moistened.

STEP 3 In a small bowl combine brown sugar, flour, melted butter, and 1 teaspoon cinnamon. Stir in pecans. Sprinkle over croissant mixture.

STEP 4 Bake in the preheated oven for 40 to 45 minutes or until a knife inserted near center comes out clean. Let stand for 30 minutes. Serve warm.

TIP: Cover and chill any leftovers. To reheat, place a single serving in a microwave-safe bowl. Microwave, covered, on 100% power (high) for 1 minute or until heated through.

PER SERVING: 273 cal., 12 g total fat (4 g sat. fat), 84 mg chol., 153 mg sodium, 37 g carbo., 2 g fiber, 6 g pro.
EXCHANGES: 2 Starch, ½ Other Carbo., 2 Fat

OFF THE SHELF TIP Find flaky, buttery croissants in the bakery or bread aisle.

Biscuit Bread Pudding with *Lemon Sauce*

Vanilla, cinnamon, and nutmeg flavor this delectable biscuit bread pudding that is served with a velvety lemon sauce.

PREP
30 MINUTES

STAND
10 MINUTES

BAKE
45 MINUTES

OVEN
350°F

RECIPE PICTURED ON PAGE 141.

FOR 12 TO 14 SERVINGS

2	16.3-ounce packages refrigerated large (flaky or southern-style) biscuits (16 total)
6	eggs, slightly beaten
1	12-ounce can (1½ cups) evaporated milk
1	5-ounce can (⅔ cup) evaporated milk
2½	cups sugar
⅓	cup butter or margarine, melted
1½	teaspoons vanilla
¾	teaspoon ground cinnamon
¾	teaspoon ground nutmeg
1	recipe Lemon Sauce

FOR 8 SERVINGS

1	16.3-ounce package refrigerated large (flaky or southern-style) biscuits
4	eggs, slightly beaten
1	12-ounce can (1½ cups) evaporated milk
	evaporated milk
1¾	cups sugar
¼	cup butter or margarine, melted
1	teaspoon vanilla
½	teaspoon ground cinnamon
½	teaspoon ground nutmeg
½	recipe Lemon Sauce

STEP 1 Bake biscuits according to package directions. Cool. Crumble biscuits into bite-size pieces; set aside.

STEP 2 Preheat oven to 350°F. In a large bowl stir together eggs, evaporated milk, sugar, melted butter, vanilla, cinnamon, and nutmeg. Place crumbled biscuits in a greased 3-quart rectangular baking dish. Pour egg mixture over biscuits, pressing to moisten evenly. Let stand for 10 minutes to thoroughly moisten biscuits.

STEP 3 Bake in the preheated oven about 45 minutes or until a knife inserted near center comes out clean. Serve warm with Lemon Sauce.

LEMON SAUCE: In a medium saucepan stir together 2 slightly beaten eggs, ¼ cup water, and ¼ cup lemon juice. Add 1 cup sugar and ½ cup cut-up butter. Cook and stir until mixture is thickened and just bubbly on edges. If desired, strain sauce. Serve warm. Store in the refrigerator. Makes about 2 cups.

PER SERVING: 577 cal., 26 g total fat (13 g sat. fat), 190 mg chol., 702 mg sodium, 80 g carbo., 0 g fiber, 10 g pro.
EXCHANGES: ½ Milk, 1½ Starch, 3½ Other Carbo., ½ Very Lean Meat, 4 Fat

FOR 8 SERVINGS: Prepare following Steps 1 to 3, except place biscuits in a 2-quart square baking dish. Bake about 35 minutes or until knife inserted in center comes out clean.

OFF THE SHELF TIP Refrigerated biscuits are available in a variety of sizes and shapes. They make a tasty base for an appetizer or topper for a casserole.

Cranberry-Pumpkin Bread Pudding
with Brandy-Butter Sauce

Rich, sweet, and full of seasonal flavors, this dessert makes a perfect holiday feast alternative to standard pie. The luscious brandy-butter sauce is festive high note.

4	eggs, slightly beaten
2	egg yolks, slightly beaten
4	cups milk
1	cup sugar
1	15-ounce can pumpkin
¼	cup brandy
1½	teaspoons pumpkin pie spice
9	slices whole wheat bread, cut into ½-inch cubes (about 8 cups)
1	cup dried cranberries
1	recipe Brandy-Butter Sauce

OFF THE SHELF TIP Not just for pumpkin pie, canned pumpkin adds moistness and texture to many baked goods.

PREP
20 MINUTES
BAKE
55 MINUTES
STAND
15 MINUTES
OVEN
350°F
MAKES
15 SERVINGS

RECIPE PICTURED
ON PAGE **130.**

STEP 1   Preheat oven to 350°F. In a very large bowl combine eggs, egg yolks, milk, sugar, pumpkin, brandy, and pumpkin pie spice. Add bread cubes and cranberries; mix well. Let stand for 15 minutes. Transfer to a lightly greased 3-quart rectangular baking dish.

STEP 2   Bake, uncovered, in the preheated oven about 55 minutes or until a knife inserted in center comes out clean. Cool slightly. Serve warm with Brandy-Butter Sauce.

BRANDY-BUTTER SAUCE: In a small saucepan melt ½ cup butter over medium heat. Stir in 1½ cups powdered sugar until mixture is smooth. Stir in 2 egg yolks; cook and stir just until bubbly. Remove from heat. Stir in 1 to 2 tablespoons brandy. Serve warm.

PER SERVING: 338 cal., 12 g total fat (6 g sat. fat), 136 mg chol., 216 mg sodium, 49 g carbo., 3 g fiber, 7 g pro.
EXCHANGES: 1 Starch, 2 Other Carbo., ½ Very Lean Meat, 2½ Fat

Orange-Ginger Baby Cheesecakes

PREP
45 MINUTES
BAKE
20 MINUTES
COOL
45 MINUTES
OVEN
350°F
MAKES
16 SERVINGS

¾ **cup finely crushed gingersnap cookies (about fourteen 1¾-inch cookies)**
1 **tablespoon packed brown sugar**
3 **tablespoons butter, melted**
1 **8-ounce package cream cheese, softened**
½ **cup orange marmalade**
1 **egg yolk**
1 **tablespoon all-purpose flour**

STEP 1 Preheat oven to 350°F. For crust, in a small mixing bowl combine crushed cookies, brown sugar, and melted butter. Divide crumb mixture evenly among sixteen 1¾-inch muffin cups. Press crumb mixture onto bottom and up sides of each cup. Bake in the preheated oven for 5 minutes.

STEP 2 Meanwhile, in a medium mixing bowl beat together cream cheese, ¼ cup of the marmalade, the egg yolk, and flour. Divide cheese mixture evenly among the muffin cups. Bake about 15 minutes more or until a knife inserted in the centers comes out clean. Cool cheesecakes in tins on a wire rack (centers will dip slightly). Remove from muffin tins. Top each cheesecake with about ½ teaspoon marmalade. Serve at once or cover and chill up to 24 hours.

MAKE-AHEAD DIRECTIONS: Bake cheesecakes as directed but do not top with additional marmalade. Place cheesecakes in a freezer container. Cover, label, and freeze up to 3 months. Before serving, thaw overnight in refrigerator. Top with marmalade before serving.

PER SERVING: 127 cal., 8 g total fat (5 g sat. fat), 34 mg chol., 104 mg sodium, 13 g carbo., 0 g fiber, 2 g pro.
EXCHANGES: 1 Other Carbo., 1½ Fat

OFF THE SHELF TIP Orange marmalade is a sparkling preserve containing pieces of orange rind. Find it with the jellies and jams.

Praline Pecan *Cheesecake*

Brown sugar, nuts, chocolate-covered toffee sprinkles, and rum flavor send this cheesecake to new heights.

PREP
30 MINUTES

BAKE
70 MINUTES

COOL
2 HOURS

CHILL
4 HOURS

OVEN
325°F

MAKES
16 SERVINGS

1	package 2-layer-size butter cake mix
½	cup butter, softened
3	8-ounce packages cream cheese, softened
⅓	cup granulated sugar
3	tablespoons all-purpose flour
1½	teaspoon rum or almond extract
3	eggs
4	1.4-ounce bars chocolate-covered English toffee, coarsely crushed
½	cup packed brown sugar
1	cup chopped pecans
⅓	cup caramel ice cream topping

STEP 1 Preheat oven to 325°F. In a large mixing bowl beat cake mix and butter together with an electric mixer on low speed until crumbly. Reserve 1 cup of crumb mixture for topping.

STEP 2 Press remaining crumb mixture into bottom and 1½ inches up the side of an ungreased 9-inch springform pan.

STEP 3 In another large mixing bowl beat the cream cheese, granulated sugar, flour, and rum extract with an electric mixer on medium speed until smooth. Add eggs; beat just until combined. Stir in crushed toffee bars. Pour into crust-lined pan.

STEP 4 In a small bowl combine reserved topping mixture, brown sugar, and pecans. Sprinkle evenly over filling.

STEP 5 Bake in the preheated oven for 70 minutes or until center is set. Remove from oven; drizzle caramel topping over top. Cool in pan on a wire rack for 15 minutes. Using a sharp small knife, loosen the crust from the sides of pan; cool for 30 minutes more. Remove the sides of the pan; cool cheesecake completely on rack. Cover and refrigerate for at least 4 hours before serving.

PER SERVING: 516 cal., 32 g total fat (16 g sat. fat), 104 mg chol., 445 mg sodium, 53 g carbo., 1 g fiber, 7 g pro.
EXCHANGES: 3½ Other Carbo., 5½ Fat

OFF THE SHELF TIP Grab a bar or a bag of chocolate-covered English toffee from the grocery checkout or candy aisle. It makes a tasty topping for many desserts.

Brownie Caramel *Cheesecake*

Melted caramel is laced through a cheesecake filling that tops a brownie crust for a scrumptious treat. Drizzled with more warm, melted caramel and chopped toffee candy, this cheesecake's simply hard to resist.

PREP
30 MINUTES

BAKE
1 HOUR

COOL
2 HOURS

CHILL
4 TO 24 HOURS

OVEN
350°F

MAKES
16 SERVINGS

1	**8-ounce package brownie mix**
1	**egg**
1	**tablespoon water**
1	**14-ounce package (²⁄₃ cup) vanilla caramels (about 48 caramels)**
1	**5-ounce can (²⁄₃ cup) evaporated milk**
3	**8-ounce packages cream cheese, softened**
1	**14-ounce can sweetened condensed milk**
3	**eggs**
¹⁄₃	**cup chopped chocolate-covered toffee bar (one 1.4-ounce bar)**

STEP 1 Preheat oven to 350°F. Grease a 10-inch springform pan; set aside. For crust, in a medium bowl stir together brownie mix, the 1 egg, and the water. Spread into the bottom of prepared springform pan. Bake in the preheated oven for 15 minutes.

STEP 2 Meanwhile, in a medium saucepan combine caramels and evaporated milk; cook and stir over medium-low heat until caramels are melted and smooth. Remove from heat. Remove ¹⁄₂ cup of the melted caramel mixture; cover and refrigerate until serving time.

STEP 3 For filling, in a large mixing bowl beat cream cheese and sweetened condensed milk with an electric mixer on medium speed until combined. Add the 3 eggs, all at once, beating on low speed just until combined.

STEP 4 Pour filling over brownie layer. Drizzle the remaining melted caramel mixture over filling. Swirl gently with a knife. Bake in the preheated oven about 45 minutes or until center appears nearly set when gently shaken.

STEP 5 Cool in pan on a wire rack for 15 minutes. Loosen edge from side of pan; cool for 30 minutes more. Remove side of the pan; cool cheesecake completely. Cover; refrigerate for at least 4 hours or up to 24 hours before serving. (Cake may crack where caramel mixture is swirled in.)

STEP 6 Before serving, heat reserved caramel mixture; drizzle over cheesecake. Sprinkle with chopped toffee bar.

PER SERVING: 433 cal., 24 g total fat (14 g sat. fat), 111 mg chol., 316 mg sodium, 48 g carbo., 1 g fiber, 9 g pro.
EXCHANGES: 2 Starch, 1 Other Carbo., 4½ Fat

OFF THE SHELF TIP Fudge brownie mix is a boxed, warm, chocolaty dessert and is usually shelved with other dessert mixes.

Chocolate-Kissed Date *Puffs*

Think s'mores, all grown up, with hazelnuts replacing marshmallows, dates joining in the fun, and puff pastry taking over for graham crackers, and wrapping the goodness into a tidy, awesome package. Get ready to swoon.

PREP
35 MINUTES

BAKE
12 MINUTES

OVEN
400°F

MAKES
18 PUFFS

1   egg
1   tablespoon water
1   17.3-ounce package frozen puff
        pastry (2 sheets), thawed
1   13-ounce jar chocolate-hazelnut
        spread
½   cup coarsely chopped hazelnuts
        (filberts), toasted
⅓   cup chopped pitted dates
⅓   cup large milk chocolate pieces

STEP 1   Preheat oven to 400°F. Lightly grease 2 baking sheets; set aside. In a small bowl beat together egg and the water; set aside.

STEP 2   On a lightly floured surface, unfold one pastry sheet. Roll to a 12-inch square. Cut into nine 4-inch squares. Spread the center of each square with about 1 tablespoon of the chocolate-hazelnut spread, leaving a 1-inch border around the edge. Divide half of the hazelnuts, dates, and chocolate pieces evenly among the prepared pastry squares, placing on top of the spread. Brush edges of squares with egg mixture. Fold each to form a triangle and crimp edges with a fork to seal. Prick tops with the fork. Transfer to one of the prepared baking sheets. Brush with egg mixture.

STEP 3   Bake in the preheated oven for 12 to 15 minutes or until golden. Repeat with remaining ingredients. Cool slightly on wire racks. Serve warm.

PER PUFF: 282 cal., 18 g total fat (1 g sat. fat), 13 mg chol., 128 mg sodium, 27 g carbo., 1 g fiber, 4 g pro.
EXCHANGES: 1 Starch, 1 Other Carbo., 3 Fat

OFF THE SHELF TIP Chocolate-hazelnut spread is a rich and creamy spread containing hazelnuts, cocoa, sugar, and milk. Look for it near the peanut butter.

Fruit-Filled Napoleons, page 162.

ABOVE: **Cranberry-Pumpkin Bread Pudding with Brandy-Butter Sauce**, page 124. BELOW: **Apple Bistro Tart**, page 184. OPPOSITE PAGE: **Dutch Almond Cherry-Filled Braids**, page 158.

CLOCKWISE FROM RIGHT:
Banana Brownie Bars, page 116. **Candy Bar Cookies**, page 98. **Coconut-Cashew Bars**, page 112. **Fudgy Brownies**, page 120. OPPOSITE PAGE: **Chocolate Goody Bars**, page 108.

CLOCKWISE FROM RIGHT:
Orange-Chocolate Cake, page 73. **Coconut-Orange Cake,** page 87. **Pumpkin Cakes,** page 196. **Cranberry-Apple Casserole,** page 150.
OPPOSITE PAGE: **Biscuit Bread Pudding with Lemon Sauce,** page 123.

CLOCKWISE FROM RIGHT: **Parmesan Rosettes,** page 43. **Broccoli Corn Bread,** page 28. **Cheddar-Corn Bread Rolls,** page 45. **Mexicitos,** page 21. OPPOSITE PAGE: **Cheese Bread,** page 38.

Waffle Breakfast Casserole, page 249.

Chocolate Chip-Peanut Butter *Cookie Pizza*

Here's a cookie to pine for: It's one you slice and eat in wedges. Chocolate chip cookie topped with a melted combo of chocolate and peanut butter that's chilled solid —but not before you add a candy bar/nut topping.

PREP
20 MINUTES
BAKE
15 MINUTES
STAND
5 MINUTES
CHILL
1 HOUR
OVEN
350°F
MAKES
16 SERVINGS

1	18-ounce roll refrigerated chocolate chip cookie dough, cut into ¼-inch slices
¾	cup semisweet chocolate pieces
¼	cup creamy peanut butter
¾	cup coarsely chopped chocolate-covered candy bars (3 to 4 ounces total) (choose your favorite)
½	cup coarsely chopped dry-roasted cashews or peanuts
¼	cup hot fudge or chocolate ice cream topping

STEP 1   Preheat oven to 350°F. Lightly grease a 12- to 13-inch pizza pan. Press cookie dough slices into prepared pan to within 1 inch of the edge of the pan.

STEP 2   Bake in the preheated oven for 15 to 20 minutes or until light brown and center appears set. Immediately sprinkle with chocolate pieces; drop peanut butter by spoonfuls over the chocolate pieces. Let stand for 5 minutes. Gently spread chocolate and peanut butter over warm crust. Top with chopped candy bars and nuts.

STEP 3   Refrigerate about 1 hour or until chocolate mixture is set. To serve, cut into wedges. If desired, heat ice cream topping; drizzle over pizza.

PER SERVING: 285 cal., 15 g total fat 8 mg chol., 114 mg sodium, 34 g carbo., 1 g fiber, 4 g pro. **EXCHANGES:** 1 Starch, 1 Other Carbo., 3 Fat

OFF THE SHELF TIP Cookie dough is sold in a roll or 18-ounce package from the refrigerator section. Choose your favorite flavor to make baking cookies a breeze.

Baked Pears *with* Almond Crunch

Dessert doesn't have to mean decadent, heavy, and guilt-producing. This one's light, smart, and elegant. You'll love pears baked in sweet white wine with a crumbled amaretti cookie topping.

EASY

PREP
10 MINUTES

BAKE
20 MINUTES

OVEN
350°F

MAKES
4 SERVINGS

2	ripe medium pears, peeled, halved lengthwise, and cored
½	cup sweet white wine (such as sauterne)
½	cup slightly crushed amaretti cookies
1	tablespoon packed brown sugar
⅛	teaspoon ground cinnamon
	Vanilla ice cream (optional)

STEP 1 Preheat oven to 350°F. Place pear halves, cut sides up, in a 2-quart square baking dish. Pour wine over pears. Combine crushed cookies, brown sugar, and cinnamon; sprinkle over pears.

STEP 2 Bake, uncovered, in the preheated oven about 20 minutes or until pears are tender. If desired, serve with ice cream.

PER SERVING: 124 cal., 1 g total fat (0 g sat. fat), 0 mg chol., 6 mg sodium, 24 g carbo., 2 g fiber, 1 g pro.
EXCHANGES: 1½ Fruit, 1 Fat

OFF THE SHELF TIP Amaretti cookies are crisp on the outside and soft on the inside. These gems are made of almond paste, sugar, and egg whites.

COOL TOOL: APPLE-POTATO PEELER-CORER-SLICER
What is it? A handcrank-operated countertop gadget. You can buy the gadget with a countertop clamp or sturdy suction base. This cool tool is smaller than a shoebox, but you may need to store it in one. Stick an apple, pear, or potato, on the three-pronged end, start turning the crank, and you'll produce ¼-inch thick slices, in a seconds flat. Set the heavy-duty gadget to peel, core, and slice, or, core and slice only, or peel only.

Cranberry-Pear Cobbler

Fresh sliced pears, cranberry sauce, and a package of cinnamon swirl complete biscuit mix commingle for a buttery, sassy-sweet favorite.

PREP
25 MINUTES

BAKE
15 MINUTES

COOL
30 MINUTES

OVEN
400°F

MAKES
8 SERVINGS

1   16-ounce can whole cranberry sauce
¼   cup sugar
2   tablespoons cornstarch
½   teaspoon finely shredded lemon peel (optional)
4   cups peeled, cored, and sliced pears
1   7.75-ounce package cinnamon swirl complete biscuit mix
½   cup chopped pecans, toasted
1   tablespoon butter or margarine, melted
1   tablespoon sugar
    Vanilla ice cream (optional)

STEP 1 Preheat oven to 400°F. In a microwave-safe 2-quart rectangular baking dish,* stir together cranberry sauce, the ¼ cup sugar, the cornstarch, and, if desired, lemon peel. Gently stir in pears. Cover with plastic wrap; microwave on 100% power (high) for 9 to 11 minutes or until mixture is bubbly and pears are just tender, stirring once halfway through cooking. Gently stir cranberry mixture again.

STEP 2 Meanwhile, prepare biscuit mix according to package directions. Stir in pecans. Drop mixture into 8 mounds on hot cranberry mixture. Drizzle with melted butter. Sprinkle with the 1 tablespoon sugar.

STEP 3 Bake in the preheated oven for 15 to 18 minutes or until biscuits are golden. Cool for 30 minutes before serving. To serve, spoon fruit and biscuits into dessert bowls. If desired, serve with ice cream.

*NOTE: Or place the fruit mixture in a large saucepan; bring to boiling over medium heat, stirring frequently. Transfer to the 2-quart rectangular baking dish and proceed as directed in Step 2.

PER SERVING: 346 cal., 10 g total fat (1 g sat. fat), 4 mg chol., 269 mg sodium, 65 g carbo., 3 g fiber, 2 g pro.
EXCHANGES: ½ Fruit, 1 Starch, 3 Other Carbo., 1½ Fat

OFF THE SHELF TIP Find this "just add water" cinnamon swirl biscuit mix with the other ready-to-use biscuit mixes.

Apricot-Peach Cobbler

EASY

PREP
10 MINUTES

BAKE
ACCORDING TO PACKAGE DIRECTIONS

MAKES
6 SERVINGS

1   15-ounce can unpeeled apricot halves
       in light syrup
1   7.75-ounce packet cinnamon swirl
       complete biscuit mix
1   21-ounce can peach pie filling
1   teaspoon vanilla
       Vanilla ice cream (optional)

STEP 1 Preheat oven according to package directions. Drain apricot halves, reserving syrup. Prepare and bake biscuit mix according to package directions, except use ½ cup of the reserved apricot syrup in place of the water called for on the package.

STEP 2 Meanwhile, in a medium saucepan combine pie filling, drained apricots, and any remaining apricot syrup. Heat through. Remove from heat; stir in vanilla. Spoon fruit mixture into bowls. Top with warm biscuits. If desired, serve with vanilla ice cream.

PER SERVING: 284 cal., 4 g total fat (0 g sat. fat), 0 mg chol., 346 mg sodium, 59 g carbo., 2 g fiber, 3 g pro.
EXCHANGES: ½ Fruit, 1 Starch, 2½ Other Carbo., ½ Fat

OFF THE SHELF TIP Canned apricot halves are a relative of the peach. They are sweet and deep orange in color and make a beautiful as well as delicious filling.

Polenta-Pecan Apple Cobbler

Cobbler is well-known as warm cooked fruit with a topper of buttery-crunchy flour or oatmeal. In this version the grain role goes to polenta, a.k.a. cooked cornmeal, and chopped pecans. So it's cobbler, same but different.

EASY

PREP
15 MINUTES
BAKE
25 MINUTES
COOL
30 MINUTES
OVEN
375°F
MAKES
6 SERVINGS

½   cup all-purpose flour
⅓   cup quick-cooking polenta mix
         or yellow cornmeal
2   tablespoons granulated sugar
1   teaspoon baking powder
½   teaspoon salt
3   tablespoons butter
½   cup chopped pecans
2   tablespoons packed brown sugar
½   teaspoon ground cinnamon
2   21-ounce cans apple pie filling
⅓   cup half-and-half or light cream
         Half-and-half or light cream
         (optional)

STEP 1 Preheat oven to 375°F. For topping, in a medium bowl stir together flour, polenta mix, granulated sugar, baking powder, and salt. Using a pastry blender, cut in butter until mixture resembles coarse crumbs; set aside. In a small bowl combine pecans, brown sugar, and cinnamon; set aside.

STEP 2 In a medium saucepan heat the apple pie filling until bubbly, stirring frequently. Cover and set aside to keep hot. Stir the ⅓ cup half-and-half into flour mixture, stirring just to moisten.

STEP 3 Transfer hot apple pie filling to a 2-quart square baking dish. Immediately drop topping by rounded teaspoons on top of filling. Sprinkle evenly with pecan mixture.

STEP 4 Bake in the preheated oven about 25 minutes or until topping is light brown. Cool for 30 minutes before serving. If desired, serve with additional half-and-half.

PER SERVING: 441 cal., 15 g total fat (6 g sat. fat), 22 mg chol., 498 mg sodium, 77 g carbo., 4 g fiber, 4 g pro.
EXCHANGES: 1 Starch, 4 Other Carbo., 3 Fat

OFF THE SHELF TIP Found in the baking aisle, cornmeal and/or polenta mix is often packaged in a tall cardboard cylinder and is the star ingredient in corn bread and polenta.

Cranberry-Apple Casserole

The few minutes it takes to assemble this sweet-tart-nutty and spiced soft concoction belie the depth of flavor that will emerge from your oven. Choose the big batch, or the small one.

PREP
20 MINUTES

BAKE
45 MINUTES

OVEN
350°F

RECIPE PICTURED
ON PAGE **140.**

FOR 8 SERVINGS

⅔	cup granulated sugar
2	tablespoons all-purpose flour
4	cups sliced, peeled apples
2	cups cranberries
2	1.23-ounce envelopes instant oatmeal with cinnamon and spice
¾	cup chopped pecans
½	cup packed brown sugar
⅓	cup all-purpose flour
⅓	cup butter, melted

FOR 4 SERVINGS

⅓	cup granulated sugar
1	tablespoon all-purpose flour
2	cups sliced, peeled apples
1	cup cranberries
1	1.23-ounce envelope instant oatmeal with cinnamon and spice
⅓	cup chopped pecans
¼	cup packed brown sugar
3	tablespoons all-purpose flour
3	tablespoons butter, melted

STEP 1 Preheat oven to 350°F. In a large bowl stir together the granulated sugar and the 2 tablespoons flour. Add apple slices and cranberries; toss to coat. Transfer the fruit mixture to a 2-quart casserole.

STEP 2 For topping, in a medium bowl combine oatmeal, pecans, brown sugar, and the ⅓ cup flour. Stir in butter until moistened. Spoon evenly over fruit.

STEP 3 Bake in the preheated oven about 45 minutes or until fruit is tender.

If necessary to prevent overbrowning, cover loosely with foil the last 10 minutes of baking. Serve warm.

PER SERVING: 372 cal., 16 g total fat (6 g sat. fat), 22 mg chol., 148 mg sodium, 58 g carbo., 4 g fiber, 3 g pro.
EXCHANGES: ½ Fruit, 1 Starch, 2½ Other Carbo., 3 Fat

FOR 4 SERVINGS: Prepare as directed at left, except assemble and bake in a 1-quart casserole.

OFF THE SHELF TIP Instant oatmeal is whole grain oats packaged plain (no added goodies) or in a variety of flavors with fruits and nuts.

Blueberry Crisp

EASY

PREP
15 MINUTES
BAKE
20 MINUTES
COOL
10 MINUTES
OVEN
350°F
MAKES
6 SERVINGS

1   21-ounce can blueberry, apple, or cherry pie filling
1   tablespoon lemon juice
¼   teaspoon ground nutmeg
1   cup quick-cooking rolled oats
¼   cup shredded coconut or chopped nuts
2   tablespoons packed brown sugar
¼   cup butter
    Half-and-half or light cream (optional)

OFF THE SHELF TIP What's your pleasure? Fruit pie filling in blueberry, apple, and cherry are standard stock, but you'll find other varieties too.

STEP 1 Preheat oven to 350°F. For filling, in a medium bowl stir together pie filling, lemon juice, and nutmeg. Spoon into six 6-ounce custard cups set in a shallow baking pan or into a 9-inch pie plate. Set aside.

STEP 2 For topping, in another medium bowl stir together oats, coconut, and brown sugar. Using a pastry blender, cut in butter until crumbly. Sprinkle topping over filling.

STEP 3 Bake in the preheated oven for 20 to 25 minutes or until edges are bubbly and topping is golden brown. Cool on a wire rack for 10 minutes. Serve warm and, if desired, pass half-and-half to pour over crisp.

PER SERVING: 294 cal., 11 g total fat (6 g sat. fat), 22 mg chol., 139 mg sodium, 47 g carbo., 4 g fiber, 3 g pro.
EXCHANGES: 1 Starch, 2 Other Carbo., 2 Fat

Blackberry & Pound Cake Crisp

Toasting and then baking slices of pound cake and serving it warm produces a crisp texture and a flavor depth that complement the berries and cream.

1   10.75-ounce frozen pound cake, thawed
1   cup all-purpose flour
¾   cup packed brown sugar
½   teaspoon ground cinnamon
¼   teaspoon salt
⅓   cup cold butter, cut up
1   cup whipping cream
2   tablespoons all-purpose flour
2   tablespoons granulated sugar
4   cups fresh or frozen blackberries

PREP
25 MINUTES
BAKE
45 MINUTES
COOL
15 MINUTES
OVEN
350°F
MAKES
6 SERVINGS

STEP 1   Cut pound cake into ½-inch slices. Place slices on a baking sheet. Broil about 4 inches from the heat about 1 minute per side or until slices are lightly toasted. (Watch carefully so they do not burn.) Cut the toasted slices into fourths. Arrange pieces in the bottom of a lightly greased 2-quart rectangular baking dish. Set aside.

STEP 2   Preheat oven to 350°F. For topping, in a medium bowl combine the 1 cup flour, the brown sugar, cinnamon, and salt. Using a pastry blender, cut in cold butter until the mixture resembles coarse crumbs. Set aside.

STEP 3   In a large bowl whisk together whipping cream, the 2 tablespoons flour, and granulated sugar until combined. Fold in blackberries. Spread the blackberry mixture over pound cake layer. Sprinkle topping over blackberry mixture.

STEP 4   Bake, uncovered, in the preheated oven for 45 to 50 minutes or until topping is golden and edges are bubbly. Cool on a wire rack for 15 minutes. Serve warm.

PER SERVING: 526 cal., 28 g total fat (16 g sat. fat), 105 mg chol., 315 mg sodium, 66 g carbo., 5 g fiber, 5 g pro.
EXCHANGES: ½ Fruit, 2 Starch, 2 Other Carbo., 5 Fat

OFF THE SHELF TIP Frozen pound cake is a fine-textured yet dense and buttery cake stored with the desserts in the freezer section.

Peach Melba Crisp

Fresh fruit is king—when it's available. That's where quality canned and frozen options become queen and jack, making delicious fruit desserts possible all year-round. Here, raspberries and peaches reign with granola and coconut crunch.

EASY

PREP
10 MINUTES

COOK
40 MINUTES

OVEN
350°F

MAKES
6 SERVINGS

5   ripe peaches, peeled, pitted, and sliced, or 5 cups frozen unsweetened peach slices, thawed but not drained
2½   teaspoons cornstarch
1   10-ounce package frozen red raspberries in syrup, thawed
1½   cups plain granola
⅔   cup flaked or shredded coconut
3   tablespoons butter, melted
     Vanilla or cinnamon-flavored ice cream (optional)

OFF THE SHELF TIP Granola is a crunchy breakfast cereal that makes a great topper for fruit crisps too.

STEP 1   Preheat oven to 350°F. Place peaches in a 2-quart square baking dish. Sprinkle with cornstarch and toss gently to coat.

STEP 2   If desired, press the undrained raspberries through a sieve; discard seeds. Spoon the whole or sieved raspberries over the peaches.

STEP 3   Bake, uncovered, in the preheated oven for 20 minutes.

STEP 4   Meanwhile, for topping, in a medium bowl combine granola, coconut, and melted butter. Stir peach mixture gently. Sprinkle topping over peaches. Bake for 20 to 25 minutes more or until topping is golden and sauce is bubbly. Serve warm. If desired, serve with ice cream.

PER SERVING: 462 cal., 16 g total fat (7 g sat. fat), 16 mg chol., 81 mg sodium, 80 g carbo., 10 g fiber, 5 g pro.
EXCHANGES: 1 Fruit, 1 Starch, 3 Other Carbo., 3 Fat

Pecan Streusel Dessert

1   cup chopped pecans
⅔   cup packed brown sugar
2   tablespoons butter, melted
1½   teaspoons ground cinnamon
1   26.5-ounce package cinnamon
           streusel coffee cake mix
½   cup dairy sour cream

PREP
20 MINUTES
BAKE
35 MINUTES
COOL
15 MINUTES
OVEN
350°F
MAKES
15 SERVINGS

RECIPE PICTURED
ON PAGE **132.**

STEP 1   Preheat oven to 350°F. Grease and flour a 13x9x2-inch baking pan; set aside. For topping, in a small bowl stir together pecans, brown sugar, butter, and cinnamon.

STEP 2   Prepare the coffee cake mix according to the package directions, except stir sour cream into prepared batter. Spread half of the batter (about 3 cups) into the prepared pan. Sprinkle batter with the streusel mix from the package of coffee cake mix. Carefully spread with the remaining batter. Sprinkle with the topping.

STEP 3   Bake in the preheated oven for 35 to 40 minutes or until a toothpick inserted near center comes out clean. Cool slightly in pan.

STEP 4   Meanwhile, prepare glaze from the coffee cake mix according to package directions. Drizzle glaze over warm cake.

PER SERVING: 395 cal., 20 g total fat (5 g sat. fat), 50 mg chol., 243 mg sodium, 50 g carbo., 1 g fiber, 4 g pro.
EXCHANGES: 3 Other Carbo., 5 Fat

OFF THE SHELF TIP Available in dozens of flavors and most commonly packaged in boxes, cake mixes are a handy alternative to the made-from-scratch method.

Peach-Raspberry *Pastry Stacks*

This recipe makes enough to serve a large dinner party, and the stacks are positively beautiful. Toasty colored pastry, sunny lemon curd whipping cream, and a crown of red berry preserves and fresh berry garnish.

PREP
35 MINUTES
BAKE
12 MINUTES
OVEN
375°F
MAKES
12 PASTRY STACKS

½   **of a 17.3-ounce package frozen puff pastry sheets (1 sheet), thawed**
2   **cups frozen unsweetened peach slices, thawed**
1   **cup whipping cream**
½   **cup purchased lemon curd**
¼   **cup seedless red raspberry preserves or strawberry jelly**
     Fresh raspberries (optional)

STEP 1   Preheat oven to 375°F. On a lightly floured surface, unfold puff pastry. Cut puff pastry into 3 rectangles along the fold lines. Cut each rectangle in half; cut each rectangle half diagonally to form a total of 12 triangles. Place triangles 1 inch apart on an ungreased baking sheet.

STEP 2   Bake in the preheated oven for 12 to 15 minutes or until golden. Transfer to a wire rack; cool. (If desired, place cooled baked pastry triangles in an airtight container; cover. Store at room temperature overnight.)

STEP 3   Coarsely chop peach slices; drain well in colander. Pat peaches dry with paper towels.

STEP 4   In a chilled large mixing bowl beat cream with chilled beaters of an electric mixer on medium speed until soft peaks form (tips curl); fold in lemon curd. Fold in chopped peaches. If desired, cover and refrigerate for up to 4 hours.

STEP 5   Spoon preserves into a small saucepan; heat over medium-low heat just until melted, stirring occasionally.

STEP 6   Split puff pastry triangles horizontally and place bottom halves on dessert plates; top with lemon curd mixture. Top with remaining puff pastry halves. Lightly drizzle with melted preserves. If desired, garnish with fresh raspberries.

PER PASTRY STACK: 232 cal., 14 g total fat (5 g sat. fat), 37 mg chol., 96 mg sodium, 17 g carbo., 2 g fiber, 1 g pro.
EXCHANGES: 1 Other Carbo., 3½ Fat

OFF THE SHELF TIP Look for lemon curd near jams and jellies. The thick, intensely flavored spread of lemons, butter, eggs, and sugar is delicious on its own and in baked goods.

Sundae-Style Pastries

In Europe, a splash of good quality balsamic vinegar is a common accent for berries. Here it joins the berries in a fruit sauce for ice cream nestled in puff pastry shells. If you have fresh mint growing in the garden, pluck a sprig to garnish the treat.

START TO FINISH
45 MINUTES
BAKE
ACCORDING TO PACKAGE DIRECTIONS
MAKES
6 PASTRIES

1	10-ounce package frozen puff pastry shells (6 shells)
¾	cup white grape juice
½	cup dried apricot halves, cut into thin strips
¼	cup balsamic vinegar
2	tablespoons light-colored corn syrup
2	teaspoons cornstarch
⅛	teaspoon ground ginger
⅛	teaspoon ground cinnamon
2	medium peaches, peeled, pitted, and sliced, and/or nectarines, pitted and sliced
1	pint vanilla or cinnamon-flavored ice cream

STEP 1 Preheat oven and prepare the puff pastry shells according to package directions. Set aside to cool.

STEP 2 In a small saucepan heat grape juice just until boiling. Remove from heat. Place apricots in a small bowl. Pour hot grape juice over apricots. Cover and let stand for 10 minutes.

STEP 3 Meanwhile, in the same saucepan bring balsamic vinegar to boiling. Boil gently for 2 to 3 minutes or until reduced to 2 tablespoons. In a small bowl stir together corn syrup, cornstarch, ginger, and cinnamon. Add syrup mixture to vinegar in saucepan, stirring to combine. Stir in apricot mixture. Cook and stir until thickened and bubbly. Cook and stir for 2 minutes more. Remove from heat. Cool slightly. Stir peach slices into thickened mixture.

STEP 4 To serve, place a scoop of ice cream in each baked puff pastry shell. Spoon warm sauce over tops of pastries.

PER PASTRY: 461 cal., 23 g total fat (5 g sat. fat), 30 mg chol., 221 mg sodium, 61 g carbo., 3 g fiber, 5 g pro.
EXCHANGES: ½ Fruit, 2 Starch, 1½ Other Carbo., 4 Fat

OFF THE SHELF TIP Ice cream is in the freezer case of course! Buy it in pints, half gallons, or by the bucket.

Shortcut Napoleons

PREP
30 MINUTES

BAKE
18 MINUTES

STAND
30 MINUTES

OVEN
400°F

MAKES
8 PASTRIES

½ of a 17.3-ounce package frozen puff pastry sheets (1 sheet), thawed
1 package 4-serving-size instant vanilla or chocolate pudding mix
1¼ cups milk
1 8-ounce carton dairy sour cream
1 cup raspberries
1 cup powdered sugar
3 to 4 teaspoons milk
1 tablespoon chocolate-flavored syrup

STEP 1 Preheat oven to 400°F. On a lightly floured surface, unfold pastry and roll into a 10-inch square. Using a sharp knife, cut pastry into eight 5x2½-inch rectangles. Arrange pastry rectangles on an ungreased baking sheet. Prick several times with a fork.

STEP 2 Bake in the preheated oven for 18 to 20 minutes or until golden. Transfer to a wire rack and let cool.

STEP 3 Meanwhile, prepare pudding mix according to package directions, except use the 1¼ cups milk and beat in sour cream along with the milk.

STEP 4 To assemble, split rectangles in half horizontally. Spoon about ⅓ cup of the pudding mixture onto bottom half of each cooled pastry rectangle; top with raspberries and top halves of pastry rectangles.

STEP 5 In a small bowl combine powdered sugar and enough of the 3 to 4 teaspoons milk to make of drizzling consistency. Spoon over pastry rectangles to glaze. Drizzle chocolate-flavored syrup over glaze. If desired, gently draw a knife through the syrup in several places to make a pretty design. Serve immediately or refrigerate for up to 2 hours.

PER PASTRY: 323 cal., 16 g total fat (4 g sat. fat), 16 mg chol., 331 mg sodium, 41 g carbo., 1 g fiber, 4 g pro.
EXCHANGES: 1 Starch, 2 Other Carbo., 3 Fat

OFF THE SHELF TIP Stock up on the variety of delicious flavors of pudding mix and use them to create a creamy filling or to make cakes and cookies moist.

Fruit-Filled Napoleons

PREP
20 MINUTES
BAKE
20 MINUTES
OVEN
375°F
MAKES
8 PASTRIES

RECIPE PICTURED
ON PAGE **129.**

½   of a 17.3-ounce package (1 sheet)
      frozen puff pastry sheets, thawed
2   cups pudding, fruit-flavored yogurt,
      or sweetened whipped cream
2   cups sliced, peeled kiwifruit,
      raspberries, and/or
      orange segments
      Sifted powdered sugar (optional)

STEP 1   Preheat oven to 375°F. On a lightly floured surface, unfold thawed pastry. Using a small sharp knife, cut pastry into 8 rectangles (each the same size). Place pastry rectangles on an ungreased baking sheet.

STEP 2   Bake in the preheated oven about 20 minutes or until puffed and golden. Cool on wire racks.

STEP 3   Just before serving, split each pastry rectangle in half horizontally. Spoon pudding into pastry bottoms. Top with fruit and pastry tops. If desired, sprinkle with powdered sugar and garnish with additional fruit. Serve immediately.

PER PASTRY: 218 cal., 11 g total fat (1 g sat. fat), 5 mg chol., 227 mg sodium, 27 g carbo., 1 g fiber, 4 g pro.
EXCHANGES: ½ Milk, 1½ Other Carbo., 2 Fat

OFF THE SHELF TIP   Check the freezer case for puff pastry. Choose shells or sheets, then store at home in the freezer. You can thaw just the sheets or shells that you need.

White Chocolate & Berries Napoleons

PREP
30 MINUTES

CHILL
2 TO 24 HOURS

BAKE
10 MINUTES

OVEN
425°F

MAKES
6 PASTRIES

½   cup sugar

2   tablespoons cornstarch or ¼ cup all-purpose flour

2   cups milk

4   egg yolks, slightly beaten

4   ounces white chocolate baking squares or white baking bars, chopped

2   teaspoons butter or margarine

½   of a 17.3-ounce package frozen puff pastry sheets (1 sheet), thawed

2   cups fresh berries (such as raspberries, blueberries, and/or blackberries)

     Sifted unsweetened cocoa powder (optional)

STEP 1   For filling, in a heavy medium saucepan, stir together sugar and cornstarch. Stir in milk. Cook and stir over medium heat until bubbly. Cook and stir for 2 minutes more. Remove from heat. Gradually stir half of the milk mixture into the beaten egg yolks. Add egg yolk mixture to milk mixture in saucepan; bring to a gentle boil. Reduce heat. Cook and stir for 2 minutes more. Remove from heat. Add chopped white chocolate and butter, stirring until melted. Pour into a medium bowl; cover surface with plastic wrap. Refrigerate for at least 2 hours or up to 24 hours. (Do not stir during chilling.)

STEP 2   Preheat oven to 425°F. On a lightly floured surface, unfold thawed puff pastry. Using a sharp knife, cut pastry in half crosswise; cut into thirds lengthwise to make 6 rectangles. Transfer rectangles

to an ungreased baking sheet. Bake in the preheated oven about 10 minutes or until golden. Remove from baking sheet; cool on a wire rack.

STEP 3   To assemble, split pastry rectangles in half horizontally. Place pastry bottoms on dessert plates. Spoon filling and berries over pastry bottoms. Add pastry tops. If desired, cover and refrigerate for up to 1 hour. If desired, sprinkle with cocoa powder before serving.

MAKE-AHEAD DIRECTIONS: Cut and bake puff pastry up to 24 hours ahead. Cool on a wire rack. Place in an airtight container. Store at room temperature.

PER PASTRY: 468 cal., 25 g total fat (7 g sat. fat), 155 mg chol., 233 mg sodium, 52 g carbo., 2 g fiber, 8 g pro.
EXCHANGES: ½ Fruit, 1 Starch, 2 Other Carbo., 1 Very Lean Meat, 4 Fat

OFF THE SHELF TIP Though not true chocolate, white chocolate baking bars are made of 20% cocoa butter plus sugar and flavors. Find it with milk and dark chocolate baking bars.

Triple-Nut Chocolate *Torte*

There's a toasted nut mixed into the cake base, another into the dark chocolate mousse middle, and yet another sprinkled over the top.

PREP
30 MINUTES
BAKE
30 MINUTES
CHILL
4 TO 24 HOURS
OVEN
350°F
MAKES
12 SERVINGS

1 **package 2-layer-size devil's food cake mix**
¾ **cup ground pecans, toasted**
2 **2.8-ounce packages milk chocolate or dark chocolate mousse dessert mix**
½ **cup chopped hazelnuts, toasted**
½ **cup slivered almonds, toasted and chopped**
Sliced almonds, toasted (optional)

STEP 1 Preheat oven to 350°F. Grease and lightly flour two 8x1½-inch round cake pans. Set aside.

STEP 2 Prepare cake mix according to package directions; fold in pecans. Divide half of the batter evenly between the prepared pans. Cover and refrigerate remaining batter while cakes bake.

STEP 3 Bake in the preheated oven about 15 minutes or until a wooden toothpick inserted near the centers comes out clean. Cool in pans on wire racks for 10 minutes. Remove from pans; cool completely on wire racks.

STEP 4 Wash pans; grease and lightly flour as in Step 1. Divide remaining batter evenly between prepared pans. Bake and cool as directed in Step 3.

STEP 5 Prepare mousse mixes according to package directions. Fold hazelnuts into half of the mousse and the chopped almonds into the other half of mousse.

STEP 6 Place 1 of the cake layers on a cake platter. Top with half of the hazelnut mousse mixture. Top with another cake layer and half of the almond mousse mixture. Repeat layers. Cover loosely and refrigerate for at least 4 hours or up to 24 hours. If desired, sprinkle with sliced almonds.

PER SERVING: 372 cal., 22 g total fat (5 g sat. fat), 3 mg chol., 374 mg sodium, 43 g carbo., 3 g fiber, 6 g pro.
EXCHANGES: 2 Starch, 2 Other Carbo., 4 Fat

OFF THE SHELF TIP Milk chocolate or dark chocolate mousse dessert mix whips up to a silky-smooth, decadent dessert or filling in an instant. Find it next to boxed cake mixes.

Like-a-Linzer Torte

PREP
25 MINUTES
BAKE
45 MINUTES
OVEN
325°F
MAKES
12 SERVINGS

1   18-ounce roll refrigerated sugar cookie dough
½   of a 12-ounce can apricot cake and pastry filling
¼   cup sliced almonds, toasted
2   tablespoons all-purpose flour
1   egg yolk
1   tablespoon water

OFF THE SHELF TIP Apricot cake and pastry filling is a canned puree of apricots and sugar found with the canned fruit pie fillings.

STEP 1   Preheat oven to 325°F. Grease a 9- to 10-inch tart pan with a removable bottom. Pat two-thirds of the cookie dough into the bottom of the prepared pan. Spread with apricot filling and sprinkle with toasted almonds.

STEP 2   On a lightly floured surface, knead the flour into the remaining cookie dough. Roll to a 9- or 10-inch circle; cut into ½-inch-wide strips. Lay strips across the filling to form a mock lattice pattern. In a small bowl stir together egg yolk and the water; brush over dough strips.

STEP 3   Bake in the preheated oven for 45 to 50 minutes or until golden. Cool on a wire rack.

PER SERVING: 239 cal., 11 g total fat (2 g sat. fat), 30 mg chol., 188 mg sodium, 33 g carbo., 1 g fiber, 3 g pro.
EXCHANGES: 1 Starch, 1 Other Carbo., 2 Fat

Lemon Poppy Seed *Shortcakes*

Shortcakes often lean to dry to soak up berry juices, but this recipe offers a moist, lemony poppyseed approach that's awesome with juicy fruit and soft cream.

PREP
20 MINUTES

BAKE
12 MINUTES

COOL
30 MINUTES

OVEN
400°F

MAKES
12 SERVINGS

1   15.6-ounce package lemon poppy seed quick bread mix
3   tablespoons butter
1   egg, slightly beaten
⅓   cup buttermilk
8   cups assorted fresh fruits, such as sliced nectarines; sliced, peeled peaches; sliced strawberries; sliced bananas; and/or blueberries
¼   cup strawberry jelly
½   cup whipping cream, whipped

STEP 1   Preheat oven to 400°F. Grease a large baking sheet; set aside.

STEP 2   Pour bread mix into a large bowl. Using a pastry blender, cut in butter until mixture resembles coarse crumbs. Combine egg and buttermilk; add to dry mixture Stir just until moistened. Drop into 12 mounds, 2 inches apart, on the prepared baking sheet.

STEP 3   Bake in the preheated oven for 12 to 15 minutes or until golden. Transfer shortcakes to a wire rack and let cool.

STEP 4   Meanwhile, place the fruits in a large bowl. In a small saucepan heat the jelly over low heat just until melted, stirring frequently. Pour jelly over fruit, tossing gently to mix. To serve, place each shortcake in an individual bowl. Divide fruit evenly among bowls and top with whipped cream.

NOTE: If you wish, prepare only half of the fruit and whipped cream. Freeze 6 of the shortcakes for another use. Before serving, thaw shortcakes at room temperature for 1 hour.

PER SERVING: 294 cal., 12 g total fat (5 g sat. fat), 5 mg chol., 198 mg sodium, 44 g carbo., 2 g fiber, 4 g pro.
EXCHANGES: 1 Fruit, 1 Starch, 1 Other Carbo., 2 Fat

OFF THE SHELF TIP   Quick bread mix is a baking aisle gem easy to dress up. Available in a variety of flavors—banana, cranberry, pumpkin, and more!

Quick Strawberry
Shortcakes

EASY

PREP
10 MINUTES
BAKE
ACCORDING TO
PACKAGE DIRECTIONS
MAKES
4 SERVINGS

4   frozen unbaked buttermilk biscuits
⅓   cup strawberry jelly
1   pint fresh strawberries, sliced
½   cup whipping cream
⅓   cup purchased lemon curd or
       strawberry curd

STEP 1   Preheat oven and bake biscuits according to package directions. Cool completely.

STEP 2   Meanwhile, in a small saucepan heat the strawberry jelly just until melted. Place berries in a bowl. Drizzle melted jelly over berries; toss to mix. Set aside.

STEP 3   In a chilled medium bowl beat whipping cream with chilled beaters of an electric mixer on medium speed just until soft peaks form (tips curl).

STEP 4   To assemble shortcakes, split each biscuit horizontally. Spread the biscuit bottoms with fruit curd; replace tops. Place each biscuit on a dessert plate. Spoon strawberry mixture over filled biscuit; top with whipped cream.

PER SERVING: 472 cal., 22 g total fat (10 g sat. fat), 61 mg chol., 619 mg sodium, 48 g carbo., 5 g fiber, 5 g pro.
EXCHANGES: 1 Fruit, 2 Starch, 4 Fat

OFF THE SHELF TIP   Refrigerated biscuits are available in a variety of sizes and shapes. They make a tasty base for an appetizer or topper for a casserole.

Tropical Fruit
Shortcakes

EASY

PREP
10 MINUTES
BAKE
ACCORDING TO
PACKAGE DIRECTIONS
MAKES
5 SHORTCAKES

1	10.2-ounce package (5) refrigerated large homestyle buttermilk biscuits
	Milk
1	to 2 teaspoons coarse sugar or granulated sugar
1	cup low-fat vanilla yogurt
¼	cup coconut
¼	of an 8-ounce container frozen whipped dessert topping, thawed
1½	cups sliced or chopped fresh fruit (such as kiwifruit, bananas, and/or refrigerated mango or papaya)

OFF THE SHELF TIP Yogurt is a creamy, tart dairy product available plain or in a wide variety of flavors with fruit.

STEP 1 Preheat oven according to package directions. Place biscuits on an ungreased baking sheet. Brush tops with milk; sprinkle with sugar. Bake according to package directions.

STEP 2 Meanwhile, in a small bowl stir together yogurt and coconut. Fold in whipped dessert topping. Split warm biscuits. Divide fruit among biscuit bottoms; top with some of the yogurt mixture. Replace biscuit tops. Top with remaining yogurt mixture.

PER SHORTCAKE: 328 cal., 13 g total fat (6 g sat. fat), 2 mg chol., 689 mg sodium, 47 g carbo., 3 g fiber, 7 g pro.
EXCHANGES: 2 Starch, 1 Other Carbo., 2 Fat

Pumpkin Pie
Dessert

Make this winner to feed a crowd or a smaller group. Creamy pumpkin filling gets decked out with crunchy topping for a memorable, delectable dessert.

PREP
20 MINUTES
BAKE
50 MINUTES
CHILL
2 HOURS
OVEN
350°F

FOR 18 SERVINGS

1	29-ounce can pumpkin
1	cup sugar
1	teaspoon ground cinnamon
½	teaspoon salt
½	teaspoon ground nutmeg
½	teaspoon ground ginger
4	eggs, slightly beaten
1	12-ounce can (1½ cups) evaporated milk
1	package 2-layer-size yellow cake mix
1	cup chopped nuts
¾	cup butter or margarine, melted
	Frozen whipped dessert topping, thawed (optional)

FOR 9 SERVINGS

1	15-ounce can pumpkin
½	cup sugar
½	teaspoon ground cinnamon
¼	teaspoon salt
¼	teaspoon ground nutmeg
¼	teaspoon ground ginger
2	eggs, slightly beaten
1	5-ounce can (⅔ cup) evaporated milk
1	package 1-layer-size yellow cake mix
½	cup chopped nuts
⅓	cup butter or margarine, melted
	Frozen whipped dessert topping, thawed (optional)

STEP 1 Preheat oven to 350°F. Grease a 13x9x2-inch baking pan; set aside.

STEP 2 In a large bowl combine pumpkin, sugar, cinnamon, salt, nutmeg, and ginger; add eggs. Beat with a wooden spoon just until mixture is combined. Gradually stir in evaporated milk; mix well. Pour into prepared pan. Sprinkle dry cake mix evenly over pumpkin mixture; sprinkle evenly with nuts. Drizzle with melted butter.

STEP 3 Bake in the preheated oven about 50 minutes or until edges are firm and top is golden. Cool in pan on a wire rack. Cover and refrigerate at least 2 hours before serving. If desired, serve with whipped dessert topping. Store in the refrigerator.

PER SERVING: 328 cal., 17 g total fat (7 g sat. fat), 75 mg chol., 364 mg sodium, 41 g carbo., 2 g fiber, 5 g pro.
EXCHANGES: 1 Starch, 1 Other Carbo., 3 Fat

FOR 9 SERVINGS: Prepare as directed in Steps 1 to 3, except pour pumpkin mixture into a greased 8x8x2-inch baking pan and bake about 40 minutes or until edges are firm and top is golden.

OFF THE SHELF TIP Not just for pumpkin pie, canned pumpkin adds moistness and texture to many baked goods.

Cherry-Pear Trifle

PREP
1 HOUR
BAKE
ACCORDING TO PACKAGE DIRECTIONS
COOL
2 HOURS
CHILL
2 TO 24 HOURS
MAKES
10 TO 12 SERVINGS

1   14- or 14.5-ounce package gingerbread mix
⅓   or ½ cup packed brown sugar
2   tablespoons cornstarch
½   teaspoon ground cinnamon
1½   cups cherry-cranberry drink or cranberry juice
1½   cups frozen pitted tart red cherries
1   recipe Easy Lemon Cream
1   29-ounce can pear slices, drained

STEP 1   Prepare and bake gingerbread mix according to package directions. Cool. (Gingerbread may be made ahead and frozen, tightly covered, for up to 4 months.) Cut into 1-inch cubes.

STEP 2   For cherry sauce, in a medium saucepan combine brown sugar (use ½ cup if using cranberry juice), cornstarch, and cinnamon. Stir in cherry-cranberry drink or cranberry juice. Add frozen cherries. Cook and stir until thickened and bubbly. Cook and stir for 2 minutes more. Cover and cool without stirring. (Cherry sauce may be made ahead and refrigerated, tightly covered, for 3 or 4 days.)

STEP 3   To assemble, spoon one-third of the Easy Lemon Cream into a 3-quart clear glass bowl. Add one-third of the cherry sauce. Top with half of the gingerbread. Spoon another third of the lemon cream over gingerbread; top with another third of the cherry sauce. Arrange pears on top of the cherry sauce.

Layer with remaining gingerbread, lemon cream, and cherry sauce. Cover and refrigerate for at least 2 hours or up to 24 hours.

EASY LEMON CREAM: In a chilled small mixing bowl beat 1 cup whipping cream and 1 teaspoon vanilla with the chilled beaters of an electric mixer on medium speed just until soft peaks form. Fold in 1 cup purchased lemon pudding; stir gently until combined. For a creamier texture, stir in 1 tablespoon lemon juice or milk.

PER SERVING: 414 cal., 14 g total fat (7 g sat. fat), 61 mg chol., 324 mg sodium, 69 g carbo., 2 g fiber, 4 g pro.

OFF THE SHELF TIP Available in dozens of flavors and most commonly packaged in boxes, cake mixes are a handy alternative to the made-from-scratch method.

Gingerbread Tumble

1   quart vanilla ice cream, softened
2   to 3 teaspoons grated fresh ginger
    or $1/2$ to 1 teaspoon ground ginger
1   14- or 14.5-ounce package
    gingerbread mix
2   cups sugar
$3/4$ cup butter
1   teaspoon ground cinnamon
9   small pears, peeled, cored,* and
    halved, or three 16-ounce cans
    pear halves, drained

PREP
30 MINUTES
FREEZE
4 HOURS
OR OVERNIGHT
BAKE
ACCORDING TO
PACKAGE DIRECTIONS
MAKES
10 TO 12 SERVINGS

STEP 1 In a large bowl combine softened vanilla ice cream with ginger. Cover and freeze at least 4 hours or overnight.

STEP 2 Prepare and bake gingerbread mix according to package directions using the 9x9x2-inch pan option. Cool. Cut into $1½$- to 2-inch chunks.

STEP 3 In a 12-inch skillet combine sugar, butter, and cinnamon. Cook and stir over medium-high heat for 3 minutes. Carefully add pears, stirring to coat. Cook and stir for 8 to 10 minutes more for fresh pears or until tender (or cook canned pears for 3 minutes).

STEP 4 To assemble, place gingerbread in a 3-quart au gratin dish or oval casserole. Top with scoops of the ginger ice cream and the warm pears. Drizzle with half of the sauce in skillet. Pass remaining sauce. Serve immediately.

MAKE-AHEAD TIP: Gingerbread can be made ahead and frozen, tightly covered, for up to 4 months.

*NOTE: If desired, leave pear stems intact.

PER SERVING: 748 cal., 36 g total fat (16 g sat. fat), 114 mg chol., 418 mg sodium, 106 g carbo., 5 g fiber, 5 g pro.
EXCHANGES: 1 Fruit, 1½ Starch, 4½ Other Carbo., 7 Fat

OFF THE SHELF TIP Ice cream is in the freezer case of course! Buy it in pints, half gallons, or by the bucket.

Berry Patch Ice Cream Dessert

PREP
30 MINUTES
BAKE
25 MINUTES
FREEZE
4 TO 24 HOURS
STAND
15 MINUTES
OVEN
325°F
MAKES
10 SERVINGS

1   19- to 22-ounce package fudge
     brownie mix
1   quart vanilla ice cream
2½   cups fresh or frozen berries
     (raspberries, blueberries, and/or
     halved strawberries)
¼   cup chocolate ice cream topping or
     raspberry syrup

STEP 1   Preheat oven to 325°F. Lightly grease two 8x1½-inch round cake pans; line bottom of each pan with waxed paper. Grease waxed paper; set pans aside. Prepare brownie mix according to package directions; divide batter evenly between prepared pans.

STEP 2   Bake in the preheated oven for 25 minutes. Cool in pans on wire racks for 10 minutes. Loosen edges, invert, and carefully remove brownie rounds from pans. Peel off waxed paper. Cool completely on wire racks. Wrap each of the brownie rounds in plastic wrap. Place 1 of the brownie rounds in an airtight freezer container and freeze for up to 2 months (use this layer to make another Berry Patch Ice Cream Dessert). Store remaining brownie round at room temperature for several hours or overnight while berry-ice cream layer is being frozen.

STEP 3   For berry-ice cream layer, line an 8x1½-inch round cake pan with plastic wrap, allowing excess to extend over edge; set aside. In a large bowl use a wooden spoon to stir ice cream just until softened. Carefully fold in 1 cup of the berries. Spread berry-ice cream mixture evenly in prepared pan. Cover and freeze for at least 4 hours or up to 24 hours.

STEP 4   To serve, place the brownie round on a serving plate. Lift berry-ice cream layer and plastic wrap from pan. Invert berry-ice cream layer onto brownie; peel off plastic wrap. Top with the remaining 1½ cups berries. Drizzle with ice cream topping. Let stand for 15 minutes before serving.

PER SERVING: 350 cal., 19 g total fat (8 g sat. fat), 58 mg chol., 141 mg sodium, 44 g carbo., 3 g fiber, 4 g pro.
EXCHANGES: 1 Starch, 2 Other Carbo., 3½ Fat

OFF THE SHELF TIP   Fudge brownie mix is a boxed, warm, chocolaty dessert and is usually shelved with other dessert mixes.

Pies & Tarts

Double-Berry Vanilla Cream Pie

PREP
40 MINUTES

BAKE
10 MINUTES

CHILL
3 HOURS

OVEN
450°F

MAKES
8 SERVINGS

1   **recipe Toasted Almond Pastry or pastry for a single-crust 9-inch pie**

1   **package 4-serving-size cook-and-serve vanilla pudding and pie filling mix**

1¾   **cups milk**

½   **cup dairy sour cream**

1   **10-ounce package frozen strawberries in syrup, thawed**

1   **tablespoon cornstarch**

5   **cups medium strawberries**

1   **cup blueberries**

    Sweetened whipped cream

STEP 1   Preheat oven to 450°F. On a lightly floured surface, roll out Toasted Almond Pastry to a 12-inch circle. Transfer pastry to a 9-inch pie plate. Trim ½ inch from edge of pie plate; fold under extra pastry and flute edge. Prick bottom and sides of crust. Bake in the preheated oven for 10 to 12 minutes. Cool on a wire rack.

STEP 2   For cream filling, cook pudding mix according to package directions, except use the 1¾ cups milk for the liquid. Cool pudding for 10 minutes. Fold in the sour cream. Spread into bottom of the cooled piecrust. Cover with plastic wrap; refrigerate for 1 hour or until filling is firm.

STEP 3   For glaze, place frozen strawberries in a blender or food processor. Cover and blend or process until smooth; transfer pureed strawberries to a small saucepan. Stir in cornstarch. Cook and stir over medium heat until thickened and bubbly. Cook for 2 minutes more.

Remove from heat. Cover surface with plastic wrap. Cool to room temperature.

STEP 4   To assemble pie, arrange half of the fresh strawberries, stems ends down, over cream layer in piecrust. Sprinkle with half of the blueberries. Drizzle ⅓ of the glaze over the berries. Arrange the remaining berries over this layer. Drizzle remaining glaze over berries. Refrigerate for 2 to 4 hours. Serve with whipped cream.

TOASTED ALMOND PASTRY: In a medium bowl combine 1¼ cups all-purpose flour, 1 tablespoon sugar, and ¼ teaspoon salt. Cut in ⅓ cup shortening until pieces are the size of small peas. Stir in ¼ cup finely chopped toasted almonds. Sprinkle 1 tablespoon water over part of the mixture; gently toss with a fork. Push to side of bowl. Repeat, using 2 to 3 tablespoons more water, until all is moistened. Form dough into a ball.

PER SERVING: 292 cal., 12 g total fat (4 g sat. fat), 10 mg chol., 238 mg sodium, 44 g carbo., 3 g fiber, 4 g pro.
EXCHANGES: 1 Fruit, 2 Starch, 0 Other Carbo., 2 Fat

OFF THE SHELF TIP   Stock up on the variety of delicious flavors of pudding mix and use them to create a creamy filling or to make cakes and cookies moist.

Fool-Your-Family Peach Pie

PREP
20 MINUTES

BAKE
50 MINUTES

OVEN
375°F

MAKES
8 SERVINGS

1   15-ounce package rolled refrigerated unbaked piecrusts (2 crusts)
1   21-ounce can peach pie filling
1½   cups fresh blueberries
⅓   cup slivered almonds, toasted
1   tablespoon milk
2   teaspoons coarse sugar or granulated sugar
     Sweetened whipped cream or vanilla ice cream (optional)

OFF THE SHELF TIP What's your pleasure? Fruit pie filling in blueberry, apple, and cherry are standard stock, but you'll find other varieties too.

STEP 1 Preheat oven to 375°F. Let piecrusts stand at room temperature for 15 minutes as directed on package. Meanwhile, in a large bowl stir together pie filling, blueberries, and almonds.

STEP 2 Line a 9-inch pie plate with 1 of the piecrusts; spoon in filling. Using a 1-inch round cutter, cut 3 holes in center of remaining piecrust; place on filled pie. Fold edge of top pastry under edge of bottom pastry. Crimp edge as desired. Brush top with milk; sprinkle with sugar. To prevent overbrowning, cover edge of pie with foil.

STEP 3 Bake in the preheated oven for 25 minutes. Remove foil; bake for 25 to 30 minutes more or until filling is bubbly and pastry is golden. Cool on a wire rack. If desired, serve pie with sweetened whipped cream.

PER SERVING: 355 cal., 17 g total fat (6 g sat. fat), 10 mg chol., 212 mg sodium, 48 g carbo., 2 g fiber, 3 g pro.
EXCHANGES: 1 Starch, 2 Other Carbo., 3 Fat

Raspberry Lattice Pie

PREP
25 MINUTES
BAKE
45 MINUTES
OVEN
375°F
MAKES
8 SERVINGS

4   cups fresh or frozen raspberries
¾   to 1 cup sugar
3   tablespoons quick-cooking tapioca
2   tablespoons butter, melted
1   15-ounce package rolled refrigerated
     unbaked piecrusts (2 crusts)

STEP 1 For filling, in a large bowl combine raspberries, sugar, tapioca, and butter. Toss until combined. (If using frozen raspberries, let the mixture stand for 15 to 30 minutes or until the fruit is partially thawed but still icy. Stir well.)

STEP 2 Preheat oven to 375°F. For bottom crust, unwrap pastry according to package directions. Fit one unbaked crust into a 9-inch pie plate. Trim pastry to ½ inch beyond edge of pie plate. For lattice top, roll remaining unbaked crust to a 12-inch diameter. Cut pastry into ½-inch strips.

STEP 3 Spoon the raspberry mixture into pastry-lined pie plate. Weave strips over the filling to make a lattice. Press the ends of the strips into the rim of the crust. Fold bottom pastry over strips; seal and flute edge. Cover edge with foil. Place pie on a baking sheet.

STEP 4 Bake in the preheated oven for 25 minutes. Remove foil. Bake for 20 to 25 minutes more or until the top is golden. (Or for frozen raspberries, bake for 50 minutes. Remove foil; bake for 20 to 30 minutes more or until top is golden.) Cool on a wire rack.

PER SERVING: 405 cal., 17 g total fat (8 g sat. fat), 18 mg chol., 231 mg sodium, 61 g carbo., 4 g fiber, 2 g pro.
EXCHANGES: ½ Fruit, 1 Starch, 2½ Other Carbo., 3 Fat

OFF THE SHELF TIP Refrigerated rolled unbaked piecrust puts the fun back in baking pies or any dessert that requires a pastry crust.

Layered Apple-Cranberry *Pie*

PREP
10 MINUTES

BAKE
40 MINUTES

STAND
15 MINUTES

OVEN
375°F

MAKES
8 SERVINGS

1   **15-ounce package rolled refrigerated unbaked piecrusts (2 crusts)**
1   **21-ounce can apple pie filling**
½   **of a 16-ounce can whole cranberry sauce**
     Granulated or coarse sugar (optional)

STEP 1   Preheat oven to 375°F. Let piecrusts stand at room temperature for 15 minutes as directed on package.

STEP 2   Line a 9-inch pie plate with 1 of the piecrusts; spoon in apple pie filling. Spoon the cranberry sauce over pie filling.

STEP 3   Cut slits in the remaining piecrust; place on filling and seal. Crimp edge as desired. If desired, sprinkle with sugar.

STEP 4   To prevent overbrowning, cover edge of pie with foil. Bake in the preheated oven for 25 minutes. Remove foil. Bake for 15 to 20 minutes more or until top is golden. Cool on wire rack.

PER SERVING: 356 cal., 14 g total fat (6 g sat. fat), 10 mg chol., 224 mg sodium, 56 g carbo., 1 g fiber, 1 g pro.
EXCHANGES: 1 Starch, 3 Other Carbo., 2½ Fat

OFF THE SHELF TIP What's your pleasure? Fruit pie filling in blueberry, apple, and cherry are standard stock, but you'll find other varieties too.

No-Peel Apple Pie

PREP
30 MINUTES

BAKE
55 MINUTES

OVEN
375°F

MAKES
8 SERVINGS

RECIPE PICTURED ON PAGE 132.

1   **15-ounce package rolled refrigerated unbaked piecrusts (2 crusts)**
4   **large cooking apples, such as Golden Delicious, Jonagold, Jonathan, McIntosh, and/or Granny Smith (2 pounds)**
2   **tablespoons lemon juice**
½   **cup granulated sugar**
2   **tablespoons all-purpose flour**
1½ **teaspoons apple pie spice**
    Milk
    Coarse or granulated sugar

STEP 1   Preheat oven to 375°F. Roll out piecrusts according to package directions. Transfer 1 piecrust to a 9-inch pie plate; set crusts aside.

STEP 2   For filling, core and thinly slice unpeeled apples (you should have about 8 cups). Place apple slices in a very large bowl. Sprinkle with lemon juice; toss gently to coat. In a small bowl stir together the ½ cup granulated sugar, the flour, and apple pie spice. Sprinkle over apple slices; toss gently to coat.

STEP 3   Spoon the apple mixture into the pastry-lined pie plate. Trim pastry to edge of pie plate. Moisten edge with water. Cut out desired shapes from center of remaining crust; set shapes aside. Center top crust over filling and seal. Crimp edge as desired. Brush the top crust with milk. If desired, top with reserved pastry cutouts; brush cutouts with milk. Sprinkle the pie with coarse or granulated sugar.

STEP 4   To prevent overbrowning, cover the edge of pie with foil. Bake in the preheated oven for 55 to 60 minutes or until apples are tender. If necessary, cover the top of the pie with foil for the last 5 to 10 minutes of baking to prevent overbrowning. Cool on a wire rack.

PER SERVING: 354 cal., 14 g total fat (6 g sat. fat), 10 mg chol., 199 mg sodium, 56 g carbo., 3 g fiber, 2 g pro.
EXCHANGES: ½ Fruit, ½ Starch, 3 Other Carbo., 2½ Fat

OFF THE SHELF TIP Simple flavor enhancers for a variety of foods, spices should be stored in airtight containers in cool, dark locations.

Parfait Pie
with Coconut Shell

PREP
20 MINUTES
BAKE
20 MINUTES
CHILL
4 HOURS
OVEN
325°F
MAKES
8 SERVINGS

2   **cups flaked coconut**
3   **tablespoons butter or margarine, melted**
1   **10-ounce package frozen red raspberries, thawed**
1   **3-ounce package raspberry-flavored gelatin**
1   **pint vanilla ice cream**

STEP 1   Preheat oven to 325°F. In a medium bowl combine coconut and melted butter. Press evenly into the bottom and up sides of a 9-inch pie plate. Bake in the preheated oven for 20 minutes. Cool on a wire rack.

STEP 2   Drain the raspberries, reserving syrup. Set aside. Add enough water to the syrup to measure 1¼ cups. In a medium saucepan combine the gelatin and the syrup mixture. Heat and stir until gelatin is dissolved. Remove from heat.

STEP 3   Add the ice cream by spoonfuls; stir until melted. Cover and refrigerate until the mixture mounds when spooned. Fold in raspberries. Pour into coconut shell. Refrigerate at least 4 hours or until set.

PER SERVING: 291 cal., 14 g total fat (10 g sat. fat), 27 mg chol., 114 mg sodium, 40 g carbo., 2 g fiber, 3 g pro.
EXCHANGES: ½ Fruit, 1 Starch, 1 Other Carbo., 2½ Fat

OFF THE SHELF TIP From the baking aisle, coconut is packaged in bags or cans and is available shredded, flaked, and even toasted.

Sweet Glazed Cherry Pie

PREP
20 MINUTES
BAKE
80 MINUTES
STAND
2 HOURS
OVEN
375°F
MAKES
8 SERVINGS

½   **cup granulated sugar**
3   **tablespoons cornstarch**
1   **16-ounce package frozen unsweetened pitted dark sweet cherries**
½   **teaspoon vanilla**
1   **15-ounce package rolled refrigerated unbaked piecrusts (2 crusts)**
¾   **cup sliced almonds, toasted**
1   **21-ounce can cherry pie filling**
¼   **cup powdered sugar**
1   **to 1½ teaspoons milk**

STEP 1   In a large bowl stir together granulated sugar and cornstarch. Add frozen cherries and vanilla. Toss. Let stand at room temperature about 1 hour or until a syrup forms; stir occasionally. Meanwhile, let piecrusts stand at room temperature for 15 minutes as directed on package.

STEP 2   Preheat oven to 375°F. Line a 9-inch pie plate with 1 of the piecrusts. Place ½ cup of the almonds in bottom of the pastry-lined pie plate. Stir cherry mixture; spoon on top of almonds. Spoon pie filling over sweet cherry mixture, spreading evenly.

STEP 3   Cut slits in remaining piecrust; place on filling and seal. Crimp edge as desired. To prevent overbrowning, cover edge of pie with foil.

STEP 4   Bake in the preheated oven for 50 minutes. Remove foil. Bake about 30 minutes more or until top is golden and filling is bubbly. Let cool on a wire rack for 1 hour.

STEP 5   In a small bowl stir together powdered sugar and enough of the milk to make of drizzling consistency. Drizzle over pie. Sprinkle remaining ¼ cup almonds on top of pie. Cool completely.

PER SERVING: 507 cal., 21 g total fat (7 g sat. fat), 10 mg chol., 211 mg sodium, 76 g carbo., 3 g fiber, 5 g pro.
EXCHANGES: ½ Fruit, 2 Starch, 2½ Other Carbo., 4 Fat

OFF THE SHELF TIP What's your pleasure? Fruit pie filling in blueberry, apple, and cherry are standard stock, but you'll find other varieties too.

Fudge Crostata *with* Raspberry Sauce

PREP
30 MINUTES
BAKE
40 MINUTES
OVEN
425°F/350°F
MAKES
12 SERVINGS

1   **15-ounce package rolled refrigerated unbaked piecrusts (2 crusts)**
1   **cup semisweet chocolate pieces (6 ounces)**
½   **cup butter**
⅔   **cup sugar**
1   **cup ground almonds**
1   **egg**
1   **egg yolk**
1   **egg white**
     Sugar (optional)
1   **recipe Raspberry Sauce**

STEP 1   Preheat oven to 425°F. Place one piecrust in a 10-inch tart pan with a removable bottom or a 9-inch pie plate; press onto bottom and up sides of pan. Trim edges, if necessary.

STEP 2   For filling, in a small saucepan melt chocolate pieces and 2 tablespoons of the butter over low heat, stirring constantly until smooth. Remove from heat. In a medium mixing bowl beat remaining 6 tablespoons butter and the ⅔ cup sugar with an electric mixer on medium speed until combined. Add almonds, 1 egg, egg yolk, and melted chocolate mixture; mix well. Spread chocolate mixture evenly over bottom of pastry-lined pan.

STEP 3   For lattice top, cut second prepared crust into ½-inch strips. Arrange strips in a lattice pattern over chocolate mixture. Trim and seal edges. Beat egg white in a small bowl until foamy; gently brush over lattice. If desired, sprinkle with sugar.

STEP 4   Bake in the preheated oven for 10 minutes; reduce oven temperature to 350°F. Bake for 30 to 35 minutes more or until crust is golden. (To prevent overbrowning, if necessary, cover edge of crust with foil after 15 to 20 minutes of baking.) Cool completely on a wire rack. To serve, cut into wedges. Serve with Raspberry Sauce.

RASPBERRY SAUCE: Place one 12-ounce package frozen lightly sweetened red raspberries (thawed) in a blender or food processor; cover and blend or process until smooth. Press through a strainer to remove seeds; discard seeds. In a small saucepan stir together the raspberry puree, $3/4$ cup sugar, and 1 teaspoon lemon juice. Bring mixture to boiling over medium-low heat. Boil for 3 minutes, stirring constantly. Transfer sauce to a bowl.

PER SERVING: 475 cal., 28 g total fat (6 g sat. fat), 66 mg chol., 230 mg sodium, 55 g carbo., 2 g fiber, 6 g pro.
EXCHANGES: 2 Starch, 1½ Other Carbo., 5 Fat

OFF THE SHELF TIP Semisweet chocolate pieces are melt-in-your-mouth chips of chocolate ready to be melted or mixed into your bread, cookie, cake, or bar recipe.

Toffee Pumpkin Pie

Pumpkin pie spins a toffee tune, thanks to a generous scattering of chopped chocolate toffee that perfectly complement the creamy filling.

PREP
30 MINUTES

BAKE
45 MINUTES

COOL
1 HOUR

CHILL
3 TO 24 HOURS

OVEN
375°F

MAKES
8 SERVINGS

½ of a 15-ounce package rolled refrigerated unbaked piecrusts (1 crust)

1 15-ounce can pumpkin

1 cup sugar

1 tablespoon all-purpose flour

1½ teaspoons ground cinnamon

2 eggs, slightly beaten

1 teaspoon vanilla

1¼ cups half-and-half or light cream

1 cup coarsely chopped chocolate-covered English toffee bars

STEP 1 Preheat oven to 375°F. Prepare pastry as directed; line a 9-inch pie plate with the pastry circle. Trim to ½ inch beyond edge of pie plate. Fold under extra pastry and flute or crimp edge. Do not prick pastry. Set aside.

STEP 2 For filling, in a large bowl stir together pumpkin, sugar, flour, and cinnamon. Add eggs and vanilla; beat with a rotary beater or fork just until combined. Gradually stir in half-and-half.

STEP 3 Place pastry-lined pie plate on the oven rack. Carefully pour filling into pastry shell. Sprinkle chopped candy over filling. To prevent overbrowning, cover pie edge with foil.

STEP 4 Bake in the preheated oven for 25 minutes. Remove foil. Bake for 20 to 25 minutes more or until a knife inserted near the center comes out clean (some chocolate from the candies may adhere to the knife but no pumpkin should). Cool on a wire rack for 1 hour. Cover and refrigerate for at least 3 hours or up to 24 hours.

PER SERVING: 444 cal., 21 g total fat (9 g sat. fat), 72 mg chol., 185 mg sodium, 58 g carbo., 3 g fiber, 6 g pro.
EXCHANGES: 4 Other Carbo., 4 Fat

OFF THE SHELF TIP Grab a bar or a bag of chocolate-covered English toffee from the grocery checkout or candy aisle. It makes a tasty topping for many desserts.

Macaroon Fruit Tart

Press macaroon cookies into service as a crust beneath a lightened cream cheese spread that holds a variety of sliced fruits in place. A glaze of melted preserves boosts the bejeweled look of this indulgence even further.

PREP
30 MINUTES

BAKE
15 MINUTES

CHILL
2 HOURS

OVEN
350°F

MAKES
12 SERVINGS

Nonstick cooking spray

1	**13-ounce package soft macaroon cookies (16 cookies)**
1	**cup ground pecans**
⅓	**cup miniature semisweet chocolate pieces (2 ounces)**
¾	**cup whipping cream**
1½	**8-ounce packages (12 ounces total) cream cheese, softened**
½	**cup sugar**
1	**tablespoon orange juice**
1½	**teaspoons vanilla**
2	**cups strawberries, halved**
2	**medium kiwifruit, peeled, halved lengthwise, and sliced**
⅓	**cup apricot preserves or jam**

STEP 1 Preheat oven to 350°F. Lightly coat the bottom and sides of a 12-inch tart pan with a removable bottom with nonstick cooking spray; set aside.

STEP 2 For crust, crumble the cookies into a medium bowl. Add pecans; mix well. Press into bottom of prepared tart pan. Bake in the preheated oven for 15 to 20 minutes or until golden. Immediately sprinkle with chocolate pieces. Cool completely.

STEP 3 In a chilled mixing bowl beat whipping cream with an electric mixer on medium speed until soft peaks form (tips curl); set aside. In another mixing bowl beat cream cheese and sugar with electric mixer on medium speed until smooth. Beat in orange juice and vanilla. Fold in whipped cream.

Spread cream cheese mixture in the prepared crust. Cover surface with plastic wrap and refrigerate up to 24 hours.

STEP 4 Arrange fruit on tart. Melt preserves and gently brush over fruit. Serve immediately or refrigerate up to 2 hours.

PER SERVING: 442 cal., 28 g total fat (15 g sat. fat), 52 mg chol., 170 mg sodium, 47 g carbo., 3 g fiber, 5 g pro.
EXCHANGES: 2 Starch, 1 Other Carbo., 5 Fat

OFF THE SHELF TIP Rich, creamy cream cheese is available in fat-free, low-fat, and regular—plus an assortment of flavors.

Apple Bistro Tart

½ of a 15-ounce package rolled refrigerated unbaked piecrusts (1 crust)

3 tablespoons granulated sugar

1 teaspoon ground cinnamon

1 teaspoon finely shredded lemon peel

2 medium tart green apples, peeled, cored, and cut into ½-inch slices

½ cup chopped pecans

½ cup caramel apple dip

Powdered sugar

OFF THE SHELF TIP Refrigerated rolled unbaked piecrust puts the fun back in baking pies or any dessert that requires a pastry crust.

PREP
30 MINUTES

BAKE
20 MINUTES

OVEN
425°F

MAKES
8 SERVINGS

RECIPE PICTURED ON PAGE **130.**

STEP 1 Preheat oven to 425°F. Let the piecrust stand according to package directions. In a bowl combine granulated sugar, cinnamon, and lemon peel. Add apple slices and pecans; toss to coat.

STEP 2 Place piecrust on a large baking sheet. Spread caramel apple dip over crust to within 2 inches of edge. Place apple mixture over caramel. Fold edges of crust 2 inches up and over apple mixture, pleating edges as necessary.

STEP 3 Bake in the preheated oven about 20 minutes or until crust is golden brown and apples are just tender. Cool slightly on a wire rack. To serve, sift powdered sugar over tart. Serve warm.

PER SERVING: 273 cal., 12 g total fat (3 g sat. fat), 5 mg chol., 174 mg sodium, 41 g carbo., 2 g fiber, 2 g pro.
EXCHANGES: 2½ Other Carbo., 2½ Fat

Lemon-Blackberry Mini Tarts

PREP
20 MINUTES
STAND
15 MINUTES
BAKE
10 MINUTES
COOL
30 MINUTES
CHILL
2 HOURS
OVEN
400°F
MAKES
4 TARTS

½ of a 15-ounce package rolled refrigerated unbaked piecrusts (1 crust)
½ of an 8-ounce package cream cheese, softened
¼ cup purchased lemon curd
1 cup fresh blackberries
2 tablespoons seedless blackberry spreadable fruit
2 teaspoons lemon juice
Powdered sugar
4 mint sprigs (optional)

STEP 1 Preheat oven to 400°F. Let piecrust stand at room temperature for 15 minutes as directed on package. Unfold piecrust. Cut four 4½- to 5-inch rounds from piecrust. Press rounds firmly into bottom and up sides of four 3½- to 4-inch individual tart pans with removable bottoms. Trim crusts even with top of pans. Prick bottoms of each crust several times with tines of a fork. Place pans on a baking sheet. Bake in the preheated oven for 10 to 12 minutes or until golden. Cool completely on wire rack.

STEP 2 In a small mixing bowl beat cream cheese and lemon curd with an electric mixer on medium speed until smooth. Divide filling among pastry shells, spreading evenly. Cover; refrigerate 2 hours or until well chilled.

STEP 3 Before serving, remove tarts from pans; arrange tarts on plates. Arrange berries on each tart. Combine spreadable fruit and lemon juice; spoon over tarts. Sift powdered sugar over tops. If desired, garnish with fresh mint.

PER TART: 448 cal., 25 g total fat (13 g sat. fat), 56 mg chol., 299 mg sodium, 54 g carbo., 4 g fiber, 3 g pro.
EXCHANGES: ½ Starch, 3 Other Carbo., 2½ Fat

OFF THE SHELF TIP Spreadable fruit is fruity and flavorful like jam or jelly without all of the sugar.

Strawberry-Banana Cheesecake Tart

1	package 1-layer-size chocolate cake mix
1	egg yolk
2	tablespoons butter, melted
1	8-ounce package cream cheese, softened
2	tablespoons sugar
2	small bananas
1	egg
1	egg white
1	cup small fresh strawberries, halved
¼	cup fudge ice cream topping

PREP
20 MINUTES

BAKE
25 MINUTES

COOL
1 HOUR

CHILL
2 TO 24 HOURS

OVEN
325°F

MAKES
10 SERVINGS

STEP 1   Preheat oven to 325°F. Grease a 9-inch tart pan with a removable bottom or a quiche dish; set aside. Set aside ⅓ cup of the dry cake mix. For crust, pour remaining dry cake mix into a small bowl. Add egg yolk and melted butter to dry mix in bowl; stir with a fork until coarse crumbs form. Pat crumbs into bottom and halfway up side of prepared pan. Set aside.

STEP 2   In a large mixing bowl combine cream cheese and sugar; beat with an electric mixer on medium speed until fluffy. Mash 1 of the bananas (about ⅓ cup mashed); beat into cream cheese mixture along with the reserved ⅓ cup dry cake mix. Stir in whole egg and egg white; pour into prepared crust.

STEP 3   Bake in the preheated oven about 25 minutes or until center is set when gently shaken. Cool in pan for 1 hour on wire rack. Cover and refrigerate for at least 2 hours or up to 24 hours.

STEP 4   Just before serving, slice the remaining banana. Arrange banana slices and strawberry halves on the tart. Remove side of tart pan. Heat fudge topping just enough so that it can be drizzled; drizzle over the fruit. Serve immediately.

PER SERVING: 277 cal., 14 g total fat (7 g sat. fat), 74 mg chol., 337 mg sodium, 35 g carbo., 1 g fiber, 4 g pro.
EXCHANGES: ½ Fruit, 2 Starch, 2 Fat

OFF THE SHELF TIP   Rich, creamy cream cheese is available in fat-free, low-fat, and regular—plus an assortment of flavors.

Pretty Pear Tart

PREP
20 MINUTES
BAKE
15 MINUTES
CHILL
1 HOUR
OVEN
375°F
MAKES
12 SERVINGS

1 18-ounce roll refrigerated gingerbread or sugar cookie dough
1 8-ounce tub cream cheese
3 ripe medium pears, peeled, cored, and very thinly sliced
1 to 2 tablespoons lemon juice
⅓ cup orange marmalade, melted
¼ cup chopped roasted, salted pistachio nuts

OFF THE SHELF TIP Cookie dough is sold in a roll or 18-ounce package from the refrigerator section. Choose your favorite flavor to make baking cookies a breeze.

STEP 1   Preheat oven to 375°F. For crust, line a 12-inch pizza pan with foil or parchment paper. Pat cookie dough into prepared pan. Build up edges slightly. Bake in the preheated oven for 15 to 20 minutes or until edge is light brown and center appears set. Cool in pan on a wire rack.

STEP 2   Invert cooled crust onto a baking sheet; remove foil. Place serving platter over inverted crust; invert platter and crust together.

STEP 3   Stir cream cheese to soften. Spread cream cheese over crust, leaving a ½-inch border. Brush pear slices with lemon juice. Arrange pear slices in concentric circles over cream cheese. Brush melted marmalade over pears. Sprinkle with pistachio nuts. Cover and refrigerate for 1 to 4 hours. Use a pizza cutter or sharp knife to cut into wedges.

PER SERVING: 249 cal., 10 g total fat (3 g sat. fat), 13 mg chol., 198 mg sodium, 38 g carbo., 2 g fiber, 3 g pro.
EXCHANGES: 1 Starch, 1½ Other Carbo., 2 Fat

Sweet Potato Tarts

½   of a 15-ounce package rolled refrigerated unbaked piecrusts (1 crust)
3   tablespoons pure maple syrup or maple-flavored syrup
3   tablespoons refrigerated or frozen egg product, thawed
1   tablespoon packed brown sugar
½   teaspoon pumpkin pie spice
⅛   teaspoon salt
¾   cup mashed cooked or canned sweet potatoes
3   tablespoons fat-free half-and-half
2   tablespoons finely chopped pecans
Chopped pecans (optional)

PREP
30 MINUTES
BAKE
15 MINUTES
OVEN
375°F
MAKES
18 TARTS

PER TART: 87 cal., 4 g total fat (1 g sat. fat), 2 mg chol., 69 mg sodium, 13 g carbo., 0 g fiber, 1 g pro. EXCHANGES: 1 Starch

OFF THE SHELF TIP Stocked alongside other canned vegetables, canned sweet potatoes are available year-round and sometimes labeled as yams.

STEP 1   Preheat oven to 375°F. On a lightly floured surface, roll piecrust into a 12-inch circle. Cut the dough into eighteen 2½-inch circles, rerolling scraps if necessary. Press dough circles onto the bottom and sides of eighteen 1¾-inch muffin cups.

STEP 2   In a small bowl stir together maple syrup, egg product, brown sugar, pumpkin pie spice, and salt. Stir in sweet potatoes and half-and-half. Spoon into piecrust-lined muffin cups. Sprinkle with the 2 tablespoons pecans.

STEP 3   Bake in the preheated oven about 15 minutes or until a knife inserted into the center of a tart comes out clean. Cool in muffin cups for 5 minutes. Remove from muffin cups. Serve warm or cover and refrigerate within 2 hours. If desired, sprinkle with additional pecans.

Holiday Baking

New Year's Money Cake

EASY

PREP
15 MINUTES
STAND
30 MINUTES
BAKE
35 MINUTES
COOL
15 MINUTES
OVEN
350°F
MAKES
16 SERVINGS

1	3-ounce package lemon-flavored gelatin
¾	cup boiling water
4	eggs
½	cup butter
	Several dimes
1	package 2-layer-size yellow cake mix
¼	cup cooking oil
1	teaspoon finely shredded lemon peel
1	teaspoon vanilla
1	recipe Lemon Icing
2	ounces chocolate-flavored candy coating, melted

STEP 1 Dissolve gelatin in the boiling water; set aside to cool. Meanwhile, allow eggs and butter to stand at room temperature for 30 minutes. Lightly grease and flour a 13x9x2-inch baking pan or 10-inch tube or fluted tube pan. Set aside.

STEP 2 To disinfect dimes, place coins in a small saucepan and cover with water; bring to boiling. Boil for 5 minutes; remove from heat and let stand for 5 minutes. Drain and dry dimes. Wrap coins in tiny pieces of foil (about 1½-inch squares).

STEP 3 Preheat oven to 350°F. Place cake mix in a large bowl; make a well in center and add oil and softened butter. Beat with an electric mixer on low speed until combined. Add eggs, 1 at time, beating well on medium speed after each. Add gelatin mixture, lemon peel, and vanilla. Beat on low speed until combined. Beat on medium speed for 2 minutes more. Pour half the batter into prepared pan; place wrapped dimes on batter evenly around the pan. Top with remaining batter.

STEP 4 Bake in the preheated oven about 35 minutes for 13x9x2-inch pan, 45 to 50 minutes for tube pan, or until a wooden toothpick inserted in center of cake comes out clean. Cool in tube pan for 15 minutes. Carefully remove from tube pan; cool completely. (Leave cake in a 13x9 pan.) Place a cake portion on each serving plate; drizzle Lemon Icing and melted candy coating over cake.

LEMON ICING: In large bowl stir together 2 cups powdered sugar and dash salt. Stir in just enough lemon juice (2 to 3 tablespoons) to make mixture thick enough to cover all traces of the dimes.

PER SERVING: 324 cal., 14 g total fat (6 g sat. fat), 69 mg chol., 310 mg sodium, 48 g carbo., 1 g fiber, 3 g pro.
EXCHANGES: 3 Starch, 2 Fat

OFF THE SHELF TIP Head for the baking aisle for little boxes of lemon-flavor gelatin. You'll find it in oodles of flavors next to pudding mixes.

Chocolate Caramel *Cheesecake*

PREP
45 MINUTES

BAKE
40 MINUTES

COOL
15 MINUTES

CHILL
4 HOURS

STAND
20 MINUTES

OVEN
350°F

MAKES
12 SERVINGS

2   **cups crushed vanilla wafers (about 50 wafers)**
6   **tablespoons butter, melted**
1   **14-ounce package vanilla caramels (about 48 caramels)**
1   **5-ounce can (⅔ cup) evaporated milk**
1   **cup chopped pecans, toasted**
2   **8-ounce package cream cheese, softened**
½   **cup sugar**
1   **teaspoon vanilla**
2   **eggs**
½   **cup semisweet chocolate pieces, melted and slightly cooled**
    Melted semisweet chocolate (optional)
    Caramel ice cream topping, (optional)
    Whipped cream (optional)
    Chopped pecans (optional)
    Chocolate curls (optional)

STEP 1 Preheat the oven to 350°F. For crust, combine crushed vanilla wafers and melted butter. Press mixture onto the bottom and about 1½ inches up the side of a 9-inch springform pan. Bake in the preheated oven for 10 minutes. Cool and set aside.

STEP 2 For caramel layer, in medium saucepan combine unwrapped caramels and evaporated milk. Cook and stir over low heat until smooth. Pour over prepared crust. Sprinkle with the 1 cup pecans. Refrigerate while preparing the filling.

STEP 3 For filling, in a large bowl combine cream cheese, sugar, and vanilla; beat with an electric mixer on medium speed until combined. Add eggs, beating on low speed just until combined (do not overbeat). Stir in melted chocolate. Pour over caramel-nut layer in pan.

STEP 4 Bake in the 350° oven about 40 minutes or until a 2½-inch area around the outside edge appears set when gently shaken. Cool cheesecake in pan on a wire rack for 15 minutes. Loosen from side of springform pan; cool completely on wire rack. Cover and refrigerate for at least 4 hours.

STEP 5 Let stand at room temperature for 20 minutes before serving. If desired, garnish with melted chocolate, caramel topping, whipped cream, additional nuts, and chocolate curls.

PER SERVING: 523 cal., 34 g total fat (16 g sat. fat), 96 mg chol., 326 mg sodium, 49 g carbo., 2 g fiber, 7 g pro.
EXCHANGES: 2 Starch, 1 Other Carbo., 7 Fat

OFF THE SHELF TIP Vanilla caramels are golden-hued soft and chewy candies individually wrapped and are sold in bags in the candy aisle.

Chocolate-Mint Meringues

PREP
20 MINUTES
BAKE
35 MINUTES
STAND
1½ HOURS
OVEN
300°F
MAKES
8 SERVINGS

3   egg whites
¼   teaspoon cream of tartar
1   cup sugar
2   tablespoons unsweetened
       cocoa powder
1   pint pink peppermint ice cream or
       other desired ice cream such as
       chocolate or coffee
     Fudge ice cream topping

STEP 1   Let egg whites stand in a large mixing bowl at room temperature for 30 minutes. Cover a baking sheet with parchment or clean plain brown paper. Draw eight 3-inch circles on the paper; set aside.

STEP 2   Preheat oven to 300°F. Add the cream of tartar to egg whites. In a small bowl stir together the sugar and cocoa powder; set aside. Beat egg white mixture with an electric mixer on medium speed until soft peaks form. Add the sugar mixture, 1 tablespoon at a time, beating about 7 minutes on high speed or until stiff peaks form and sugar is almost dissolved.

STEP 3   Using a pastry bag, pipe the meringue onto the circles on the paper, building up the sides to form shells. (Or use the back of a spoon to spread the meringue over the circles, building up the sides.)

STEP 4   Bake in the preheated oven for 35 minutes. Turn off oven. Let shells dry in oven, with door closed, for 1 hour. Remove from paper. Cool completely.

STEP 5   Place 1 scoop of ice cream in each shell. Drizzle each with fudge topping.

PER SERVING: 250 cal., 6 g total fat (4 g sat. fat), 15 mg chol., 106 mg sodium, 46 g carbo., 0 g fiber, 3 g pro.
EXCHANGES: 3 Other Carbo., 1½ Fat

OFF THE SHELF TIP   Ice cream is in the freezer case of course! Buy it in pints, half gallons, or by the bucket.

HOLIDAY BAKING TIP   When baking several kinds of cookies for the holidays or a special occasion, spread the fun over three days. Day 1: mix and chill dough. Day 2: bake cookies. Day 3: decorate. Day 3 is a good one to bring friends and family in to join the creative effort.

DOUGH-FREEZING TIP   Wrap dough tightly and freeze it if you don't plan to bake the next day. Frozen dough thaws in 2 to 3 hours. Cut it in sections to speed the thaw.

Hearts & Cherries

Heart-shape, chocolate-dusted tortilla crisps and cherry sauce are a great way to dress up ice cream for Valentine's Day or a birthday.

EASY *FAST*

PREP
15 MINUTES

BAKE
8 MINUTES

OVEN
350°F

MAKES
4 SERVINGS

2   8- to 10-inch flour tortillas
     Butter-flavored nonstick
       cooking spray
2   tablespoons sugar
½   teaspoon unsweetened cocoa powder
1   15.5-ounce can pitted dark sweet
       cherries, well drained
½   cup black cherry spreadable fruit
1   cup (½ of a pint) butter pecan
       or butter brickle ice cream
       (or other desired flavor)
½   cup whipping cream, whipped

STEP 1   Preheat oven to 350°F. Cut each tortilla into 6 wedges. Fold each wedge in half lengthwise; trim top edge with scissors to form a heart shape.

STEP 2   Open hearts and place them close together on an ungreased baking sheet. Coat hearts lightly with cooking spray; sprinkle with a mixture of sugar and cocoa powder. Bake in the preheated oven for 8 to 10 minutes or until light brown. Cool on a wire rack.

STEP 3   For cherry sauce, combine drained cherries and spreadable fruit in a small saucepan or in a microwave-safe bowl. Heat over low heat or microwave oven on 100% power (high) about 1 minute or until heated.

STEP 4   To serve, place one tortilla heart on each of 4 dessert plates. Spoon some cherry sauce on top. Top with several small scoops of ice cream, then with another tortilla heart and a spoonful of whipped cream. Cover with a third heart. Pass remaining sauce.

PER SERVING: 716 cal., 37 g total fat (20 g sat. fat), 158 mg chol., 171 mg sodium, 95 g carbo., 3 g fiber, 5 g pro.
EXCHANGES: 1 Fruit, 1½ Starch, 4 Other Carbo., 7 Fat

OFF THE SHELF TIP   Spreadable fruit is fruity and flavorful like jam or jelly without all of the sugar.

Fourth of July Cherry-Cola Cake

Citrus and ginger produce a refreshing cola-spiced cake that's perfect for midsummer celebrations with its festive icing and whole cherries.

PREP
30 MINUTES

BAKE
ACCORDING TO PACKAGE DIRECTIONS

COOL
1 HOUR

CHILL
5 TO 24 HOURS

OVEN
350°F

MAKES
10 TO 12 SERVINGS

1   package 2-layer-size German chocolate cake mix
    Cherry cola
1½ teaspoons ground ginger
1   teaspoon finely shredded lime peel
1   recipe Celebration Icing
10 to 12 dark sweet cherries with stems

STEP 1   Preheat oven to 350°F. Grease and flour a 13x9x2-inch baking pan; set aside.

STEP 2   Prepare cake mix according to package directions, except substitute cherry cola for the liquid called for and add ginger and lime peel. Pour batter into the prepared pan. Bake according to package directions. Cool for 10 minutes on a wire rack. Remove from pan; cool completely on wire rack.

STEP 3   Use a serrated knife to cut top of cake level. Trim edges of cake. Discard trimmed pieces. Cut cake in half lengthwise into two 13x4½-inch rectangles. Place one rectangle on a serving platter. Spread with tinted Celebration Icing. Top with second rectangle. Spread with white icing. Refrigerate cake for 1 hour or until icing is set. Wrap cake in plastic wrap. Refrigerate for 4 to 24 hours before serving. Top each slice with a cherry.

CELEBRATION ICING: This recipe is based on a 1-pound package (about 4½ cups) of powdered sugar. In a medium mixing bowl beat ⅓ cup butter with an electric mixer on medium speed until smooth. Gradually add 1 cup powdered sugar, beating well. Slowly beat in 3 tablespoons milk and 1 teaspoon vanilla. Gradually beat in an additional 2 cups powdered sugar. Divide the mixture in half. To half of the icing, beat in 2 tablespoons cherry spreadable fruit and red food coloring to make a pink icing. Gradually beat in enough powdered sugar until of spreading consistency. To remaining half of the icing, add enough powdered sugar to make spreading consistency.

PER SERVING (WITH FROSTING): 554 cal., 19 g total fat (6 g sat. fat), 81 mg chol., 457 mg sodium, 96 g carbo., 0 g fiber, 5 g pro.
EXCHANGES: 1½ Starch, 5 Other Carbo., 3 Fat

OFF THE SHELF TIP Available in dozens of flavors and most commonly packaged in boxes, cake mixes are a handy alternative to the made-from-scratch method.

Tombstone Brownies

PREP
45 MINUTES

BAKE
28 AND 40 MINUTES

OVEN
350°F

MAKES
36 SERVINGS

2   15- to 23.5-ounce packages fudge brownie mix
    Aluminum foil
2   teaspoons powdered sugar
½   teaspoon unsweetened cocoa powder
¾   cup canned vanilla frosting
1   cup canned chocolate frosting
    Purple, black, and green paste food coloring
    Resealable small plastic bags
¼   cup chocolate cookie crumbs
3   2½- to 4-inch wooden skewers
½   cup shredded coconut

STEP 1   Line an 8x8x2-inch and a 13x9x2-inch pan with foil. Prepare each brownie mix according to package directions. Bake one mix in the 13x9-inch pan following package directions. Bake second mix in the 8x8-inch pan for 40 to 45 minutes. Cool in pans. Use edges of foil to lift and transfer brownies to a cutting board. Remove foil. From the 13x9-inch brownie, cut 1½x3-inch rectangles for tombstones. Trim the top corners off of some of the rectangles.

STEP 2   Combine powdered sugar and cocoa powder; sprinkle some of the mixture over the tombstones. Tint half the vanilla frosting with black and half with purple paste food coloring. Place each tinted icing into a resealable plastic bag. Snip a tiny hole in one corner of each bag and squeeze the icing to decorate the tombstones. Lightly sprinkle tombstones again with the powdered sugar-cocoa mixture.

STEP 3   Frost the top and sides of the 8x8-inch brownie with chocolate frosting and sprinkle top with cookie crumbs. Insert about half of each wooden skewer into the frosted brownie; press a tombstone onto other end of skewer. Add two more tombstones to the frosted brownie. (Place remaining tombstones on a platter for people to eat right away!)

STEP 4   For the grass, place some paste green food coloring and a few drops of water into a screw-top jar; stir to mix. Add coconut, seal the container, and shake the mixture to color the coconut. Sprinkle the green coconut around the base of each tombstone on top of the graveyard brownie.

PER SERVING: 162 cal., 6 g total fat (2 g sat. fat), 0 mg chol., 108 mg sodium, 27 g carbo., 0 g fiber, 1 g pro.
EXCHANGES: 1 Starch, 1 Other Carbo., 1 Fat

OFF THE SHELF TIP   Fudge brownie mix is a boxed, warm, chocolaty dessert and is usually shelved with other dessert mixes.

Pumpkin Cakes

PREP
1 HOUR
BAKE
20 MINUTES
OVEN
350°F
MAKES
6 CAKES
(2 SERVINGS EACH)

RECIPE PICTURED ON PAGE 140.

1   16-ounce package pound cake mix
1   cup canned pumpkin
2   eggs
⅓   cup water
2   teaspoons pumpkin pie spice
1   teaspoon baking soda
1   16-ounce can vanilla or cream
     cheese frosting
     Orange food coloring
     Large gumdrops (optional)

STEP 1   Preheat oven to 350°F. Grease and lightly flour six 4-inch individual fluted tube pans.

STEP 2   In large bowl combine cake mix, pumpkin, eggs, water, pumpkin pie spice, and baking soda. Beat with an electric mixer on medium speed for 3 minutes., Pour about ⅓ cup of the batter into each tube pan. (Refrigerate remaining batter.)

STEP 3   Bake in the preheated oven for 10 to 12 minutes or until a wooden toothpick inserted near centers comes out clean. Cool in pans on wire racks for 10 minutes. Remove cakes from pans. Cool completely on wire racks. Repeat with remaining batter to make six more cakes. If necessary, trim flat sides of cakes evenly with serrated knife. Tint frosting orange.

STEP 4   For each pumpkin cake, spread about 2 rounded tablespoons of the frosting on flat side of one cake. Add another cake, pressing flat sides together to form a round pumpkin-shape cake.

Frost outside of cake with orange frosting. If desired, make stems by trimming sides of green gumdrops straight with knife; place stem in center of each cake. Make leaves and vines; place on top and around bottom of each cake.

PER SERVING (½ CAKE): 349 cal., 11 g total fat (4 g sat. fat), 36 mg chol., 290 mg sodium, 62 g carbo., 1 g fiber, 3 g pro.
EXCHANGES: 2½ Other Carbo., 1 Fat

OFF THE SHELF TIP   Not just for pumpkin pie, canned pumpkin adds moistness and texture to many baked goods.

Witch Hat Cake

PREP
40 MINUTES
BAKE
ACCORDING TO PACKAGE DIRECTIONS
MAKES
12 SERVINGS

1   **package 2-layer-size white cake mix**
     Green or orange food coloring (optional)
1   **8-inch wooden skewer**
1   **rolled sugar ice cream cone**
2   **16-ounce cans chocolate fudge frosting**
     Halloween candies and/or large yellow and white gumdrops
     Gumdrop Moons and Stars (optional)

STEP 1   Preheat oven according to package directions. Grease and flour one 9x1$\frac{1}{2}$-inch round cake pan and one 9x9x2-inch square baking pan. Prepare cake mix according to package directions, adding, if desired, green or orange food coloring to batter. Bake according to package directions. Remove from pans and cool completely on wire racks. Trim tops of cakes as necessary to make even thickness.

STEP 2   Cut a 5-inch circle, 3$\frac{1}{2}$-inch circle, 2$\frac{1}{2}$-inch circle, and 2-inch circle from the square cake layer. Stuff some of the cake scraps into the ice cream cone to fill.

STEP 3   Place a small amount of frosting in the middle of a cake plate. Place the 9-inch round cake layer on frosting and press gently to secure (this helps hold cake in place while frosting).

STEP 4   Place about $\frac{1}{3}$ cup of the frosting in the center of the cake layer and spread to a 5-inch circle. Place the 5-inch round of cake on top. Spread about $\frac{1}{4}$ cup frosting in the center of this cake layer and top with the 3$\frac{1}{2}$-inch round of cake. Spread more frosting and add the 2$\frac{1}{2}$- and 2-inch cake rounds. Insert the 8-inch wooden skewer down through cake layers for added support. Attach the ice cream cone on top with additional frosting.

STEP 5   Frost cake and ice cream cone with remaining frosting. Decorate if desired, with Halloween candies and/or Gumdrop Moons and Stars.

PER SERVING: 589 cal., 23 g total fat (6 g sat. fat), 0 mg chol., 507 mg sodium, 89 g carbo., 1 g fiber, 3 g pro.
EXCHANGES: 6 Other Carbo., 5 Fat

GUMDROP MOONS AND STARS: Use a rolling pin to roll out large yellow and white gumdrops on sugar-coated waxed paper. Cut out moon and star shapes with hors d'oeuvre cutters. Dip cutters into sugar to prevent sticking.

OFF THE SHELF TIP   Canned frosting is now available in a rainbow of flavors and colors and makes putting the icing on the cake a snap!

Pumpkin Praline Cake

PREP
25 MINUTES

BAKE
50 MINUTES

STAND
15 MINUTES

OVEN
350°F

MAKES
16 SERVINGS

¾   cup pecans, chopped
¼   cup butter, softened
¼   cup packed brown sugar
1   package 2-layer-size yellow cake mix
1   15-ounce can pumpkin
½   cup cooking oil
½   cup packed brown sugar
¼   cup water
1   teaspoon ground cinnamon
1   teaspoon ground allspice
½   teaspoon ground nutmeg
3   eggs
1   16-ounce can cream cheese frosting

STEP 1   Preheat oven to 350°F. Grease and flour a 10-inch fluted tube pan; set aside. In a bowl stir together the pecans, butter, and ¼ cup brown sugar; set aside.

STEP 2   In a mixing bowl combine cake mix, pumpkin, cooking oil, ½ cup brown sugar, water, cinnamon, allspice, and nutmeg. Beat with an electric mixer on medium speed for 1 minute. Add eggs and beat well. Pour half of the batter into the prepared pan. Drop small mounds of the pecan mixture over the batter. Spread the remaining batter over the pecan mixture.

STEP 3   Bake in the preheated oven for 50 to 60 minutes or until a wooden toothpick inserted near the center comes out clean. Cool the cake in the pan on a wire rack for 15 minutes. Remove from pan and cool completely. Drizzle with the frosting. Cover and refrigerate to store.

TRICK OR TREAT BAG CAKES: Prepare cake as at left, except omit the pecan mixture. Divide batter into two greased and floured 9x9x2-inch baking pans. Bake in a 350°F oven for 30 to 35 minutes or until a wooden toothpick inserted near the center of cakes comes out clean. Cool cakes in pans for 10 minutes. Remove cakes from the pans and cool completely. Wrap and freeze cake layers 2 hours or until partially frozen. Level cakes layers by slicing off the rounded top parts with a long serrated knife. Cut each cake layer vertically into four squares. Tint two 16 ounce cans cream cheese frosting with desired paste food coloring. Spread about ¼ cup frosting over the top of one of the cake squares. Place another cake square on top and frost. Repeat two more times, forming a rectangular "bag shape." Secure by inserting four 4-inch wooden picks vertically down through the cake layers near the four corners. Repeat with remaining cake squares and frosting. Frost tops and sides of cakes. Decorate with Halloween candies and suckers. Remove wooden picks before serving.

PER SERVING: 436 cal., 25 g total fat (7 g sat. fat), 96 mg chol., 278 mg sodium, 51 g carbo., 1 g fiber, 5 g pro.
EXCHANGES: 1½ Starch, 2 Other Carbo., 4½ Fat

OFF THE SHELF TIP Simple flavor enhancers for a variety of foods, spices should be stored in airtight containers in cool, dark locations.

Harvest Pudding

This hearty gem is studded with oats, walnuts, pears, and apples. Enjoy it in the fall when cool weather begins.

PREP
25 MINUTES

BAKE
45 MINUTES

COOL
30 MINUTES

OVEN
350°F

MAKES
12 SERVINGS

⅓   cup quick-cooking rolled oats
¼   cup all-purpose flour
2   tablespoons packed brown sugar
⅛   teaspoon ground cinnamon
¼   cup butter
2   tablespoons chopped walnuts
1   package 2-layer-size sour cream
     white cake mix
3   eggs
     Dairy sour cream
     Pear nectar
2   medium pears, cored and finely
     chopped (2 cups)
1   medium cooking apple, cored and
     finely chopped (⅔ cup)

STEP 1   Preheat oven to 350°F. Grease a 3-quart rectangular baking dish; set aside. For the topping, in a small bowl combine the oats, flour, brown sugar, and cinnamon. With a pastry blender, cut in butter until pieces are pea size. Stir in the walnuts. Set aside.

STEP 2   Prepare the cake mix according to package directions, except use whole eggs instead of egg whites, use sour cream instead of oil, use half of the water called for, and use pear nectar for the other half of the water. Stir in chopped pears and apple. Pour into the prepared baking dish, spreading evenly.

STEP 3   Bake in the preheated oven for 20 minutes. Carefully pull oven rack out slightly and very carefully sprinkle topping mixture over cake. Return to oven and bake for 25 to 30 minutes more or until a wooden toothpick inserted near the center comes out clean. Cool on a wire rack 30 minutes. Serve warm.

PER SERVING: 333 cal., 12 g total fat (6 g sat. fat), 65 mg chol., 409 mg sodium, 54 g carbo., 1 g fiber, 5 g pro.
EXCHANGES: 2 Starch, 1½ Other Carbo., 2 Fat

OFF THE SHELF TIP Find nectar, a fruit puree, water, and sugar mixture with canned juices.

Tree-Topped *Brownies*

EASY

PREP
15 MINUTES
BAKE
ACCORDING TO
PACKAGE DIRECTIONS
MAKES
36 BROWNIES

1   19- to 22-ounce package fudge
     brownie mix
20   holiday marshmallows or ½ cup
     (about 50) tiny marshmallows
     Purchased frosting (optional)
     Nonpareils or other small candies
     for decorating (optional)

STEP 1   Grease a 13x9x2-inch baking pan (or use a foil pan for gift giving); set aside.

STEP 2   Preheat oven and prepare brownie mix according to package directions; spread into the prepared pan.

STEP 3   Bake according to package directions, adding holiday marshmallows in a tree shape the last 4 to 5 minutes of baking. Cool in pan on a wire rack. If desired, decorate with frosting and nonpareils or other small candies.

PER BROWNIE: 107 cal., 5 g total fat (1 g sat. fat), 12 mg chol., 63 mg sodium, 16 g carbo., 0 g fiber, 1 g pro.
EXCHANGES: 1 Other Carbo., 1 Fat

OFF THE SHELF TIP Bags of fluffy, sweet marshmallows are available in regular and miniature sizes and in traditional white or pastel colors.

Quick Panforte Bars

EASY

PREP
15 MINUTES
BAKE
30 MINUTES
OVEN
350°F
MAKES
32 BARS

1   18-ounce roll refrigerated sugar
      cookie dough
1   10- to 12-ounce can unsalted mixed
      nuts, coarsely chopped
½   cup butterscotch-flavor pieces or
      semisweet chocolate pieces
½   cup mixed dried fruit bits, coarsely
      chopped dried apricots, or golden
      raisins (optional)
½   cup shredded coconut

STEP 1   Preheat oven to 350°F. Lightly
grease a 9x9x2-inch baking pan; set aside.

STEP 2   In a large bowl stir cookie dough
with a wooden spoon until soft. Add nuts,
butterscotch-flavor pieces, and, if desired,
dried fruit. Stir until well mixed. Pat dough
evenly into the prepared pan. Sprinkle
coconut over top, pressing in lightly.

STEP 3   Bake in the preheated oven
about 30 minutes or until a wooden
toothpick inserted near center comes out
clean. Cool completely in pan on a wire
rack. Cut into bars.

PER BAR: 109 cal., 6 g total fat (2 g sat. fat), 2 mg
chol., 70 mg sodium, 13 g carbo., 0 g fiber, 2 g pro.
EXCHANGES: 1 Other Carbo., 1 Fat

OFF THE SHELF TIP You'll find all sorts
of salted and unsalted nuts in the baking
aisle (look for pieces and already-chopped)
or chips section.

Pistachio Chip Cookies

Topped with cherries and studded with chocolate, these festive, pretty cookies are jewels on the cookie tray.

EASY

PREP
15 MINUTES

BAKE
12 MINUTES

OVEN
350°F

MAKES
ABOUT 30 COOKIES

½   cup butter
1   package 4-serving-size instant
    pistachio pudding mix
1   egg
1   cup all-purpose flour
½   teaspoon baking soda
    Several drops green food coloring
    (optional)
1   cup miniature semisweet
    chocolate pieces
15 green or red candied cherries, halved

OFF THE SHELF TIP Stock up on the variety of delicious flavors of pudding mix and use them to create a creamy filling or to make cakes and cookies moist.

STEP 1   Preheat oven to 350°F. Lightly grease baking sheets; set aside.

STEP 2   In medium bowl beat butter and pudding mix with an electric mixer on medium to high speed for 30 seconds. Beat in egg. Beat in flour and baking soda. If desired, stir in food coloring. Stir in chocolate pieces. Drop by rounded teaspoonfuls 2 inches apart on prepared baking sheets. Press one cherry half into center of each cookie.

STEP 3   Bake in the preheated oven about 12 minutes or until bottoms are light brown. Transfer to a wire rack and let cool.

PER COOKIE: 87 cal., 5 g total fat (2 g sat. fat), 15 mg chol., 101 mg sodium, 11 g carbo., 0 g fiber, 1 g pro.
EXCHANGES: ½ Starch, 1 Fat

Peanut Butter Fudge *Tarts*

PREP
20 MINUTES

BAKE
11 MINUTES

OVEN
350°F

MAKES
24 TARTS

Nonstick cooking spray
½   of an 18-ounce roll refrigerated peanut butter cookie dough
½   cup semisweet chocolate pieces
¼   cup sweetened condensed milk

STEP 1   Preheat oven to 350°F. Coat twenty-four 1³/₄-inch muffin cups with nonstick cooking spray; set aside.

STEP 2   For tart shells, cut cookie dough into 6 equal pieces. Cut each piece into 4 equal slices. Place each slice of dough in a prepared cup.

STEP 3   Bake in the preheated oven about 9 minutes or until edges are light brown and dough is slightly firm but not set. Remove tart shells from oven. Gently press a shallow indentation in each tart shell with the back of a round ½ teaspoon measuring spoon.

STEP 4   Bake for 2 minutes more or until the edges of tart shells are firm and light golden brown. Let tart shells cool in cups on a wire rack for 15 minutes. Carefully remove tart shells from cups. Cool completely on wire racks.

STEP 5   For filling, in a small saucepan combine chocolate pieces and sweetened condensed milk. Cook and stir over medium heat until chocolate is melted. Spoon a slightly rounded teaspoon of filling into each cooled tart shell. Cool, allowing filling to set.

PER TART: 75 cal., 4 g total fat (1 g sat. fat), 4 mg chol., 46 mg sodium, 10 g carbo., 0 g fiber, 1 g pro. **EXCHANGES:** ½ Other Carbo., 1 Fat

OFF THE SHELF TIP   Sweetened condensed milk is a thick and syrupy milk-and-sugar combo sold in 14-ounce cans on the baking aisle shelves.

Mince Pastry Twists

PREP
20 MINUTES

BAKE
12 MINUTES PER BATCH

OVEN
375°F

MAKES
24 TWISTS

1   **8-ounce package (8) refrigerated crescent rolls**

½   **cup prepared mincemeat**

½   **cup chopped pecans**

½   **cup powdered sugar (optional)**

⅛   **teaspoon vanilla (optional)**

     Milk (optional)

STEP 1   Preheat oven to 375°F. Lightly grease two baking sheets; set aside.

STEP 2   Unroll crescent rolls and separate into triangles; cut each triangle lengthwise into thirds to make three triangles (24 total). In a small bowl combine mincemeat and pecans. Spoon about 1 teaspoon of the mixture onto each dough triangle, spreading to cover surface of dough. Fold in corners, overlapping slightly in the center. Place 1 inch apart on prepared baking sheets.

STEP 3   Bake in the preheated oven about 12 minutes or until golden brown. Transfer to a wire rack and let cool.

STEP 4   If desired, for icing, in a small bowl stir together powdered sugar, vanilla, and enough milk (1 to 2 teaspoons) to make an icing of drizzling consistency. Drizzle over cooled twists. To store, place twists in layers separated by waxed paper in an airtight container; cover. Store at room temperature for up to 3 days or freeze for up to 3 months.

PER TWIST: 61 cal., 4 g total fat (0 g sat. fat), 0 mg chol., 94 mg sodium, 7 g carbo., 0 g fiber, 1 g pro.
EXCHANGES: ½ Other Carbo., ½ Fat

OFF THE SHELF TIP Prepared mincemeat is a rich preserve made of apples, raisins, citrus peel, sugar, and spices. Find it by canned pie fillings.

Kids' Baking

The Magic Pancake

This pancake puffs high while it bakes, then falls in the middle to make a perfect crater for cheese and bacon.

PREP
10 MINUTES

BAKE
20 MINUTES

OVEN
400°F

MAKES
4 SERVINGS

4	eggs, slightly beaten
2/3	cup all-purpose flour
2/3	cup milk
1	cup finely shredded Swiss, cheddar, or Monterey Jack cheese (4 ounces)
2	tablespoons cooked bacon pieces

STEP 1 Preheat oven to 400°F. Grease a 10-inch ovenproof skillet. Place the skillet in the oven to heat.

STEP 2 Meanwhile, in a medium bowl beat together the eggs, flour, and milk until smooth. Pour into the hot skillet.

STEP 3 Bake in the preheated oven about 20 minutes or until pancake is puffed and golden. Sprinkle with cheese and bacon pieces. Cut into wedges.

PER SERVING: 289 cal., 15 g total fat (8 g sat. fat), 244 mg chol., 207 mg sodium, 18 g carbo., 1 g fiber, 19 g pro.
EXCHANGES: 1 Starch, 2½ Lean Meat, 1½ Fat

OFF THE SHELF TIP Save time and mess by stocking up on a variety of ready-to-use shredded cheeses.

Goof Balls

PREP
20 MINUTES
BAKE
15 MINUTES
OVEN
350°F
MAKES
20 BISCUITS

2   10- to 12-ounce packages (20 total) refrigerated biscuits
20 milk chocolate kisses
²/₃ to ¾ cup tiny marshmallows
¼   cup sugar
2   teaspoons ground cinnamon

STEP 1 Preheat the oven to 350°F. Flatten biscuits with the palm of your hand. Place 1 chocolate kiss and 3 or 4 marshmallows in the center of each biscuit. Bring edges of biscuit up and around chocolate kiss and marshmallows to enclose; pinch well to seal.

STEP 2 In a small bowl stir together the sugar and cinnamon. Roll each biscuit ball in the sugar mixture to coat. Place biscuit balls on an ungreased large baking sheet.

STEP 3 Bake in the preheated oven about 15 minutes or until bottoms are golden brown. Serve warm.

PER BISCUIT: 139 cal., 6 g total fat (2 g sat. fat), 1 mg chol., 331 mg sodium, 20 g carbo., 1 g fiber, 2 g pro.
EXCHANGES: 1½ Starch, ½ Fat

OFF THE SHELF TIP Refrigerated biscuits are available in a variety of sizes and shapes. They make a tasty base for an appetizer or topper for a casserole.

Gooey Brownie Cups

4   purchased unfrosted chocolate
     brownies, cut into irregular-size
     chunks
1   cup tiny marshmallows
¼   cup peanut butter-flavor pieces
     and/or milk chocolate pieces
2   tablespoons chopped cocktail peanuts
     Chocolate or vanilla ice cream
     Chocolate-flavored syrup

OFF THE SHELF TIP Bags of these
fluffy, sweet marshmallows are available
in regular and miniature sizes and in
traditional white or pastel colors.

PREP
10 MINUTES
BAKE
7 MINUTES
OVEN
350°F
MAKES
4 SERVINGS

STEP 1   Preheat oven to 350°F. In a
large bowl toss together brownie chunks,
marshmallows, peanut butter-flavored
pieces, and peanuts. Divide among
4 individual baking dishes.

STEP 2   Bake in the preheated oven
for 7 to 8 minutes or until warm and
marshmallows are golden brown.
Serve with ice cream and drizzle with
chocolate syrup.

PER SERVING: 581 cal., 28 g total fat (9 g sat.
fat), 63 mg chol., 280 mg sodium, 78 g carbo.,
3 g fiber, 9 g pro.
EXCHANGES: 3 Starch, 2 Other Carbo., 5 Fat

Caramel Bubble Ring

PREP
25 MINUTES

BAKE
35 MINUTES

STAND
1 MINUTE

OVEN
350°F

MAKES
10 TO 12 SERVINGS

RECIPE PICTURED
ON PAGE **133.**

⅓ **cup chopped pecans**
¾ **cup sugar**
4 **teaspoons ground cinnamon**
2 **11-ounce packages (24 total) refrigerated breadsticks**
⅓ **cup butter or margarine, melted**
½ **cup caramel ice cream topping**
2 **tablespoons maple-flavor syrup**

STEP 1 Preheat oven to 350°F. Generously grease a 10-inch fluted tube pan. Sprinkle half of the pecans in the bottom of the prepared pan; set aside. In a small bowl stir together sugar and cinnamon; set aside.

STEP 2 Separate each package of breadstick dough on the perforated lines into 6 spiral pieces, making 12 pieces total. Do not unroll. Cut the pieces in half crosswise. Dip each piece of dough into melted butter; roll in sugar mixture to coat. Arrange dough pieces in the prepared pan.

STEP 3 Sprinkle with remaining pecans. In a measuring cup stir together caramel topping and maple-flavored syrup; drizzle over dough pieces in pan.

STEP 4 Bake in the preheated oven about 35 minutes or until dough is light brown, covering with foil the last 10 minutes to prevent overbrowning.

STEP 5 Let stand for 1 minute only. (If it stands for more than 1 minute, the ring will be difficult to remove from pan.) Invert onto a serving platter. Spoon any topping and nuts remaining in the pan onto rolls. Serve warm.

PER SERVING: 367 cal., 13 g total fat (4 g sat. fat), 17 mg chol., 567 mg sodium, 58 g carbo., 2 g fiber, 5 g pro.
EXCHANGES: 2 Starch, 2 Other Carbo., 2 Fat

OFF THE SHELF TIP A staple for any off-the-shelf cook, refrigerated breadsticks come in a variety of savory flavors such as garlic, Parmesan, and corn bread to make any meal special.

Pumpkin Spice Whoopies

PREP
35 MINUTES

BAKE
15 MINUTES PER BATCH

OVEN
375°F

MAKES
15

1   cup canned pumpkin
⅓   cup butter, softened
1   package 2-layer-size spice cake mix
2   eggs
½   cup milk
1   recipe Marshmallow-Spice Filling

STEP 1   Preheat oven to 375°F. Line a baking sheet with foil (grease foil, if using) or parchment paper; set aside.

STEP 2   In a large mixing bowl beat pumpkin and butter with an electric mixer on medium speed until smooth. Add cake mix, eggs, and milk; beat on low speed until combined. Beat on medium speed for 1 minute. Drop batter by heaping tablespoons 3 inches apart on prepared baking sheet. Refrigerate remaining batter.

STEP 3   Bake in the preheated oven about 15 minutes or until set and light brown around edges. Carefully remove from foil or parchment paper; let cool on wire rack. Repeat with remaining batter, lining cooled baking sheets each time with new foil or parchment paper. If desired, place cookies in a covered storage container with waxed paper between layers to prevent sticking. Store cookies at room temperature for 24 hours.

STEP 4   To serve, prepare Marshmallow-Spice Filling. Spread about 2½ tablespoons of the the filling on the flat side of one cookie; top with a second cookie. Repeat with remaining filling and cookies. Serve immediately or cover and refrigerate for up to 2 hours.

MARSHMALLOW-SPICE FILLING: In a medium mixing bowl beat together ½ cup softened butter and one 8-ounce package softened cream cheese with an electric mixer on medium speed until smooth. Add 2 cups powdered sugar, ½ of a 7-ounce jar marshmallow crème, 1 teaspoon vanilla, ½ teaspoon ground cinnamon, and ¹/₂ teaspoon ground nutmeg. Beat until well combined.

PER PIE: 379 cal., 19 g total fat (11 g sat. fat), 75 mg chol., 387 mg sodium, 49 g carbo., 1 g fiber, 3 g pro. **EXCHANGES:** 3 Other Carbo., 4½ Fat

OFF THE SHELF TIP Marshmallow crème is a thick, fluffy marshmallow-based creme available in jars and plastic tubs.

After-School Snack Cake

PREP
20 MINUTES

BAKE
30 MINUTES

OVEN
350°F

MAKES
8 SERVINGS

1	package 1-layer-size chocolate or yellow cake mix
¼ cup	packed brown sugar
½ cup	almond butter or peanut butter
½ cup	water
1	egg
½ cup	almond toffee pieces
¼ cup	chopped almonds or peanuts

STEP 1 Preheat oven to 350°F. Grease and flour an 8x8x2-inch baking pan; set aside.

STEP 2 In a large mixing bowl combine cake mix and brown sugar; add almond butter. Beat with an electric mixer on low speed just until crumbly. Set aside ⅓ cup of the crumb mixture. Add the water and egg to remaining crumb mixture; beat on low speed for 30 seconds, scraping side of bowl constantly. Beat on high speed for 2 minutes. Stir in ¼ cup of the almond toffee pieces. Pour into the prepared baking pan.

STEP 3 Bake in the preheated oven for 20 minutes. Stir the remaining ¼ cup almond toffee pieces and the almonds into the reserved crumb mixture; carefully sprinkle over cake. Bake for 10 to 20 minutes more or until a toothpick inserted into center comes out clean. Cool in pan on wire rack.

PER SERVING: 366 cal., 22 g total fat (5 g sat. fat), 37 mg chol., 406 mg sodium, 41 g carbo., 2 g fiber, 6 g pro.
EXCHANGES: 2½ Other Carbo., 1 High-Fat Meat, 2½ Fat

OFF THE SHELF TIP Look for jars of almond butter next to the peanut butter.

Peanut Butter Pizzas

PREP
20 MINUTES
COOK
10 MINUTES
PER BATCH
OVEN
375°F
MAKES
5 OR 6
INDIVIDUAL PIZZAS

1   10- to 13.8-ounce package refrigerated pizza dough
⅔   cup chunky peanut butter
2   cups assorted toppers, such as grape jelly or strawberry preserves, marshmallow creme, tiny marshmallows, chocolate-hazelnut spread, sliced strawberries, peanuts, and/or sliced bananas
       Cinnamon-sugar (optional)

STEP 1   Preheat oven to 375°F. Lightly grease two baking sheets. Divide dough into five or six pieces. Cover; let rest for 10 minutes. Roll each piece into a 6-inch circle. Place circles on the prepared baking sheets. Prick dough generously with a fork (do not allow to rise). Bake, one baking sheet at a time, in the preheated oven for 10 to 12 minutes or until light brown.

STEP 2   Remove crusts from oven. While still warm, spread with peanut butter. Arrange on serving board or platter. Serve warm with remaining toppings. If desired, sprinkle with cinnamon-sugar.

PER PIZZA: 523 cal., 26 g total fat (4 g sat. fat), 0 mg chol., 490 mg sodium, 62 g carbo., 4 g fiber, 15 g pro.
EXCHANGES: 1 Starch, 3 Other Carbo., 2 High-Fat Meat, 1½ Fat

OFF THE SHELF TIP   Refrigerated pizza dough is commonly found in a tube with other refrigerated bread products. These unbaked crusts are ready to unroll, top, and bake for a perfect pizza.

Monster Morsels

PREP
10 MINUTES
BAKE
10 MINUTES
OVEN
350°F
MAKES
12 SERVINGS
(48 PIECES)

¼   **cup sugar or orange-colored sugar**
½   **teaspoon pumpkin pie spice**
1   **11.5-ounce package (8) refrigerated breadsticks**

STEP 1 Preheat oven to 350°F. In a shallow dish stir together sugar and pumpkin pie spice. Unroll breadsticks. Separate and cut into 1-inch pieces. Roll each piece in the sugar mixture, coating pieces on all sides. Place on an ungreased baking sheet.

STEP 2 Bake in the preheated oven about 10 minutes or until bottoms are light brown. Serve warm.

PER SERVING (4 PIECES): 92 cal., 2 g total fat (0 g sat. fat), 0 mg chol., 202 mg sodium, 17 g carbo., 0 g fiber, 2 g pro.
EXCHANGES: 1 Starch

OFF THE SHELF TIP A staple for any off-the-shelf cook, refrigerated breadsticks come in a variety of savory flavors such as garlic, Parmesan, and corn bread to make any meal special.

Banana-Chocolate *Bites*

PREP
20 MINUTES
BAKE
11 MINUTES
COOL
10 MINUTES
OVEN
375°F
MAKES
16 BITES

RECIPE PICTURED ON PAGE **134.**

1   **8-ounce package (8) refrigerated crescent rolls**
3   **tablespoons chocolate-hazelnut spread**
2   **medium bananas, cut into sixteen ¾-inch slices**
4   **teaspoons lemon juice**
1   **egg yolk**
1   **tablespoon water**

STEP 1   Preheat oven to 375°F. Grease a baking sheet; set aside.

STEP 2   Unroll crescent roll dough and separate into 8 triangles. Cut each triangle in half lengthwise, forming 16 long, narrow triangles. Place about ½ teaspoon of chocolate-hazelnut spread on wide end of each triangle. Brush each banana slice with some of the lemon juice. Place a banana slice on top of spread. Roll dough around bananas. Place bites on prepared baking sheet. In a small bowl beat together egg yolk and water. Brush egg yolk mixture onto dough of each bite.

STEP 3   Bake in the preheated oven for 11 to 15 minutes or until golden brown. Remove bites from baking sheet and cool on a wire rack for 10 minutes. Serve warm or within 4 hours.

PER BITE: 80 cal., 4 g total fat (1 g sat. fat), 13 mg chol., 118 mg sodium, 11 g carbo., 1 g fiber, 1 g pro. **EXCHANGES:** 1 Other Carbo., 1 Fat

OFF THE SHELF TIP   Crescent rolls are a flaky dough, ready to be shaped into rolls or used as the base of an appetizer, dessert, or main dish.

Shark Bites

These meat pies can be a meal's main dish. They get their "bite" from your favorite barbecue sauce, mixed up the way you like it: sweet, spicy, or hot.

PREP
20 MINUTES

BAKE
15 MINUTES

OVEN
375°F

MAKES
8 SERVINGS

8   ounces lean ground beef
¼   cup bottled barbecue sauce
¼   cup purchased shredded carrot
2   8-ounce packages (16 rolls total) refrigerated crescent rolls
4   slices American cheese, halved (optional)
        Milk
        Sesame seeds (optional)

OFF THE SHELF TIP Choose your favorite barbecue sauce from the condiment section—mild, sassy, or devilishly hot.

STEP 1   Preheat oven to 375°F. In a large skillet cook ground beef over medium heat until brown. Drain off fat. Stir in barbecue sauce and carrot; set aside.

STEP 2   Separate each package of dough into 4 rectangles. Pinch together at perforations to seal. Place a rounded spoonful of beef mixture onto one half of each rectangle. If using cheese, put a half slice on top of beef on each dough rectangle. Use a pastry brush to brush edges of dough with milk. Bring the other end of dough up and over filling. Use a fork to seal the edges of the dough. Prick tops with a fork several times. Place the bites on a baking sheet; brush with milk. If desired, sprinkle with sesame seeds.

STEP 3   Bake in the preheated oven about 15 minutes or until golden brown. Serve warm.

PER SERVING: 240 cal., 11 g total fat (3 g sat. fat), 18 mg chol., 724 mg sodium, 27 g carbo., 0 g fiber, 9 g pro.
EXCHANGES: 2 Starch, ½ Lean Meat, 1½ Fat

Home Run
Garlic Rolls

A spritz of Parmesan cheese kicks up the flavor of these impressive rolls. They're terrific for a supper of make-your-own deli sandwiches or as an accompaniment to grilled meat.

PREP
20 MINUTES

RISE
30 MINUTES

BAKE
13 MINUTES

OVEN
350°F

MAKES
24 ROLLS
(12 SERVINGS)

1   16-ounce loaf frozen white or whole wheat bread dough, thawed
1   tablespoon butter or margarine, melted
⅛   teaspoon garlic powder
2   tablespoons grated Parmesan cheese

STEP 1   Lightly grease a 13x9x2-inch baking pan; set aside.

STEP 2   Shape dough into 24 balls. Place balls in prepared pan. Cover; let rise in a warm place until nearly double (about 30 minutes). After 20 minutes, preheat oven to 350°F.

STEP 3   Bake in the preheated oven for 13 to 15 minutes or until golden. Meanwhile, in a small bowl combine melted butter and garlic powder. Brush butter mixture over hot rolls; sprinkle with Parmesan cheese. Serve warm.

PER SERVING (2 ROLLS): 102 cal., 1 g total fat (1 g sat. fat), 3 mg chol., 26 mg sodium, 16 g carbo., 0 g fiber, 3 g pro.
EXCHANGES: 1 Starch, ½ Fat

OFF THE SHELF TIP Found in the freezer section in loaves, this frozen bread dough is ready to thaw, re-form (if desired), and bake.

Potluck

Baked Beef Ravioli

PREP
15 MINUTES

BAKE
20 MINUTES

OVEN
375°F

MAKES
8 TO 10 SERVINGS

2	9-ounce packages refrigerated 4-cheese ravioli
1½	pounds lean ground beef
1	cup chopped onion (1 large)
1	tablespoon bottled minced garlic (6 cloves)
1	14-ounce can diced tomatoes, undrained
1	10.75-ounce can condensed tomato soup
1	teaspoon dried basil, crushed
1	teaspoon dried oregano, crushed
1½	cups shredded mozzarella cheese (6 ounces)
½	cup shredded Parmesan cheese (2 ounces)

PER SERVING: 503 cal., 20 g total fat (9 g sat. fat), 113 mg chol., 854 mg sodium, 40 g carbo., 3 g fiber, 40 g pro.
EXCHANGES: 1 Vegetable, 2½ Starch, 4 Medium-Fat Meat

OFF THE SHELF TIP Refrigerated ravioli can be found filled with cheese, meat, or even squash.

STEP 1 Cook pasta according to package directions; drain. Set aside and keep warm.

STEP 2 Meanwhile, preheat oven to 375°F. In a large skillet cook ground beef, onion, and garlic over medium heat until meat is brown and onion is tender; drain off fat. Stir in undrained tomatoes, soup, basil, and oregano. Gently stir in cooked pasta. Transfer to an ungreased 3-quart rectangular baking dish. Sprinkle with mozzarella cheese and Parmesan cheese.

STEP 3 Bake, uncovered, in the preheated oven about 20 minutes or until heated through.

TO TOTE: Cover casserole tightly. Transport in an insulated carrier.

Hot Chicken Salad

PREP
25 MINUTES
BAKE
30 MINUTES
STAND
10 MINUTES
OVEN
400°F
MAKES
12 SERVINGS

1   cup coarsely crushed potato chips
⅔   cup finely chopped almonds
6   cups cubed cooked chicken
       (2 pounds)
3   cups chopped celery (6 stalks)
1   8-ounce package shredded
       mozzarella cheese (2 cups)
2   8-ounce cartons dairy sour cream
       or 2 cups plain yogurt
1   10.75-ounce can condensed cream
       of chicken soup
¼   cup chopped onion
1   teaspoon dried thyme or basil,
       crushed
4   hard-cooked eggs, chopped

OFF THE SHELF TIP Grab a can of cream soup from the soup section. Make sure your choice is "condensed" and not "ready to serve."

STEP 1 Preheat oven to 400°F. In a small bowl combine potato chips and almonds; set aside. In a large bowl combine chicken, celery, mozzarella cheese, sour cream, soup, onion, and thyme. Gently fold in hard-cooked eggs. Transfer to an ungreased 3-quart rectangular baking dish. Sprinkle with potato chip mixture.

STEP 2 Bake, uncovered, in the preheated oven for 30 to 35 minutes or until heated through. Let stand for 10 minutes before serving.

TO TOTE: Do not let stand after baking. Cover tightly. Transport in an insulated carrier.

PER SERVING: 398 cal., 25 g total fat (10 g sat. fat), 168 mg chol., 437 mg sodium, 9 g carbo., 2 g fiber, 33 g pro.
EXCHANGES: ½ Starch, 4½ Lean Meat, 2½ Fat

Buffet Chicken *Scallop*

Chopped chicken, stuffing, and sour cream combine for a saucy, sensational main dish that's a sure hit.

PREP
25 MINUTES

BAKE
25 MINUTES

STAND
10 MINUTES

OVEN
350°F

MAKES
12 SERVINGS

1	cup chopped onion (1 large)
¾	cup chopped green sweet pepper (1 medium)
2	tablespoons butter or margarine
3	cups packaged herb-seasoned stuffing mix
1	cup chicken broth
3	eggs, slightly beaten
1	10.75-ounce can condensed cream of celery soup
4	cups chopped cooked chicken or turkey (about 1¼ pounds)
1½	cups cooked rice*
1	10.75-ounce can condensed cream of chicken soup
½	cup dairy sour cream
¼	cup milk

STEP 1 Preheat oven to 350°F. In a large skillet cook onion and sweet pepper in hot butter over medium heat until tender; remove from heat.

STEP 2 In large bowl combine stuffing mix and chicken broth; stir in eggs and cream of celery soup. Stir in onion mixture, chicken, and rice. Spread in a lightly greased 3-quart rectangular baking dish.

STEP 3 Bake, uncovered, in the preheated oven for 25 to 30 minutes or until an instant-read thermometer inserted in the center registers 160°F. Let stand for 10 minutes.

STEP 4 Meanwhile, for sauce, in a small saucepan combine cream of chicken soup, sour cream, and milk; heat and stir until smooth and heated through. Serve sauce with baked chicken mixture.

*NOTE: For 1½ cups cooked rice, in a medium saucepan combine 1 cup water and ½ cup uncooked long grain rice. Bring to boiling; reduce heat. Simmer, covered, for 15 to 18 minutes or until rice is tender.

TO TOTE: Cover baking dish tightly. Transfer sauce to a tightly covered container. Transport casserole and sauce in an insulated carrier.

PER SERVING: 286 cal., 12 g total fat (5 g sat. fat), 106 mg chol., 758 mg sodium, 23 g carbo., 2 g fiber, 19 g pro.
EXCHANGES: 1½ Starch, 2 Lean Meat, 1 Fat

OFF THE SHELF TIP Look in the refrigerated meat section for precooked chicken or turkey seasoned or unseasoned strips, cubes, and whole pieces.

Tuna-Macaroni Casserole

Mayo-inspired snap, sweet red pepper flavor, and a buttery crumb topping transform this dish from standby to standout.

PREP
25 MINUTES
BAKE
40 MINUTES
OVEN
350°F
MAKES
4 SERVINGS

4   **ounces dried small shell macaroni (1 cup)**

1   **10.75-ounce can condensed cream of onion soup**

⅓   **cup milk**

¼   **cup mayonnaise or salad dressing**

½   **teaspoon dry mustard**

1   **6-ounce can tuna, drained and flaked**

1   **cup shredded American or cheddar cheese (4 ounces)**

½   **cup chopped bottled roasted red sweet peppers**

¼   **cup fine dry bread crumbs**

1   **tablespoon butter or margarine, melted**

½   **teaspoon paprika**

    Snipped fresh parsley (optional)

STEP 1   Cook macaroni according to package directions; drain.

STEP 2   Meanwhile, preheat oven to 350°F. In a large bowl stir together soup, milk, mayonnaise, and mustard. Stir in tuna, American cheese, and roasted red peppers. Gently fold in cooked macaroni. Spoon into an ungreased 1½-quart casserole.

STEP 3   In a small bowl combine bread crumbs, melted butter, and paprika; sprinkle evenly over casserole.

STEP 4   Bake, uncovered, in the preheated oven for 40 to 45 minutes or until heated through. If desired, sprinkle with parsley.

TO TOTE: Cover casserole tightly. Transport in an insulated carrier. If desired, transport parsley in an insulated cooler with ice packs.

PER SERVING: 498 cal., 29 g total fat (11 g sat. fat), 72 mg chol., 1394 mg sodium, 36 g carbo., 2 g fiber, 23 g pro.
EXCHANGES: 2½ Starch, 2 Lean Meat, 4 Fat

OFF THE SHELF TIP These mild and sweet gems are a real time-saver, and roasted red sweet peppers can be found in jars in the grocery aisle.

Cheesy Tuna-Noodle *Casserole*

Ripe olives and cheddar update this comfort food favorite.

PREP
25 MINUTES

BAKE
30 MINUTES

OVEN
375°F

MAKES
6 SERVINGS

8   **ounces dried medium noodles (4 cups)**
⅓   **cup chopped onion (1 small)**
2   **tablespoons butter**
2   **tablespoons all-purpose flour**
1   **10.75-ounce can condensed cheddar cheese soup**
¾   **cup milk**
1   **10-ounce package frozen chopped broccoli**
1   **9-ounce can tuna, drained and flaked**
1   **2.25-ounce can sliced, pitted ripe olives, drained**
½   **cup shredded cheddar cheese (2 ounces)**

PER SERVING: 358 cal., 14 g total fat (7 g sat. fat), 79 mg chol., 769 mg sodium, 38 g carbo., 3 g fiber, 23 g pro.
EXCHANGES: ½ Vegetable, 2½ Starch, 2 Lean Meat, 1 Fat

OFF THE SHELF TIP Grab a can of cream soup from the soup section. Make sure your choice is "condensed" and not "ready to serve."

STEP 1 Cook noodles according to package directions; drain. Return noodles to saucepan.

STEP 2 Meanwhile, preheat oven to 375°F. In a medium saucepan cook onion in hot butter over medium heat until tender. Stir in flour, then soup. Gradually stir in milk. Cook and stir until thickened and bubbly. Gently stir in broccoli, tuna, and olives. Add tuna mixture to noodles; toss gently to coat. Transfer to an ungreased 2-quart casserole.

STEP 3 Bake, covered, in the preheated oven for 25 minutes. Top with cheddar cheese. Bake, uncovered, about 5 minutes more or until cheese is melted and mixture is heated through.

TO TOTE: Cover tightly. Transport in an insulated carrier.

Brunch Turnovers

Plump pastry is packed with brunch good—Swiss and bacon or ham—and a little sweet stuff to make a delicious handheld meal. They're great to make ahead and reheat in the oven or on a grill.

PREP
30 MINUTES

BAKE
12 MINUTES

CHILL
8 TO 24 HOURS

OVEN
400°F

MAKES
9 TURNOVERS

1   **13.8-ounce package refrigerated pizza dough**
¼   **cup orange marmalade**
¾   **cup chopped Canadian-style bacon or cooked ham**
¾   **cup shredded Swiss cheese (3 ounces)**
¼   **cup thinly sliced green onion (2)**
    Freshly ground black pepper
    Milk
    Poppy seeds and/or sesame seeds

STEP 1   Preheat oven to 400°F. Line a baking sheet with foil; grease foil. Set aside. Unroll pizza dough onto a lightly floured surface. Roll dough into a 12-inch square. Spread orange marmalade evenly over dough. Cut dough into nine 4-inch squares.

STEP 2   For filling, in a medium bowl stir together Canadian bacon, Swiss cheese, and green onion. Place about 3 tablespoons of the filling on each dough square. Sprinkle each lightly with pepper. Fold one corner of each dough square over filling to opposite corner. Use the tines of a fork to seal edges. Prick tops of turnovers with the fork. Place turnovers on prepared baking sheet. Brush with milk and sprinkle with poppy and/or sesame seeds.

STEP 3   Bake in the preheated oven for 12 to 15 minutes or until golden (filling will leak out slightly).

TO TOTE: Cool turnovers on a wire rack. Place turnovers in a covered container.

Refrigerate for 8 to 12 hours. Tote in an insulated cooler with ice packs. To serve, arrange medium-hot coals around the outside edge of a grill with a cover. Test for medium heat in center of the grill. Place turnovers on grill rack in center of the grill (not over coals). Cover and grill for 6 to 8 minutes or until heated through, turning once.

PER TURNOVER: 149 cal., 5 g total fat (2 g sat. fat), 16 mg chol., 326 mg sodium, 18 g carbo., 1 g fiber, 8 g pro.
EXCHANGES: ½ Starch, ½ Other Carbo., 1 Medium-Fat Meat

OFF THE SHELF TIP Orange marmalade is a sparkling preserve containing pieces of orange rind. Find it with the jellies and jams.

Scalloped Potatoes & Ham

This stick-to-your-ribs classic comfort dish can be a hearty accompaniment to simple grilled meat, roasted veggies, or a plain salad of mixed greens.

EASY

PREP
15 MINUTES
BAKE
45 MINUTES
STAND
10 MINUTES
OVEN
350°F
MAKES
6 TO 8 SERVINGS

1   10.75-ounce can condensed cream of onion or cream of celery soup
½   cup milk
⅛   teaspoon black pepper
3   cups cubed cooked ham (about 1 pound)
1   20-ounce package refrigerated diced potatoes with onion
¾   cup shredded Swiss or cheddar cheese (3 ounces)

OFF THE SHELF TIP Save time and mess by stocking up on a variety of ready-to-use shredded cheeses.

STEP 1   Preheat oven to 350°F. In a large bowl stir together soup, milk, and pepper. Stir in ham and potatoes. Transfer to an ungreased 2-quart rectangular baking dish.

STEP 2   Bake, covered, in the preheated oven for 40 minutes. Stir mixture. Sprinkle with Swiss cheese. Bake, uncovered, for 5 to 10 minutes more or until heated through and cheese is melted. Let stand for 10 minutes before serving.

TO TOTE: Do not let stand after baking. Cover tightly. Transport in an insulated carrier.

PER SERVING: 332 cal., 14 g total fat (6 g sat. fat), 64 mg chol., 1613 mg sodium, 29 g carbo., 2 g fiber, 21 g pro.
EXCHANGES: 2 Starch, 2 Medium-Fat Meat, ½ Fat

Hash Brown *Casserole*

1   16-ounce carton dairy sour cream

1   10.75-ounce can condensed cream
      of chicken soup

1   32-ounce package frozen diced
      hash brown potatoes

2   cups diced cooked ham (10 ounces)

2   cups cubed American cheese
      (8 ounces)

½   cup chopped onion (1 medium)

¼   teaspoon black pepper

2   cups crushed cornflakes

⅓   cup butter or margarine, melted

OFF THE SHELF TIP Grab a can of
cream soup from the soup section. Make
sure your choice is "condensed" and not
"ready to serve."

PREP
20 MINUTES

BAKE
50 MINUTES

CHILL
8 TO 24 HOURS

OVEN
350°F

MAKES
12 SERVINGS

STEP 1   In a very large bowl combine sour cream and soup. Stir in the frozen potatoes, ham, cheese, onion, and pepper. Spread the mixture evenly in an ungreased 3-quart rectangular baking dish. Cover and refrigerate for at least 8 hours or up to 24 hours.

STEP 2   To bake, preheat oven to 350°F. In a small bowl combine cornflakes and melted butter. Sprinkle over the potato mixture. Bake casserole, uncovered, in the preheated oven for 50 to 55 minutes or until hot in center and bubbly around edges.

TO TOTE: Cover tightly. Transport in an insulated carrier.

PER SERVING: 388 cal., 24 g total fat (14 g sat. fat), 64 mg chol., 968 mg sodium, 31 g carbo., 1 g fiber, 13 g pro.
EXCHANGES: 2 Starch, 1½ Medium-Fat Meat, 3 Fat

Cinnamon-Swirl Bread Pudding

Bright, sparkling apricot or peach fruit sauce turns the old-fashioned favorite bread pudding into a vibrant breakfast or brunch experience.

PREP
20 MINUTES
BAKE
35 MINUTES
STAND
15 MINUTES
OVEN
325°F
MAKES
6 SERVINGS

6   slices cinnamon-swirl bread or cinnamon-raisin bread

     Nonstick cooking spray

1½   cups fat-free milk

¾   cup refrigerated or frozen egg product, thawed

3   tablespoons sugar

1   teaspoon vanilla

¼   teaspoon ground nutmeg

1   5.5-ounce can apricot or peach nectar

2   teaspoons cornstarch

STEP 1   To dry bread, preheat oven to 325°F. Place bread slices in a single layer on a baking sheet. Bake in the preheated oven for 10 minutes, turning once. Turn off oven. Cool on a wire rack. Cut into ½-inch cubes (should have 4 cups).

STEP 2   Preheat oven to 325°F. Coat six 6-ounce custard cups with nonstick cooking spray. Divide the bread cubes among the cups. In a medium bowl beat together milk, egg product, sugar, vanilla, and nutmeg with a wire whisk or rotary beater. Pour the milk mixture evenly over the bread cubes. Lightly press cubes down with fork or back of a spoon.

STEP 3   Place the custard cups in a 13x9x2-inch baking pan. Place pan in oven. Carefully pour hottest tap water available into the baking pan around the custard cups to a depth of 1 inch.

STEP 4   Bake in the preheated oven for 35 to 40 minutes or until a knife inserted near center comes out clean. Remove the cups from the baking pan. Let stand for 15 to 20 minutes.

STEP 5   Meanwhile, for sauce, in a small saucepan stir together nectar and cornstarch. Cook and stir over medium heat until thickened and bubbly. Reduce the heat. Cook and stir for 2 minutes more.

STEP 6   To serve, loosen edges of puddings with a knife. Invert into dessert dishes. Serve topped with about 1 tablespoon warm sauce.

TO TOTE: Cover puddings tightly. Transfer sauce to a tightly covered container. Transport puddings and sauce in an insulated carrier.

PER SERVING: 164 cal., 2 g total fat (1 g sat. fat), 1 mg chol., 189 mg sodium, 28 g carbo., 0 g fiber, 8 g pro.
EXCHANGES: 1 Milk, 1 Starch

OFF THE SHELF TIP   Find nectar, a fruit puree, water, and sugar mixture with canned juices.

Marble Cake

Imagine soft, buttery cake topped with sublime chocolate frosting and given a kick with chopped toffee bars. Whoops, it's all gone!

PREP
30 MINUTES

BAKE
30 MINUTES

COOL
2 HOURS

OVEN
350°F

3	cups all-purpose flour
2½	teaspoons baking powder
¾	teaspoon baking soda
¼	teaspoon salt
¾	cup butter, softened
2	cups sugar
1	tablespoon vanilla
3	eggs
1½	cups milk
½	cup chocolate-flavored syrup
1	recipe Chocolate Butter Frosting
2	1.4-ounce bars chocolate-covered English toffee, chopped (optional)

STEP 1 Preheat oven to 350°F. Grease a 13x9x2-inch baking pan; set aside. In a medium bowl combine flour, baking powder, baking soda, and salt; set aside.

STEP 2 In a large mixing bowl beat butter for 30 seconds. Add sugar and vanilla; beat until fluffy. Add eggs, 1 at a time, beating well after each. Add flour mixture and milk alternately to beaten mixture, beating on low speed after each addition just until combined.

STEP 3 Transfer 1½ cups of the batter to a medium bowl; stir in chocolate-flavored syrup. Pour light batter into the prepared pan. Spoon chocolate batter over light batter. Gently cut through batters to marble.

STEP 4 Bake in the preheated oven for 30 to 35 minutes or until a wooden toothpick inserted near the center comes out clean. Cool in pan on a wire rack. Frost with Chocolate Butter Frosting.

If desired, sprinkle top of the cake with chopped candy bars.

CHOCOLATE BUTTER FROSTING: In a large mixing bowl beat 6 tablespoons butter and ½ cup unsweetened cocoa powder with an electric mixer on medium speed until fluffy. Gradually add 2 cups powdered sugar, beating well. Slowly beat in ¼ cup milk and 1½ teaspoons vanilla. Slowly beat in an additional 2 cups powdered sugar. If necessary, beat in additional milk to reach spreading consistency. Makes 2 cups.

TO TOTE: Cover and transport in the baking pan.

PER SERVING: 453 cal., 16 g total fat (9 g sat. fat), 79 mg chol., 332 mg sodium, 74 g carbo., 1 g fiber, 5 g pro.
EXCHANGES: 2 Starch, 3 Other Carbo., 3 Fat

OFF THE SHELF TIP Grab a bar or a bag of chocolate-covered English toffee from the grocery checkout or candy aisle. It makes a tasty topping for many desserts.

Pineapple *Sheet Cake*

PREP
20 MINUTES

BAKE
20 MINUTES

COOL
1 HOUR

OVEN
350°F

MAKES
24 SERVINGS

2   cups all-purpose flour
2   cups granulated sugar
1½   teaspoons baking soda
½   teaspoon salt
1   15.5-ounce can or two 8-ounce cans crushed pineapple (in heavy syrup)
2   eggs, slightly beaten
1   teaspoon vanilla
½   cup chopped nuts
1   8-ounce package cream cheese, softened
½   cup butter or margarine, softened
1   teaspoon vanilla
1   16-ounce box powdered sugar
½   cup chopped nuts

STEP 1   Preheat oven to 350°F. Lightly grease a 15x10x1-inch baking pan; set aside. In a large bowl stir together the flour, granulated sugar, baking soda, and salt. Stir in undrained pineapple, eggs and 1 teaspoon vanilla until combined. Stir in ½ cup nuts. Spread mixture into the prepared pan. Pan will be full.

STEP 2   Bake in the preheated oven for 20 to 25 minutes or until a wooden toothpick inserted near the center comes out clean. Cool in pan on a wire rack.

STEP 3   For frosting, in a large mixing bowl beat the cream cheese, butter, and 1 teaspoon vanilla with an electric mixer on medium speed until combined. Gradually beat in the powdered sugar until frosting is smooth.

STEP 4   Spread frosting over cooled cake. Sprinkle with the remaining ½ cup nuts.

TO TOTE: Cover cake with plastic wrap. Transport cake in pan.

PER SERVING: 293 cal., 11 g total fat (5 g sat. fat), 39 mg chol., 202 mg sodium, 47 g carbo., 1 g fiber, 3 g pro.
EXCHANGES: 1 Starch, 2 Other Carbo., 2 Fat

OFF THE SHELF TIP Powdered sugar is granulated sugar that has been crushed into a fine powder. Because it dissolves readily, it is often used in icings and candy.

Peach Upside-Down Cake

Upside-down cake is an American tradition, originally browned as it bakes in a cast-iron skillet. Try a fresh twist by baking it with peaches instead of pineapple. You choose fresh or canned based on what's available. This cake's excellent with either.

PREP
40 MINUTES

BAKE
30 MINUTES

OVEN
350°F

FOR 16 SERVINGS

1	package 2-layer-size yellow cake mix
½	cup butter
1	cup packed brown sugar
1½	cups sliced, peeled peaches or frozen unsweetened peach slices
½	cup pecan halves (optional)
12	halved maraschino cherries (optional)

FOR 8 SERVINGS

1	package 1-layer-size yellow cake mix
¼	cup butter
½	cup packed brown sugar
¾	cup sliced, peeled peaches or frozen unsweetened peach slices
¼	cup pecan halves (optional)
6	halved maraschino cherries (optional)

STEP 1 Preheat oven to 350°F. Prepare cake batter according to package directions; set cake batter aside.

STEP 2 Divide the butter between two 9x1½-inch round cake pans. Place pans in the preheated oven about 5 minutes or until butter is melted. Remove pans from oven.

STEP 3 Stir half of the brown sugar into the butter in each pan and spread evenly over bottoms of cake pans. Arrange peach slices over brown sugar mixture. If desired, arrange pecan halves and/or cherries in spaces between peach slices. Spoon cake batter over fruit, dividing evenly.

STEP 4 Bake in the preheated oven for 30 to 35 minutes or until a wooden toothpick inserted near the centers comes out clean. Cool in pan on a wire rack for 5 minutes. Loosen sides; invert onto serving plates. Serve warm.

TO TOTE: Cover tightly. Transport in an insulated carrier.

PER SERVING: 261 cal., 10 g total fat (4 g sat. fat), 17 mg chol., 282 mg sodium, 43 g carbo., 1 g fiber, 2 g pro.
EXCHANGES: 3 Other Carbo., 2 Fat

FOR 8 SERVINGS: Follow Steps 1 to 4 above, except assemble in one 9x1½-inch round cake pan.

OFF THE SHELF TIP Available in dozens of flavors and most commonly packaged in boxes, cake mixes are a handy alternative to the made-from-scratch method.

Crescent Fruit Pizza

Fresh fruit pressed into a citrus-spiked pudding base on a pastry crust makes an attractive dessert that's full of flavor too.

PREP
35 MINUTES

BAKE
11 MINUTES

CHILL
1 HOUR

OVEN
375°F

MAKES
8 SERVINGS

1	8-ounce package (8) refrigerated crescent rolls
1	tablespoon butter or margarine, melted
½	teaspoon almond extract
4	teaspoons sugar
1	package 4-serving-size instant vanilla pudding and pie filling mix
1½	cups milk
1	teaspoon finely shredded orange peel
¼	of an 8-ounce container frozen whipped dessert topping, thawed
3	cups fresh fruit (such as blueberries; sliced kiwifruit; sliced strawberries; raspberries; and/or sliced, peeled peaches)

STEP 1 Preheat oven to 375°F. Press rolls into the bottom of a 12-inch pizza pan or a 13x9x2-inch baking pan. In a small bowl combine butter and almond extract; brush over dough. Sprinkle with sugar.

STEP 2 Bake in the preheated oven for 11 to 13 minutes or until golden. Cool completely in pan on wire rack.

STEP 3 In a medium mixing bowl combine pudding mix and milk. Beat with an electric mixer on low speed for 1 minute. Stir in orange peel. Cover and refrigerate for 10 minutes. Fold in dessert topping.

STEP 4 Spread pudding mixture over crust. Arrange fruit over pudding. Cover and refrigerate for at least 1 hour or up to 3 hours before serving.

TO TOTE: Cover pizza tightly with plastic wrap. Transport in an insulated cooler with ice packs.

PER SERVING: 231 cal., 10 g total fat (4 g sat. fat), 7 mg chol., 434 mg sodium, 33 g carbo., 2 g fiber, 4 g pro.
EXCHANGES: ½ Fruit, 1½ Other Carbo., 2½ Fat

OFF THE SHELF TIP Crescent rolls are a flaky dough, ready to be shaped into rolls or used as the base of an appetizer, dessert, or main dish.

Casseroles

Nacho Casserole

PREP
20 MINUTES
BAKE
45 MINUTES
OVEN
350°F
MAKES
6 SERVINGS

1	pound lean ground beef
½	cup chopped onion (1 medium)
1	15-ounce can pork and beans in tomato sauce
1	11-ounce can whole kernel corn with sweet peppers, drained
1	10.75-ounce can condensed tomato soup
1	4-ounce can diced green chile peppers
2	teaspoons chili powder
2	cups shredded Monterey Jack cheese or Monterey Jack cheese with jalapeño peppers (8 ounces)
2	cups coarsely crushed tortilla chips

OFF THE SHELF TIP Grab a can of cream soup from the soup section. Make sure your choice is "condensed" and not "ready to serve."

GOTTA-HAVE BAKEWARE FOR CASSEROLES Casserole-type dishes in transparent or opaque oven-to-freezer glass are versatile, hardy, and produce good results. 11x13-inch and 8x12-inch rectangular sizes and a 9-inch square in oven-to-freezer-glass make a good starter set. A 1½-quart and 2-quart soufflé dish will serve you well.

STEP 1 In a large skillet cook ground beef and onion over medium heat until meat is brown and onion is tender; drain. Stir in pork and beans, corn, soup, chile peppers, and chili powder. Transfer to an ungreased 2-quart rectangular baking dish.

STEP 2 Bake, covered, in a 350°F oven about 40 minutes or until heated through. Sprinkle with Monterey Jack cheese and tortilla chips. Bake, uncovered, for 5 minutes more. Serve immediately.

PER SERVING: 555 cal., 32 g total fat (14 g sat. fat), 94 mg chol., 1,194 mg sodium, 42 g carbo., 7 g fiber, 30 g pro.
EXCHANGES: ½ Vegetable, 2½ Starch, 3 Medium-Fat Meat, 2½ Fat

Creamy Meatball *Casserole*

Frozen cooked meatballs join your favorite veggie blend, potatoes, and sour cream for a tangy hot dish to bring to the table.

EASY

PREP
15 MINUTES

BAKE
1 HOUR

OVEN
350°F

MAKES
6 SERVINGS

1	10.75-ounce can condensed cream of mushroom or cream of onion soup
1	cup milk
½	cup dairy sour cream
½	teaspoon salt
⅛	teaspoon black pepper
32	frozen cooked meatballs (0.5 ounce each)
1	20-ounce package refrigerated red-skinned potato wedges
1	16-ounce package frozen stir-fry vegetables (any combination)

STEP 1 Preheat oven to 350°F. In a large bowl combine soup, milk, sour cream, salt, and pepper. Stir in meatballs, potato wedges, and vegetables. Transfer to an ungreased 3-quart rectangular baking dish.

STEP 2 Bake, covered, in the preheated oven about 1 hour or until heated through.

PER SERVING: 423 cal., 28 g total fat (12 g sat. fat), 37 mg chol., 1,291 mg sodium, 28 g carbo., 6 g fiber, 17 g pro.
EXCHANGES: 1 Vegetable, 1½ Starch, 2 Medium-Fat Meat, 3 Fat

OFF THE SHELF TIP Frozen cooked meatballs are a time-saving ingredient, making easy work for casseroles, hot sandwiches, appetizers, and pasta dishes.
MAKE-AHEAD STRATEGIES Try these tasks to filling your freezer with casseroles to thaw and serve when you're short on time.
DO 2: Instead of making just one casserole, prepare one for the freezer, too. Doing so will hardly—if at all—increase your prep time or cleanup, and you'll make use of partial ingredients.
SWAP: Partner with a friend, use the Do 2 (or 3) tip, but swap the spares with your friend.
INDULGE: When mood or opportunity strikes, spend the afternoon or evening preparing casseroles—a favorite or two and an intriguing new one—for the freezer. No rush! Put on your favorite tunes; enjoy your kitchen creativity.
BATCH TASKS: Lay out your recipes and combine like tasks for each. Brown meats on the stovetop simultaneously and make sauces simultaneously, too.

Cheese-Burger Casserole

PREP
25 MINUTES

BAKE
30 MINUTES

STAND
10 MINUTES

OVEN
375°F

MAKES
6 SERVINGS

4	ounces dried penne pasta (2 cups)
1	pound lean ground beef or ground pork
½	cup chopped onion (1 medium)
½	teaspoon bottled minced garlic (1 clove)
2	10.75-ounce cans condensed cheddar cheese soup
½	cup milk
1	teaspoon dried basil, crushed
⅛	teaspoon black pepper
1½	cups shredded Swiss or American cheese (6 ounces)
1	cup chopped tomato (2 medium)

OFF THE SHELF TIP Packed in oil and found in the grocery aisle, bottled minced garlic couldn't get much easier to use.

STEP 1 Cook pasta according to package directions; drain. Set aside.

STEP 2 Meanwhile, preheat oven to 375°F. In a large skillet cook ground beef, onion, and garlic until meat is brown and onion is tender; drain off fat. Stir in soup, milk, basil, and pepper. Stir in cooked pasta and 1 cup of the Swiss cheese. Spoon mixture into an ungreased 2-quart rectangular baking dish.

STEP 3 Bake, covered, in the preheated oven for 30 to 35 minutes or until heated through. Sprinkle with remaining ½ cup cheese and the tomatoes. Let stand for 10 minutes before serving.

PER SERVING: 519 cal., 34 g total fat (15 g sat. fat), 103 mg chol., 944 mg sodium, 32 g carbo., 2 g fiber, 28 g pro.
EXCHANGES: 2 Starch, 3 Medium-Fat Meat, 3 Fat

Turkey-Wild Rice Bake

PREP
35 MINUTES
BAKE
15 MINUTES
OVEN
350°F
MAKES
6 SERVINGS

1	6-ounce package long grain and wild rice mix
1	cup chopped onion (1 large)
1½	teaspoons bottled minced garlic (3 cloves)
1	tablespoon butter
1	10.75-ounce can condensed cream of chicken soup
1	cup milk
1½	teaspoons dried basil, crushed
2	cups shredded Swiss cheese (8 ounces)
3	cups chopped cooked turkey (about 1 pound)
1	4.5-ounce jar (drained weight) sliced mushrooms, drained
½	cup finely shredded Parmesan cheese (2 ounces)
⅓	cup sliced almonds, toasted

PER SERVING: 700 cal., 36 g total fat (19 g sat. fat), 132 mg chol., 1,400 mg sodium, 37 g carbo., 4 g fiber, 56 g pro.
EXCHANGES: 2½ Starch, 7 Lean Meat, 2½ Fat

OFF THE SHELF TIP Wild rice mix is a savory mix containing wild rice, long grain rice, and herbs.

STEP 1 Prepare rice mix according to package directions, except discard the seasoning packet. Set aside.

STEP 2 Preheat oven to 350°F. In a 12-inch skillet cook onion and garlic in hot butter over medium heat until onion is tender. Stir in soup, milk, and basil; heat through. Slowly add Swiss cheese, stirring until cheese is melted. Stir in cooked rice, turkey, and mushrooms. Transfer to an ungreased 3-quart rectangular baking dish. Sprinkle with Parmesan cheese.

STEP 3 Bake, uncovered, in the preheated oven for 15 to 20 minutes or until heated through. Sprinkle with almonds before serving.

Turkey-Broccoli Casserole

Tap this recipe for a superb way to enjoy holiday turkey leftovers. Stock your pantry with the ingredients ahead of time, and you'll save yourself a trip to the store.

PREP
25 MINUTES

BAKE
35 MINUTES

OVEN
350°F

MAKES
6 SERVINGS

2   **cups dried medium noodles (4 ounces)**

2   **cups frozen cut broccoli**

1   **10.75-ounce can condensed cream of onion or cream of celery soup**

1   **8-ounce carton dairy sour cream**

½   **cup milk**

2   **cups refrigerated chopped cooked turkey or chicken (10 ounces)**

1   **8-ounce can sliced water chestnuts, drained**

½   **cup shredded Swiss cheese (2 ounces)**

⅓   **cup fine dry bread crumbs**

2   **tablespoons butter, melted**

OFF THE SHELF TIP Look in the refrigerated meat section for precooked chicken or turkey seasoned or unseasoned strips, cubes, and whole pieces.

STEP 1   Cook noodles according to package directions, adding the broccoli during the last 2 minutes of cooking; drain. Set aside.

STEP 2   Preheat oven to 350°F. In a large bowl combine soup, sour cream, and milk. Stir in turkey, water chestnuts, Swiss cheese, and noodle mixture. Transfer to an ungreased 2-quart square baking dish.

STEP 3   In a small bowl combine bread crumbs and melted butter. Sprinkle over noodle mixture.

STEP 4   Bake, uncovered, in the preheated oven about 35 minutes or until heated through.

PER SERVING: 441 cal., 23 g total fat (11 g sat. fat), 100 mg chol., 656 mg sodium, 38 g carbo., 3 g fiber, 24 g pro.
EXCHANGES: 1 Vegetable, 2 Starch, 2½ Lean Meat, 2½ Fat

Monterey Turkey Casserole

EASY

PREP
15 MINUTES

BAKE
30 MINUTES

OVEN
350°F

MAKES
8 SERVINGS

5	cups slightly crushed tortilla chips
4	cups cubed cooked turkey or chicken (about 1¼ pounds)
2	16-ounce jars salsa
1	10-ounce package frozen whole kernel corn
½	cup dairy sour cream
2	tablespoons all-purpose flour
1	cup shredded Monterey Jack cheese with jalapeño peppers or mozzarella cheese (4 ounces)

STEP 1 Preheat oven to 350°F. Place 3 cups of the tortilla chips in the bottom of a lightly greased 3-quart rectangular baking dish. In a large bowl combine turkey, salsa, corn, sour cream, and flour; spoon over tortilla chips.

STEP 2 Bake, uncovered, in the preheated oven for 25 minutes. Sprinkle with the remaining 2 cups tortilla chips and the cheese. Bake for 5 to 10 minutes more or until heated through.

PER SERVING: 444 cal., 17 g total fat (7 g sat. fat), 74 mg chol., 1,127 mg sodium, 46 g carbo., 4 g fiber, 29 g pro.
EXCHANGES: 1 Vegetable, 2½ Starch, 3 Lean Meat, 1 Fat

OFF THE SHELF TIP Ranging in spiciness from mild to mouth-searing, salsa adds unique flavor to lots of dishes. If unopened, salsa can be kept at room temperature for six months; once opened, refrigerate for up to one month.

FREEZING TIP Whether you're making a dish that's headed for the fridge or freezer, keep your food safe by cooling it quickly after cooking. Doing so reduces the opportunity for harmful bacteria to grow. What's more, a fast chill reduces the likelihood of large ice crystals forming that can mess with your casserole's flavor and texture. These tips help:

First, put the cooked food in the fridge. Put it in whole, or, if you're going to divide it in half or into individual portions, do so prior to the first chilldown. Doing so hastens the release of heat.

Next, move tightly sealed and wrapped cooled casseroles from fridge to freezer once cooled. If space allows, arrange the containers in a single layer for faster freezing. You can stack the goods once they are frozen.

Chicken & Orzo Casserole

Seasoned cooked chicken breast strips make this south-of-the-border casserole a snap to make. Orzo is a small pasta often mistaken for rice because of its shape.

EASY

PREP
15 MINUTES
BAKE
20 MINUTES
STAND
10 MINUTES
OVEN
350°F
MAKES
4 TO 6 SERVINGS

2   teaspoons cumin seeds
1   14-ounce can chicken broth
1   14.5-ounce can Mexican-style stewed
    tomatoes or one 10-ounce can diced
    tomatoes and green chile peppers,
    undrained
¼   cup oil-packed dried tomatoes,
    drained and cut up
1   cup dried orzo pasta
2   9-ounce packages Southwestern-
    flavored frozen cooked chicken
    breast strips, thawed, or two
    5.5-ounce packages Southwestern-
    flavored refrigerated cooked
    chicken breast strips
    Paprika (optional)
    Fresh jalapeño or serrano chile
    peppers, seeded and chopped
    (optional)*

STEP 1 Preheat oven to 350°F. Place cumin seeds in a large saucepan. Heat over medium heat for 3 to 4 minutes or until seeds are toasted and aromatic, shaking pan occasionally. Carefully stir in the chicken broth, undrained tomatoes, dried tomatoes, and uncooked orzo. Bring to boiling. Transfer to a 2-quart baking dish. Top with chicken breast strips.

STEP 2 Bake, covered, in the preheated oven about 20 minutes or until orzo is tender. Let stand, covered, for 10 minutes before serving. To serve, if desired, sprinkle with paprika and top with chopped chile peppers.

PER SERVING: 388 cal., 7 g total fat (2 g sat. fat), 60 mg chol., 1,227 mg sodium, 44 g carbo., 3 g fiber, 35 g pro.
EXCHANGES: 1 Vegetable, 2½ Starch, 3½ Very Lean Meat, 1 Fat

*NOTE: Because chile peppers contain volatile oils that can burn your skin and eyes, avoid direct contact with them as much as possible. When working with chile peppers, wear plastic or rubber gloves. If your bare hands do touch the chile peppers, wash them well with soap and water.

OFF THE SHELF TIP Precooked chicken breast strips are a true time-saver. These strips come seasoned or unseasoned and are ready to add to a salad, stir-fry, or casserole.

Bean Enchilada Casserole

PREP
25 MINUTES
BAKE
40 MINUTES
STAND
5 MINUTES
OVEN
350°F
MAKES
4 TO 6 SERVINGS

1 15-ounce can red kidney beans, pinto beans, or black beans, rinsed and drained

1 15-ounce can garbanzo beans (chickpeas), navy beans, or Great Northern beans, rinsed and drained

1 10.75-ounce can condensed cheddar cheese soup or one 10-ounce can condensed nacho cheese soup

1 10-ounce can enchilada sauce

1 8-ounce can tomato sauce

2 cups corn chips or tortilla chips, broken

¾ cup shredded Monterey Jack cheese with jalapeño peppers or Monterey Jack cheese (3 ounces)

Toppers: sliced pitted ripe olives, sliced green onions, chopped tomatoes, chopped green sweet pepper, and/or shredded lettuce (optional)

PER SERVING: 426 cal., 18 g total fat (7 g sat. fat), 28 mg chol., 2,037 mg sodium, 54 g carbo., 13 g fiber, 23 g pro.
EXCHANGES: ½ Vegetable, 2 Starch, 1 Other Carbo., 2 High-Fat Meat

OFF THE SHELF TIP Enchilada sauce is a tomato-based sauce containing red chiles and spices and is available in mild, medium, and hot.

STEP 1 Preheat oven to 350°F. For filling, in a large bowl combine beans and soup; set aside. In a medium bowl combine enchilada sauce and tomato sauce. Spoon bean mixture into a greased 2-quart rectangular baking dish; pour sauce mixture over bean mixture. Sprinkle with chips. Cover with lightly greased foil.

STEP 2 Bake in the preheated oven about 40 minutes or until heated through. Remove foil; sprinkle with Monterey Jack cheese. Let stand about 5 minutes or until cheese melts. If desired, serve with toppers.

Pork & Apple Casserole

Sweet crunchy apples make a lovely partner for pork. Toss them with corn bread stuffing for a fall-flavored dish.

1	pound bulk pork sausage
1⅓	cups chopped apple (2 medium)
1⅓	cups packaged corn bread stuffing mix
1	tablespoon dried minced onion
2	eggs
1¼	cups apple juice or apple cider
½	cup shredded cheddar cheese (2 ounces)

OFF THE SHELF TIP Corn bread stuffing mix is made with crumbled savory corn bread, white bread cubes, and herbs. This stuffing is a tasty break from the traditional.

DO THE THAW Thaw frozen casseroles safely in the fridge overnight or during the workday.

PREP
25 MINUTES
BAKE
30 MINUTES
OVEN
400°F
MAKES
6 SERVINGS

STEP 1 Preheat oven to 400°F. In a large skillet cook sausage until brown. Drain off fat. Stir in chopped apple, dry stuffing mix, and dried minced onion. In a small bowl whisk together eggs and apple juice; add to sausage mixture. Toss to coat. Transfer mixture to a greased 2-quart square baking dish.

STEP 2 Bake, covered, in the preheated oven for 20 minutes. Uncover; stir stuffing mixture and sprinkle with cheddar cheese. Bake, uncovered, about 10 minutes more or until hot in center (160°F).

PER SERVING: 429 cal., 29 g total fat (11 g sat. fat), 138 mg chol., 776 mg sodium, 24 g carbo., 2 g fiber, 17 g pro.
EXCHANGES: 1 Fruit, ½ Starch, 2½ High-Fat Meat, 2 Fat

Ham-Sauerkraut Casserole

If your taste buds crave ham-and-Swiss but you don't want a sandwich, this creamy casserole brings home that tang flavor.

EASY

PREP
15 MINUTES

BAKE
25 MINUTES

OVEN
375°F

MAKES
6 SERVINGS

2   cups diced cooked ham (10 ounces)
1   14-ounce can Bavarian-style sauerkraut, rinsed, drained, and snipped*
1   10.75-ounce can condensed cream of potato soup
1   cup shredded Swiss cheese (4 ounces)
½   cup milk
1   tablespoon yellow mustard
¾   cup rye bread crumbs**
1   tablespoon butter, melted

STEP 1   Preheat oven to 375°F. In a large bowl combine ham, sauerkraut, soup, Swiss cheese, milk, and mustard. Transfer mixture to an ungreased 1½-quart casserole. In a small bowl combine bread crumbs and melted butter; sprinkle over ham mixture.

STEP 2   Bake, uncovered, in the preheated oven about 25 minutes or until heated through.

*NOTE: If Bavarian-style sauerkraut is not available, substitute one 14.5-ounce can sauerkraut plus 2 tablespoons packed brown sugar and ½ teaspoon caraway seeds.

**NOTE: Use a blender or food processor to make fluffy soft bread crumbs. One slice yields ¾ cup.

PER SERVING: 236 cal., 13 g total fat (7 g sat. fat), 53 mg chol., 1,611 mg sodium, 13 g carbo., 2 g fiber, 17 g pro.
EXCHANGES: ½ Vegetable, ½ Other Carbo., 2 Medium-Fat Meat, ½ Fat

OFF THE SHELF TIP Bavarian-style sauerkraut is fermented shredded cabbage, salt, and caraway seeds making up this tasty side dish and condiment. Find it in jars or cans in the canned vegetable aisle.

Triple Seafood Bake

PREP
25 MINUTES

BAKE
40 MINUTES

OVEN
350°F

MAKES
5 OR 6 SERVINGS

2½ cups half-and-half, light cream, or milk

1 10.75-ounce can condensed cream of mushroom with roasted garlic soup

⅓ cup dry sherry

1⅓ cups uncooked instant rice

1 6.5-ounce can minced clams, drained

1 6-ounce can crabmeat, drained

6 ounces cooked, peeled, and deveined medium shrimp, halved lengthwise

1 4-ounce (drained weight) can sliced mushrooms, drained

¼ cup sliced almonds

Snipped fresh parsley (optional)

OFF THE SHELF TIP A boon for the busy cook, instant rice comes plain and flavored.
SERVING TIP After baking, let your casserole stand, covered, for ten minutes before serving. This allows time for the dish to firm and makes serving much easier!

STEP 1 Preheat oven to 350°F. In a large saucepan combine half-and-half, soup, and sherry. Bring to boiling. Stir in rice, clams, crabmeat, shrimp, and mushrooms. Transfer to an ungreased 2-quart casserole. Sprinkle with almonds.

STEP 2 Bake, uncovered, in the preheated oven about 40 minutes or until rice is tender. If desired, sprinkle with parsley before serving.

PER SERVING: 476 cal., 20 g total fat (9 g sat. fat), 168 mg chol., 780 mg sodium, 37 g carbo., 2 g fiber, 32 g pro.
EXCHANGES: 2 Starch, ½ Other Carbo., 3½ Very Lean Meat, 3½ Fat

Crab-Mushroom Bake

PREP
20 MINUTES

BAKE
25 MINUTES

OVEN
350°F

MAKES
4 SERVINGS

½   cup finely chopped celery (1 stalk)
1   tablespoon butter
1   10.75-ounce can condensed cream
     of shrimp soup
¾   cup soft bread crumbs*
1   4-ounce can (drained weight) sliced
     mushrooms, drained
⅓   cup milk
2   tablespoons dry sherry
1   6.5-ounce can pasteurized crabmeat,
     drained, or one 6.5-ounce can
     crabmeat, drained, flaked, and
     cartilage removed
⅓   cup finely shredded Parmesan cheese
     Lemon wedges (optional)

PER SERVING: 276 cal., 10 g total fat (6 g sat. fat), 83 mg chol., 1,260 mg sodium, 26 g carbo., 2 g fiber, 17 g pro.
EXCHANGES: ½ Other Carbo., 2½ Very Lean Meat, 1½ Fat

OFF THE SHELF TIP Canned crabmeat is a sweet, succulent meat from crabs and is found near the canned tuna and salmon.

STEP 1   Preheat oven to 350°F. In a medium saucepan cook celery in hot butter over medium heat until tender. Stir in soup, ½ cup of the bread crumbs, the mushrooms, milk, and sherry. Bring mixture just to boiling, stirring constantly. Stir in crabmeat. Transfer to an ungreased 9-inch pie plate.

STEP 2   In a small bowl combine the remaining ¼ cup bread crumbs and the Parmesan cheese. Sprinkle over crab mixture.

STEP 3   Bake, uncovered, in the preheated oven about 25 minutes or until mixture is bubbly and top is golden. If desired, serve with lemon wedges.

***NOTE:** Use a blender or food processor to make fluffy soft bread crumbs. One slice yields ¾ cup crumbs.

Greek Pasta Casserole

PREP
25 MINUTES

BAKE
20 MINUTES

STAND
10 MINUTES

OVEN
375°F

MAKES
6 SERVINGS

12   ounces dried rotini pasta (3½ cups)
1   15-ounce can tomato sauce
1   10.75-ounce can condensed tomato soup
1   15-ounce can white kidney (cannellini) beans or garbanzo beans (chickpeas), rinsed and drained
2   cups crumbled feta cheese (8 ounces)
1   cup coarsely chopped, pitted Greek black olives
½   cup seasoned fine dry bread crumbs
2   tablespoons butter, melted
2   tablespoons grated Parmesan cheese

STEP 1 Cook pasta according to package directions; drain.

STEP 2 Preheat oven to 375°F. In a very large bowl combine the cooked pasta, the tomato sauce, and soup; toss to coat. Stir in beans, feta cheese, and olives. Spoon pasta mixture into a lightly greased 3-quart rectangular baking dish. In a small bowl combine bread crumbs, melted butter, and Parmesan cheese; sprinkle over pasta mixture.

STEP 3 Bake, uncovered, in the preheated oven for 20 to 25 minutes or until heated through and top is light brown. Let stand for 10 minutes before serving.

PER SERVING: 553 cal., 19 g total fat (10 g sat. fat), 52 mg chol., 1,890 mg sodium, 74 g carbo., 7 g fiber, 24 g pro.
EXCHANGES: ½ Vegetable, 4 Starch, 1 Other Carbo., 1½ Medium-Fat Meat, 1 Fat

OFF THE SHELF TIP Don't look for seasoned bread crumbs in the bread section. It will be near stuffing and mac 'n' cheese mixes.
REHEATING TIP The casserole you baked yesterday for serving today (and meanwhile have stored in the fridge) should be reheated in the oven at 325 degrees Fahrenheit for about 45 to 60 minutes. You can also reheat a few portions of leftovers, lightly covered, in the microwave on high. Though timing will depend on the amount and type of food being warmed, start with 5 or 10 minutes and then check every five thereafter.

If the food seems dry, add a little broth or sauce to the dish to rehydrate.

California Vegetable Casserole

PREP
15 MINUTES

BAKE
70 MINUTES

OVEN
350°F

MAKES
8 SIDE-DISH SERVINGS

1   10.75-ounce can condensed cream
      of mushroom soup
1   cup uncooked instant white rice
½   of a 15-ounce jar cheese dip
      (about ¾ cup)
1   cup milk
⅓   cup chopped onion (1 small)
¼   teaspoon dried oregano, crushed
1   16-ounce package frozen cauliflower,
      broccoli, and carrots

STEP 1   Preheat oven to 350°F. In a large bowl combine soup, rice, cheese dip, milk, onion, and oregano. Stir in frozen vegetables. Transfer to an ungreased 1½-quart casserole.

STEP 2   Bake, covered, in a preheated oven about 70 minutes or until heated through, stirring once. Stir before serving.

PER SERVING: 179 cal., 8 g total fat (4 g sat. fat), 26 mg chol., 723 mg sodium, 21 g carbo., 2 g fiber, 6 g pro.
EXCHANGES: ½ Vegetable, 1½ Starch, 1½ Fat

OFF THE SHELF TIP A boon for the busy cook, instant rice comes plain and flavored.

Spinach & Artichoke Casserole

1   10.75-ounce can reduced-fat condensed cream of mushroom soup

1   8-ounce package reduced-fat cream cheese (Neufchâtel), cubed

2   10-ounce packages frozen chopped spinach, thawed and well drained

1   14-ounce can artichoke hearts, drained and coarsely chopped

1   2.8-ounce can french-fried onions, coarsely crushed

2/3   cup crushed crackers (such as rich round or saltine crackers)

2   tablespoons butter, melted

OFF THE SHELF TIP Tender and meaty marinated artichoke hearts are packed in oil and herbs. You can find them in the canned vegetable aisle of your store.

PREP
20 MINUTES
BAKE
40 MINUTES
OVEN
350°F
MAKES
8 SIDE-DISH SERVINGS

STEP 1 Preheat oven to 350°F. In a large saucepan combine soup and cream cheese. Cook and stir over medium heat until cream cheese melts. Remove from heat. Stir in spinach, chopped artichokes, and french-fried onions. Transfer to a greased 2-quart casserole.

STEP 2 In a small bowl combine crushed crackers and melted butter. Sprinkle over top of spinach mixture.

STEP 3 Bake, uncovered, in the preheated oven about 40 minutes or until heated through.

PER SERVING: 247 cal., 17 g total fat (7 g sat. fat), 33 mg chol., 637 mg sodium, 17 g carbo., 4 g fiber, 7 g pro.
EXCHANGES: 1 Vegetable, 1 Starch, 3 Fat

Waffle Breakfast Casserole

Tired of turning out the same breakfast or brunch casserole? Try this version that uses prepared, toasted waffles in place of bread.

EASY

PREP
15 MINUTES

CHILL
4 TO 24 HOURS

BAKE
50 MINUTES

STAND
10 MINUTES

OVEN
350°F

MAKES
8 SERVINGS

RECIPE PICTURED ON PAGE **144.**

1   **pound bulk pork sausage**
6   **frozen waffles, toasted and cubed**
1   **cup shredded cheddar cheese (4 ounces)**
6   **eggs, slightly beaten**
2   **cups milk**
1   **teaspoon dry mustard**
⅛   **teaspoon black pepper**
    Frozen waffles, toasted (optional)
    Maple-flavor or maple syrup (optional)

STEP 1   Preheat oven to 350°F. In a large skillet cook sausage until brown; drain off fat.

STEP 2   Arrange half of the cubed waffles in an ungreased 2-quart rectangular baking dish. Top with half of the sausage and ⅔ cup of the cheddar cheese. Top with remaining cubed waffles and then remaining sausage.

STEP 3   In a medium bowl combine eggs, milk, mustard, and pepper. Pour over layers in dish. Cover and refrigerate for at least 4 hours or up to 24 hours.

STEP 4   Bake in the preheated oven for 50 to 60 minutes or until a knife inserted near the center comes out clean. Sprinkle with remaining ⅓ cup cheese. Let stand for 10 minutes before serving. If desired, serve on toasted waffles and drizzle with maple syrup.

PER SERVING: 413 cal., 28 g total fat (12 g sat. fat), 217 mg chol., 668 mg sodium, 15 g carbo., 1 g fiber, 19 g pro.
EXCHANGES: ½ Milk, 1 Starch, 2 High-Fat Meat, 2 Fat

OFF THE SHELF TIP Grab a can of cream soup from the soup section. Make sure your choice is "condensed" and not "ready to serve."

FOIL, WRAPS, BAGS & PLASTIC CONTAINER TIP Don't let a bad wrap undo your make-ahead efforts in the freezer. When preparing make-aheads and leftovers for a stay in the freezer, insulate them well using freezer grade products. There is a difference in their performance, and it adds up in preventing moisture loss and protecting the texture and flavor of your food. So choose heavy-duty rather than light-duty aluminum foil and freezer-grade plastic wrap and zip bags. For leftovers, choose plastic—freezer-grade—containers sized to match the food portion as closely as possible.

Metric Information

The charts on this page provide a guide for converting measurements from the U.S. customary system, used throughout this book, to the metric system.

Product Differences

Most of the ingredients called for in the recipes in this book are available in most countries. However, some are known by different names. Here are some common American ingredients and their possible counterparts:

- Sugar (white) is granulated, fine granulated, or castor sugar.
- Powdered sugar is icing sugar.
- All-purpose flour is enriched, bleached or unbleached white household flour. When self-rising flour is used in place of all-purpose flour in a recipe that calls for leavening, omit the leavening agent (baking soda or baking powder) and salt.
- Light-colored corn syrup is golden syrup.
- Cornstarch is cornflour.
- Baking soda is bicarbonate of soda.
- Vanilla or vanilla extract is vanilla essence.
- Bell peppers are capsicums.
- Golden raisins are sultanas.

Volume & Weight

The United States traditionally uses cup measures for liquid and solid ingredients. The chart below shows the approximate imperial and metric equivalents. If you are accustomed to weighing solid ingredients, the following approximate equivalents will be helpful.

- 1 cup butter, castor sugar, or rice = 8 ounces = 1/2 pound = 250 grams
- 1 cup flour = 4 ounces = 1/4 pound = 125 grams
- 1 cup icing sugar = 5 ounces = 150 grams

Canadian and U.S. volume for a cup measure is 8 fluid ounces (237 ml), but the standard metric equivalent is 250 ml.

1 British imperial cup is 10 fluid ounces.

In Australia, 1 tablespoon equals 20 ml, and there are 4 teaspoons in the Australian tablespoon.

Spoon measures are used for smaller amounts of ingredients. Although the size of the tablespoon varies slightly in different countries, for practical purposes and for recipes in this book, a straight substitution is all that's necessary. Measurements made using cups or spoons should be level unless stated otherwise.

Common Weight Range Replacements

Imperial / U.S.	Metric
1/2 ounce	15 g
1 ounce	25 g or 30 g
4 ounces (1/4 pound)	115 g or 125 g
8 ounces (1/2 pound)	225 g or 250 g
16 ounces (1 pound)	450 g or 500 g
1 1/4 pounds	625 g
1 1/2 pounds	750 g
2 pounds or 2 1/4 pounds	1,000 g or 1 Kg

Oven Temperature Equivalents

Fahrenheit Setting	Celsius Setting*	Gas Setting
300°F	150°C	Gas Mark 2 (very low)
325°F	160°C	Gas Mark 3 (low)
350°F	180°C	Gas Mark 4 (moderate)
375°F	190°C	Gas Mark 5 (moderate)
400°F	200°C	Gas Mark 6 (hot)
425°F	220°C	Gas Mark 7 (hot)
450°F	230°C	Gas Mark 8 (very hot)
475°F	240°C	Gas Mark 9 (very hot)
500°F	260°C	Gas Mark 10 (extremely hot)
Broil	Broil	Grill

*Electric and gas ovens may be calibrated using celsius. However, for an electric oven, increase celsius setting 10 to 20 degrees when cooking above 160°C. For convection or forced air ovens (gas or electric) lower the temperature setting 25°F/10°C when cooking at all heat levels.

Baking Pan Sizes

Imperial / U.S.	Metric
9×1 1/2-inch round cake pan	22- or 23×4-cm (1.5 L)
9×1 1/2-inch pie plate	22- or 23×4-cm (1 L)
8×8×2-inch square cake pan	20×5-cm (2 L)
9×9×2-inch square cake pan	22- or 23×4.5-cm (2.5 L)
11×7×1 1/2-inch baking pan	28×17×4-cm (2 L)
2-quart rectangular baking pan	30×19×4.5-cm (3 L)
13×9×2-inch baking pan	34×22×4.5-cm (3.5 L)
15×10×1-inch jelly roll pan	40×25×2-cm
9×5×3-inch loaf pan	23×13×8-cm (2 L)
2-quart casserole	2 L

U.S. / Standard Metric Equivalents

1/8 teaspoon = 0.5 ml	
1/4 teaspoon = 1 ml	
1/2 teaspoon = 2 ml	
1 teaspoon = 5 ml	
1 tablespoon = 15 ml	
2 tablespoons = 25 ml	
1/4 cup = 2 fluid ounces = 50 ml	
1/3 cup = 3 fluid ounces = 75 ml	
1/2 cup = 4 fluid ounces = 125 ml	
2/3 cup = 5 fluid ounces = 150 ml	
3/4 cup = 6 fluid ounces = 175 ml	
1 cup = 8 fluid ounces = 250 ml	
2 cups = 1 pint = 500 ml	
1 quart = 1 litre	

introducing a brand-new

by Better Homes and Gardens®

off the shelf

creative convenience
delectable taste and
guaranteed success!

Little time to cook? *Every recipe in the Off the Shelf series is quick and easy, kitchen-tested and taste-approved, for today's busy cooks.*

Combine fresh ingredients
with convenience foods for
meals made simple!

Available where cookbooks are sold.

ADT0147_0406